SHIFT HAPPENS

HAPPENS

THE HISTORY OF LABOR IN THE UNITED STATES

J. ALBERT MANN

HARPER

An Imprint of HarperCollinsPublishers

Written with love and admiration
for the other J. Albert Mann,
Jackson Albert Mann

Library of Congress Control Number: 2023944811
ISBN 978-0-06-327348-1

Typography by Torborg Davern
24 25 26 27 28 LBC 5 4 3 2 1

First Edition

CONTENTS

SECTION THREE:

THE PROGRESSIVE ERA 1900–1916

SECTION FOUR:

WORLD WAR I AND THE FIRST RED SCARE 1917–1920

SECTION ONE

The Age of Discovery
to the Civil War
1492–1865

IS SHE REALLY GOING TO START WITH MARCO POLO AND CHRISTOPHER COLUMBUS?

Marco Polo traveled to Asia in the thirteenth century on an epic journey. He encountered cultures and nations Europeans barely knew existed. He returned to write a book about his adventures—stories full of amazing art, architecture, and animals, as well as cool innovations like eyeglasses and the postal service.

Polo's book topped everybody's TBR list, including Christopher Columbus's.

Columbus fanboyed Polo hard. He dreamed of being just like him one day. So when he grew up, he set sail—heading west, not east—hoping to bump into the lands Marco Polo described from the opposite direction. Not only did Columbus have Polo's amazing stories dancing in his head, he had the man's actual book on board his ship.

We all know what happened next—instead of bumping into Asia, he bumped into North America.

Kind of.

He really landed in the Bahamas.

Columbus's trip was paid for by the king and queen of Spain during a time in history called "the Age of Discovery." A better name for it would have been "the Age of Stealing Other People's Shit" because these Spanish royals fronted Columbus the money for one reason only: gold.

Gold was their version of cash. And the only way to get it was to "find" it.

The "Age of Discovery" with its hunt for gold is the beginning of capitalism—an economy controlled by private owners (in this case, the king and queen of Spain) seeking personal profit (gold for themselves).

So Columbus docked in the Bahamas and met the folks who lived there—the people of the Lokono Nation (called the Arawak by the Europeans). The Lokono were friendly and showered Columbus with gifts. Unfortunately, the gifts were parrots and glass—not gold.

Noticing the Indigenous people did not carry weapons, he enslaved them. Every Lokono citizen fourteen years or older was placed in chains and put to work mining for gold. At the end of each day, anyone who hadn't found gold had their hands cut off and bled to death.

The "New World's" first working class had a huge problem—there *wasn't* much gold in the Bahamas. What could they do? They bravely fought back. But without swords or guns, it was pretty hopeless. They were burned alive or hanged, and they began to engage in mass suicide using poison and self-starvation.

When Columbus arrived in the Bahamas in 1492, there were an estimated 300,000 Indigenous people from the Lokono and Carib nations living on the islands. By 1548, after fifty-five years of violent enslavement and harsh labor, only about 500 people survived.

Welcome to the history of labor in the United States.

CHAPTER 2

SOMEBODY'S GOTTA WORK

During the 150 years of the Lokono and Carib genocide, Europeans were moving to North America in ever-increasing numbers. When they arrived, they got right to work.

Just kidding. Most of the first settlers weren't the nose-to-the-grindstone type. They were men of leisure who had never picked up a shovel or hammer in their entire lives. John Smith, leader of the settlement of Jamestown, Virginia, had to establish martial law, forcing the colonists into the fields at gunpoint for their own survival.

And that survival wasn't easy.

Food was rationed because there wasn't much of it. What food did exist was moldy and filled with maggots. If someone got caught taking more than their share, a needle was jammed through their tongue and they were tied to a tree until they starved.

Unhappy with both the working and the starving, the colonists looked for a "next steps" kind of plan. They decided to go with Christopher Columbus's idea: enslave the people who already live there.

But Columbus had done this on an island with guns and

swords against a people who had neither. The colonists' plan was to enslave the nations surrounding them on a large continent, where they were seriously outnumbered. They did have guns and they did use them to massacre some of the Indigenous people around them in hopes of coaxing the ones they didn't kill into the fields. But those Indigenous people just returned to kill them right back. As desperate as the colonists were, they quickly realized the "Indians" were not the answer to their labor shortage.

And eating wasn't the colonists' only problem.

Just like the king and queen of Spain had financed Columbus's trip in return for gold, corporations that functioned very much like our corporations today were forming in England and financing the trips of the colonists with one thing in mind—profit.

This "new world" was supposed to be supplying the shareholders of these companies with wealth. If there wasn't any gold to steal, then the colonists had better start mining stuff, trapping some animals, or planting a ton of crops. But all these things required workers. In a letter to shareholders written in 1616, the Virginia Company promised "*great profit*" as soon as there were "*more hands.*"

After failing to enslave the local people (whose land they were about to start making "great profit" from), they turned their eye toward folks back home.

To quickly sum up the population in England (and Scotland and Ireland, which England owned): these folks were flat-out miserable.

The old European economic system called feudalism, where the royals owned the land and the peasants lived and worked on it, was dying. The new system of capitalism was rising to take feudalism's place.

In the feudalist system, land was used to house and feed people. In the capitalist system, land would be used to produce profit for the people who owned it. Royals kicked the people off the land, built fences or "enclosures" around it, and filled it with sheep to sell wool. Then they hired a guy or two to tend the sheep.

Kicking the people off the land and enclosing it caused massive homelessness. Thousands and thousands of people were now roaming the countryside looking for work. Lots of workers but not a lot of jobs meant low wages. And once you found employment, you were locked in because it was against the law to leave your job, no matter what your employer paid you. "*Servants served masters,*" said English law, and that was that. If you tried to run and they caught you, there was jail time, a fine, *and* they cut off one of your ears.

Hungry, overworked, and missing a lot of ears, the working class began to come together in order to solve their problems (today this is called organizing). But organized labor isn't good for profit. The growing rich in England looked to the "New World" to "*drain from the Mother-Country the disaffected and the vicious.*" In other words, they decided to ship people they didn't like to the colonies.

This was easy-peasy when it came to anyone in jail—especially anyone who had been organizing labor or had run away from their jobs. The courts simply waived their jail sentence if they agreed to get on a ship. If they didn't, they made the jail sentence longer.

But there was no money to be made by shipping so-called criminals to the American colonies to work—at least not until they *reached* the colonies. If the growing rich wanted to make big profits, they needed many hands, and they just hadn't arrested enough people. So they hatched a second plan.

They filled newspapers and plastered the streets with propaganda—information used to sell a particular viewpoint. That viewpoint?

The "New World" is a land of milk and honey!

It wasn't.

Jobs are plentiful and wages high!

The first was true, but the second was dead wrong.

This propaganda flooded across Ireland, Scotland, and Germany, where workers were starving for food and jobs.

"Go!" said the landowners . . . who owned the land over there too.

"How?" asked the poor . . . who had no money.

And now comes the real cruelty in the landowners' plan: the poor were made to pay for the passage to the colonies by signing a contract to do *"any work in which the employer shall employ them"* for a certain number of years (mostly two to seven). They became known as indentured servants.

Things didn't go well for these folks right from the get-go. The boats were a floating misery of rotten food, sloshing waste, and killer disease. Lots of people died, which was terrible. And if watching your fellow passengers suffer and die wasn't bad enough, the folks who survived found out the contracts they'd signed had been written so that the years of those who died on the trip were doled out to those who lived. So the two to seven years thing was more like an estimate.

Once they landed, the contracts of those still alive were sold to different business owners, and off the servants went to serve.

Masters could be cruel and cheap, since profits were the

goal. If indentured servants complained, employers took them to court. Each complaint the employer won (and the employers mostly won) added six months to the worker's contract. Most servants lived new miserable lives in the New World that weren't very different from their old miserable lives in the Old World.

Joining these indentured folks was a host of child workers. Kidnapping was big business in Europe. People who stole children— called "crimps" or "spirrits"—whisked them from street to boat, getting paid per child.

Europe was no stranger to putting children as young as six years old to work. But stealing children from their families to sell to merchants on another continent was something new. One woman *seduced children using gingerbread*—sounding very much like a fairy tale, but without a happily ever after for the kids.

Once the children reached colonial shores, they were sold under contract like adults and put straight to work. At first, children mostly worked in the shipping business—preparing meals, swabbing decks, and even carrying gunpowder during battle. Over the years, working children would be a common sight in the colonies in almost all aspects of industry. The poet Sarah Norcliffe Cleghorn would go on to immortalize them in verse.

> *The golf links lie so near the mill*
> *That almost every day*
> *The laboring children can look out*
> *And see the men at play.*

Convicts, indentured servants, kidnapped children—all

landed in the colonies and were put to work. Hard work. But if these workers had it bad—and they did—there were others who had it worse. Much worse.

The "more hands" needed by the Virginia Company also came shackled together on ships—African people brought over as slaves. Owning a person's life for years was one thing; owning a person's life forever was quite another. The enslavement of Black people was flourishing across most of the globe at this time in history, but it thrived particularly well in the American colonies.

With hands supplied, the hard work of producing profit got underway. Planting rice, picking tobacco, harvesting lumber, building ships, and mining iron—you name it, these workers did it. And did it, and did it, and did it.

Along with growing profits, towns, and cities came a growing despair.

CHAPTER 3

RUNNING, RIOTING, AND REVOLTING

Capitalists stopped chopping off hands, since workers needed them to make profit. But whipping, branding, beating, maiming, starving, and—every once in a while—burning or hanging were all legally permissible possibilities.

Workers responded by running, rioting, and revolting. In Virginia, the farmers, slaves, and servants who followed a man named Nathaniel Bacon did all three.

Ironically, Bacon's Rebellion began with pigs. A few people from the Indigenous Doeg Nation took some pigs from a white farmer to remedy a wrong done by the farmer. The farmer went after the pigs and ended up killing two Doeg citizens. Things seriously fell apart after that.

White farmers had been craving war with the Doeg Nation because war meant the Virginian army would likely remove the Doeg people from Doeg land, allowing white farmers to have it. But the Virginian government didn't want war for two reasons: One, the government was made up of rich folks who already had lots of great land far from the Doeg Nation. And two, the Virginian government was still England's government, and

England had treaties with the Indigenous nations to keep the colonists off Indigenous land.

England wasn't being nice by honoring these treaties. It was about money.

The fur trade was hopping. England was making big bucks selling beaver, muskrat, and fox fur. How much? The royally owned Hudson's Bay Company made more than $31 million in today's dollars in less than ten years . . . and the fur trade went on for more than two centuries. Corporations like this needed the Indigenous nations to allow them to operate on their lands. They also needed those lands to stay wild to keep trapping beaver, muskrat, and fox.

What they didn't need was a bunch of farmers plowing it under.

The Virginia government told the colonists to stay the hell off the Doeg Nation's land. But all those people who had been shut out by enclosures in the Old World were now pouring into the New World with the understanding that they'd soon be farmers again. Why? Because farming was what people did. Without it, what would they do? Keep working for other folks? This wasn't what any of them had signed up for. They'd signed up to own their own land in two to seven years.

Let's talk about land for a second. It was a place to grow food and live. It was also the only way to have a say in government. If you didn't own land, you couldn't vote. If you couldn't vote, you had no say in making laws. It's no wonder that all the laws in the land favored those people who owned it.

Unfortunately for wannabe farmers, the land that the colonies sat on was all taken up. The English Crown owned the land, along with rich corporations like the Dutch West India Company and the Hudson's Bay Company—land that had been either "bought" or stolen from Indigenous nations. The Crown and the companies granted this land to people they knew and liked. In other words, rich folks gave it to other rich folks.

In New York, three-fourths of the land was granted to just thirty people. The governor of New York once gave a friend of his half a million acres for 30 shillings. In today's dollars, that comes to about 120 bucks . . . not per acre but for half a million acres.

If you were a poor white farmer, you had to take your land directly from the other people who already owned it—Indigenous nations—without military aid or government "purchases." Of course, this taking of land further benefited wealthy landowners by creating a buffer between them and Indigenous nations. Both poor white farmers and Indigenous nations understood they were being exploited, and resentment ran high. It was easy to see why (1) the farmers wanted war, (2) the Doeg wanted the farmers gone, and (3) the Virginian government couldn't care less about either of them.

Back to Bacon.

Bacon wasn't a poor man. He had land—he just wanted more. But he represented a lot of poor white farmers and was elected to the government, where he quickly began organizing a war against the Doeg Nation. The government proclaimed him a rebel and threw him in jail. Thousands of farmers, runaway servants, and enslaved people marched into town to support him.

The jailers did not love the look of the gathering crowd. They released Bacon and warned him to chill out. Instead, he took off like a jackrabbit into the backwoods to organize his war.

Dammit, now the government had to send the army after him.

Bacon was definitely a bit of an asshole, but in the summer of 1676, folks were willing to follow him. It had been hot and dry, and the crops were dying. People were desperate, dirt poor, and fast becoming poorer. Land was hard to come by, and the less of it you had, the more you were taxed. Bacon's followers wanted equality. They wanted a say in government. And if they were slaves, they wanted freedom, which Bacon promised to those who joined him.

In the middle of the battle between Bacon and the army, Virginia granted free white men without land the right to vote. This was about to be a mini-democratic moment, but then Bacon got sick and died and the whole thing fell apart. White rebels were hanged. Black rebels were given back to their enslavers. And the right to vote was revoked.

Only the demoralization of working people remained.

Enslaved people were the most demoralized workers of all. A few years after Bacon, an enslaved man named Sam was busy organizing rebellions in Virginia. He certainly wasn't alone. There were over forty substantially organized revolts— those with extensive and detailed plots that made it into court records—before the outbreak of the Revolutionary War. But of course, smaller revolts were an everyday occurrence because life as a slave sucked.

Court records from May of 1688 reveal just how good Sam was at organizing. Local officials whipped him in public squares across two counties "*to deter him & others from the like evil practice for time to come*," and ruled that afterward "*hee have a strong Iron collar affixed about his neck with four spriggs [which] collar he is never to take or gett off nor to goe off his master or masters plantacon during all the time he shall live."*

But *rebelling for freedom* was the evil practice?

A year after Sam and ten years after Bacon, a man named Jacob Leisler led an army of artisans and laborers against the merchant aristocracy in New York City. Leisler ended up capturing Fort James in lower Manhattan. The governor of New York called the rebel group *"the scum of the people."*

Leisler led his scum right into power by arresting the governor and shipping him back to England. Now in control of the government, these men enacted a bit of democracy . . . like giving free white men without property the right to vote. Leisler was eventually overthrown and hanged, but unlike Bacon, the liberties he helped win stuck around.

Unfortunately, liberties won for free white men are not liberties won for all.

CAPITALISM GOES VIRAL

The American colonies were like an oppression factory. Indigenous people's land was invaded by white farmers. White farmers were controlled by the elite of the colonies. The colonies were exploited by England. And together, the colonies and England used and abused indentured servants and Black people. Out of this mess rose the free laborer—workers as we know them today.

The fastest-growing industry in the colonies was shipbuilding, and the best places for this industry were seaports and cities. Shipbuilding needed carpenters, rope makers, sailmakers, and more. In turn, these workers needed to eat and live—which brought in tradespeople to make houses, shoes, tools, and food.

Farming was still king, but farmers were like little family factories. They didn't need tradespeople. They made their own stuff. But in the cities, the population grew and the tradespeople settled in. The more work the tradespeople received, the more of their own workers they needed to employ.

More slaves? More indentured servants? Astoundingly, no. Not because anyone suddenly grew a conscience. But because . . . guess.

Money.

Enslaved people and indentured servants were workers who had to be fed, clothed, and housed all year long. The trades were seasonal. Masons didn't build in the middle of winter. Neither did carpenters repair the hulls of ships. It was much more economical to pay a worker a wage for a few months than it was to contract an indentured servant or buy a slave and need to care for them all year long or forever. Out of this need, the free laborer (or wage-earning worker) was born.

Since the big money was being made in ports and cities, farmers began traveling into town to sell their extra crops, using the money to buy some of the stuff they needed instead of making it all themselves. Today we call this the commodity market. Commodities are products that are bought and sold (like corn and coffee) instead of being consumed by the people who grew them.

So, the northern colonies were bustling . . . in the warmer months. People were working . . . in the warmer months. And in the colder months? People were freezing and starving.

Besides these very real winter doldrums, the price fluctuation for goods and services also wreaked havoc on the new wage-earning workers. When the price of goods fell, wages fell. When the price of goods rose, wages did not rise. If you're wondering why, well, so were the workers. They took their question to court. Pay attention to the answer, because it's still used today.

When prices fell, the colonial court told workers they should "*be content to abate their wages according to the fall of the commodities.*" When prices rose, workers were not given more because it was necessary, said the court, "*to save the American Workingman from himself.*" Or as one employer put it: "*high wages more frequently make laboring people miserable; they too commonly employ their spare time and cash, in debauching their morals and ruining their health."*

In other words, workers couldn't *handle* the money. Unlike the extremely moral wealthy class, who lived in mansions, traveled through the streets in sedan chairs carried by servants, and wore expensive white periwigs while people went hungry.

It's not surprising that the rioting and rebellions continued:

. . . over bread in Boston, when merchants sold all their grain to the Caribbean for a higher profit while Bostonians starved . . .

. . . over wages in Maine, when an employer withheld the pay of fishermen because he thought they wouldn't notice . . .

. . . and over being enslaved down in South Carolina.

Folks weren't looking to be carried around in chairs through the streets—they were looking for the bare minimum of equality, stability, and justice. To get it—like Nathaniel, Sam, and Jacob—they organized . . . but this time, at their jobs.

Guilds and benevolent societies formed around certain skills, as they'd been doing in Europe since the Middle Ages—carpenters, tailors, blacksmiths (and other trades) came together in groups to promote fair business practices, educate themselves in their fields, set wages and hours, create safe working conditions, and help fellow members and their families in times of need. These were very much the beginning of what we now call labor unions.

The guilds and benevolent societies struggled to stay together because they were widely scattered and had no real means of communication. Even so, they did see some small successes.

In 1734, a guild of maids in New York bought a page in a

newspaper to announce they were organizing for better working conditions: *we think it reasonable we should not be beat by our Mistrisses Husbands.* And in 1741, the Journeymen Caulkers of Boston—workers who sealed the hulls of ships to make them waterproof—organized to demand payment in cash instead of credit at stores. By sticking together, the maids experienced fewer beatings and the caulkers made actual money.

These budding groups even engaged in early strikes: walking off the job together in protest. A strike is a huge risk for working folks. It means throwing your entire life, and that of your family, into total uncertainty.

Will you lose your home?

Will you eat?

Will you ever work again?

Truckmen—workers who removed dirt from the street—refused to work until they were paid more per load. They were all fired "*for not obeying the Command and doing their Dutyes as becomes them in their Place.*"

Their place = their class.

Class in the American colonies was alive and well, and lots of people didn't like it.

When the governor of Massachusetts was riding his carriage into Boston, he came upon a group of carters on the road—workers who "carted," or carried, produce from the country into the city to sell. The governor ordered them out of the way so he could pass.

They refused. One of them shouted:

"*I am as good flesh and blood as you, you may go out of the way.*"

The carters were immediately arrested.

The incident was widely discussed among the wealthy and powerful. The working class seemed to be forgetting *their place.*

The working class hadn't forgotten their place. They just didn't like it. And the only way to change it was to change the laws that allowed them to be tossed into jail if they didn't get out of a rich man's way.

Working people needed in on government to have their interests represented. But democracy had not yet been established. The Revolutionary War had not yet happened, even if a few of the colonies did allow some free white men to vote.

Thanks to Leisler's Rebellion, New York was one of them. In 1734, a group of New York City's free white working men formed a group called the Popular Party, with the goal of electing working-class men to office. The Popular Party used the *New York Journal*—run by a man named John Peter Zenger—to get out its message with headlines like: "*A poor honest man is preferable to a rich knave.*"

Just how powerful is the press? For the first time in the history of the colonies, workers elected workers, and were now in control of a government. Into office came a baker, a bricklayer, a house painter, and a mechanic (an eighteenth-century name for a person who worked with their hands).

The upper class went ballistic. They howled that the people had been "*misled*" and the city was in the hands of "*men of the Low class.*" John Peter Zenger was arrested. The goal of the upper class? Stop the presses . . . they didn't own.

The press is where the stories that end up in our history textbooks are first recorded. The freer the press, the more perspectives are published; the wider the scope in history books, the more open we become to different people's points of view.

Zenger's lawyer argued the importance of freedom of the press before the United States was even the United States. And he won. But the battle against a free press would go on.

A few years later, the rich regained control of New York City's government. But then they lost it in Boston in 1740. These working white men were seriously turned up. Farmers, chimney sweeps, and mechanics began cooperating with each other to change their circumstances. In one instance, they voted for a land bank to print paper money, which would make it easier for them to engage in the economy. They got it passed. The rich opposed it—because it made it easier for the working class to engage in the economy—and ran to the British government, who held the last say in the American colonies. Great Britain terminated the land bank.

The working class might have lost their bank, but the solidarity they were forging—between farmers and urban workers, between carters and house painters, between bricklayers and bakers—was about to come in handy. When the Founding Fathers proposed a revolution in response to unfair British taxation, they would use this solidarity to forge something even better: a more democratic country.

A RIOTOUS MOB FOUNDS
A NATION

The American colonies existed for one reason only: to increase the profits of British manufacturing, merchants, and landlords. According to Harvard historian John C. Miller: *"A handful of English capitalists carried more weight at Westminster [the seat of government in England] than the welfare of millions of Americans."*

The colonies could only sell to Great Britain, and at prices fixed by Great Britain. They also couldn't buy anything from any other country but Great Britain. On top of this, they weren't allowed to build certain kinds of mills, forges, or furnaces—to keep from competing with Great Britain. And they weren't allowed to move west into Indigenous lands because of the fur trade making the British all that money.

These rules were hurting just about every white man in the colonies—merchants, farmers, dockworkers, sailors—but it was the well-off whose chatter about Great Britain's "economic tyranny" edged the colonies toward war.

White working men already knew a thing or two about economic tyranny—and they began to organize against Great Britain the way they'd organized against the rich in the colonies. This new development made the upper-class colonials pretty nervous.

Gouverneur Morris—the writer who would ten years later pen the famous "we the people" part of the United States Constitution—was one of these nervous rich men, saying: *"The mob begin to think and to reason. I see, and I see with fear and trembling, that if the disputes with Britain continue, we shall be under the domination of a riotous mob. It is to the interest of all men, therefore, to seek for reunion with the parent state."*

"Seek reunion" with Great Britain? From the "we the people" guy?

Gouverneur Morris may have started pulling back on his revolutionary rhetoric, but "the mob" of whom he spoke—those white working men—were on a roll and continued to push the cause.

Forget guilds and benevolent societies. Farmers and laborers now formed their own military organizations: the Regulators, the Associators, the United Company. In history books we often refer to them as a single group called the Sons of Liberty.

Morris called them *"reptiles."*

Led by merchants and the professional class, the Sons of Liberty rallied against the British in the streets. They got the hated Stamp Act (a law taxing just about every piece of paper in the colonies, from wills to newspapers) repealed. They succeeded in boycotting British tea. They educated one another inside taverns, where everything was read aloud for people who couldn't read. Plus, they did a lot of singing.

They sang songs against the tyranny of British rule, but they also sang songs against the tyranny of those at home.

White working women joined in too, creating the Daughters of Liberty. These radical societies, which had started inside northern cities, soon spread—bringing into the fold farmers and white workers as far south as Charleston. They were essentially an intercolonial union of white working-class people creating white working-class solidarity.

When the British tried to hire workers to build soldier barracks in Boston, workers refused. The British increased the wages. The workers still wouldn't build. When more workers were called in from other areas . . . they too declined to build the barracks.

The wealthy and powerful attempted to control the *reptiles* by creating their own organizations. But working folks continued to remind these lofty fellows just what it was working people were after: equality. In the words of a mechanic from Philly: "*Have we not an equal Right of electing or being elected? I think it absolutely necessary that one or two Mechanics be elevated to represent so large a Body of the Inhabitants.*"

The guy had a point. Working-class people should be represented in government. They weren't back then—the reason this man was about to fight a war—and they aren't today. Out of our forty-six presidents, thirty-seven of them were/are millionaires (or wealthier). At the writing of this book, the median net worth of members in Congress is over $1 million. The working class rarely holds public office.

Back in the colonies with war approaching, the mechanics forced the wealthy and powerful to work with them, from local meetings straight up to electing the Continental Congress (the first governing body in the budding nation). In Boston, an aristocrat wrote that their town meeting "*was carried on by a mob of the lowest sort of people,*" where "*the lowest Mechanicks discuss upon the most important points of government with the utmost freedom.*"

This idea, that anyone can stand up and speak—that the democratic experience should actually be democratic—is what we say makes this country great today. But it wasn't what the wealthy and powerful had in mind back then. The working class led the colonies into revolution for all the good things we tell ourselves about being Americans: liberty, democracy, happiness, and equality. These once radical ideas ended up becoming our most celebrated norms.

AN ORGY OF FRAUD

The working class fought and won, and the United States was born. What had workers learned from revolution?

Collective action.

Militancy.

Communication.

Collaboration.

Lessons they'd put to good use as they turned away from one foe (England) to face the next (industry).

Trade with other countries boomed now that British rule was no more. France and Great Britain were at war with one another and, on top of this, both were experiencing crop failure. American capitalists took advantage of the situation and invested heavily in taking over the French and British trade of commodities—grain, cotton, tobacco, peas, corn, etc.—to Europe and Asia.

Industry—the making of goods—was slower out of the gate. The number one reason was because goods were still being made in Great Britain. The United States also lacked roads to support industrial growth. Southern elites piled on by forbidding taxa-tion on goods coming in and out of the country, since they were busy importing enslaved people and exporting cotton and tobacco and didn't want either taxed. This made goods coming into the country cheap and therefore hard to compete with. Finally, individual farms were still tiny industrial centers all to themselves, making their own tools and clothes and growing their own food. They didn't need to purchase much of anything outside their little worlds.

Slowly, the transportation infrastructure began to develop, just as that war between the French and British messed things up for American foreign trade.

Hang on here as we go through this.

First, Britain and France kept stealing American stuff off ships, including the sailors, who they forced into their war. The US responded by stopping all foreign trade with the Embargo Act. But this cost capitalists money, and since they were in charge of the government, they nixed the Embargo Act and instituted the Non-Intercourse Act. This might sound like they tried to stop people from having sex, but what it really did was reopen American foreign trade to everybody *but* Great Britain and France. Capitalists were back in business . . . until that Non-Intercourse Act pissed off Great Britain and led to the War of 1812, a second war between Great Britain and the United States. That war with Great Britain meant no stuff like clothes and shoes coming from Great Britain, which meant the United States needed to create its own. Industry was on its way.

American industry started in the north, while the economy in the south stayed completely based on agriculture and the abundance of enslaved labor. A mutually beneficial partnership formed as the budding textile mills of northern industry were fed by the cotton from southern fields, fueling the profit and growth of both.

This north-south alliance, combined with the growing market economy and the theft of Indigenous lands (following two centuries of war with Indigenous nations), swelled into a perfect storm for capitalism. It provided a giant labor force of which a large part went unpaid, as well as an abundance of cheap/free (stolen) land that contained raw materials and the space to build mills and factories. Between the end of the Revolutionary War and the beginning of the Civil War—approximately eighty years—the United States went from not having any industry to being number four in the entire world.

Thirty years after that, it was number one.

The first factory was built in Pawtucket, Rhode Island, by a thief named Samuel Slater. Slater stole plans for the machinery to spin yarn from his boss in England and then quickly took off for the United States. It was against the law to do this, but no one prosecuted Slater. Instead, he became fabulously rich.

Slater's first hires were young children—handing the title of first American factory workers to seven-year-olds. Young women were its second. Slater wasn't alone in his success. Other factories were cropping up all over the north: shoes, iron, steel. And with them came the growth of another institution: the corporation.

A corporation is a group of individuals authorized by law to exist as a person. The corporation was born in Europe and sailed over to North America as early as 1587 with English colonizers. The first permanent settlements—in Virginia and New England—were both corporate ventures.

Corporations are only alive on paper, although right from their beginning, the law has treated them as people. A corporation has a name (like a person). It has the right to hold property (like a person). It can sue and be sued (like a person), but—incredibly—the owners of the corporation (who are people) are not personally responsible for anything the corporation does. So they can rack up lawsuits and debt that not a single real person is responsible for. Corporations also have the right to free speech (like a person). A corporation can't cast an actual vote, yet it can use its profits to support the candidate it chooses (just like a person). Between the Revolutionary War and the Civil War, over 22,000 corporations were born in America.

Iron companies were the first to be incorporated in large numbers, and pretty much invented what would become known as the "company town." This was a town completely owned by the corporation—the land, the factories, the schools, the churches, the houses, and the stores. The iron companies were also the first to pay wages without handing someone a check or money. Instead, they paid workers by giving them a number on a piece of paper that they could then take to stores to buy things they needed. The catch was that the paper was only good at company stores, where the corporation fixed prices and made a profit off their workers a second time. It also locked workers inside the company town, as moving somewhere else with a number on a piece of paper didn't work. These iron company towns made so much money for their shareholders that the idea would take off across the United States following the Civil War.

The power of corporations was first seen in 1850, when the Boston Associates—an early American corporation of fifteen families—controlled 20 percent of the entire nation's cotton spindle industry, while also owning 30 percent of the railroads, 39 percent of the insurance industry, and 40 percent of the banking industry in the state of Massachusetts. With this ownership, they controlled the press, the churches, the schools, the factories, and the legislature in not just a town—but the entire state of Massachusetts. That is one powerful "person."

Next, business associations formed. These were groups of owners of the corporations in a single industry who met to discuss stuff. Unfortunately, some of that stuff was price and wage fixing, which is agreeing together to price goods at a certain amount and pay workers a certain amount to discourage competition.

Hanging out together in these associations gave these corporations another idea called monopolies. This is when companies buy up other companies, becoming one gigantic company. With competition gone, corporations have free rein to lift prices, lower wages, and sell inferior products.

Railroads were known for their monopolies, which engaged in what one historian called "*an orgy of fraud.*" During their heyday, railroads spent hundreds of thousands of dollars bribing congressmen for land grants, cheap loans, and tax subsidies.

These years of growth between the wars weren't all economic heaven. In fact, this unchecked capitalism caused severe crises in 1819, 1837, 1854, 1857, and 1860. When these recessions and depressions took place, capitalists blamed it on overproduction. The factories fell silent, and workers went home to starve and freeze.

Overproduction: too many shoes, too much cloth, too much coal and steel and iron.

What went unsaid was that many of the workers who made all this "too much" didn't earn enough to purchase it. And that Samuel Slater made $700,000 in forty years, which is many millions in our time. And that iron companies reported dividends—money given to their stockholders—of between 40–100 percent.

What also went unsaid was that if capitalists took less and paid workers more, those workers could then afford to purchase the goods they themselves had made, eliminating the "over" part of overproduction, stemming misery, and avoiding the economic recessions and depressions.

Wasn't America rich enough to provide for everyone?

The working class knew it was working hard for the country's prosperity. It also knew it was not experiencing that prosperity.

Another thing it knew?

The United States did not need more capitalists.

CHAPTER 7

FATAL FLAW

O nto the scene walked more capitalists.

These fellows, called merchant capitalists, stood between the small shops and the market to take a cut. They spelled the beginning of the end for those small shops, which were also helped out history's door by growing factories and machines. But before small shops disappeared, workers inside them would organize in the same way the guilds and benevolent societies of pre–Revolutionary War times did: around their specific skills.

The small shop was filled with "skilled" workers—people who had spent years learning to do something specific, like make shoes. If you made shoes, you were called a cordwainer, and you didn't just walk into a shop and train in a day to cordwain. It took years to master the skills.

The Philadelphia cordwainers created an organization where an oath was taken to stand by a worker-agreed wage scale, keep all conversations of the workers secret, and help other cordwainers in times of need. The idea took off in other shops, and for a bit, they seemed to work.

But the Philadelphia Cordwainers' Organization had a fatal

flaw—they did not allow "unskilled" workers called apprentices to join. (Note: *unskilled* is a terrible term, although a historic one, because it always, always takes skill to do a job.)

When the organization went on strike, the merchant capitalists didn't miss a beat: they immediately had the shopkeeper hire the apprentices in their place.

Sure, things were slow for a bit as the apprentices learned to make shoes, but they were also paid way less, so the shopkeepers and the merchant capitalists made way more. The merchant capitalists told the cordwainers that if they wanted their jobs back, they would now have to work at apprentice-level pay. And they didn't stop there.

They took the Philadelphia cordwainers to court. At the time, our laws were still based on English common law, which made it illegal for workers to gather together to ask for higher wages (now called collective bargaining). It was considered *"conspiracy against the good of society."* The law was upheld and the cordwainer organization was crushed. Having skills had given the cordwainers a false sense of security.

(In case you were wondering about those business organizations where owners of corporations got together to set prices and wages . . . no, they were not against English common law.)

Not being allowed to organize was just *one* of the two big problems facing workers in the new country. The other was the argument going on in the government between the Federalists and the Democratic Republicans over what our United States Constitution should and should not say. This argument surrounded the biggest word of the day.

Slavery.

In most history books, this fight is explained as Alexander Hamilton and the Federalists vying for a powerful central government against Thomas Jefferson and the Democratic Republicans vying for powerful state governments. This is true, but what did it mean?

It meant a fight between the northern wealthy capitalists (Federalists) and the southern wealthy plantation owners (Democratic Republicans).

The Federalists' strong central government included a lifetime appointment of the president, like a king. It called democracy a *"government of the worst."* And John Jay, a Founding Father and a Federalist, said: *"Those who own the country ought to govern it."*

Oh, John Jay.

But they were also the party calling for the end of slavery. Not because they cared about Black folks, but because the end of slavery would mean the end of southern power, giving all the power to them.

The Democratic Republicans' "states' rights" simply meant the right to keep slavery going. Ironically, these were also the folks who championed the Bill of Rights to protect freedom of speech, freedom of the press, freedom of religion, etc.

Slavery vs. No Slavery.

If anyone is thinking that this was a different time and that these folks just didn't get that enslaving people was wrong, think again.

Alexander Hamilton, a slave owner, said that slavery was *"fatal to religion and morality,"* and Thomas Jefferson, a slave owner, wrote: *"This abomination must have an end, and there is a superior bench reserved in heaven for those who hasten it."*

Jefferson is not sitting on that bench.

The bottom line here is that neither party was anything to write home about. But for white male workers, the choice was clear, because one party—the southern Democratic Republicans—included them in its Bill of Rights.

Not legally allowed to organize around their jobs, white working men pulled another "Sons of Liberty." But instead of forming military organizations, now they formed political groups called Democratic Societies or Republican Clubs. They loudly supported Thomas Jefferson and the Democratic Republicans.

The Federalists fought back against what they called the "*people's movement*" with colorful lies, stating that if these workers won, "*the Bible will be cast into a bonfire and the wives and daughters of Americans would become the victims of legal prostitution.*"

How did this turn out?

The Democratic Republicans won. The Bill of Rights became law. And white working men's ability to vote exploded. White wives and daughters did not become sex workers, but neither did hundreds of thousands of Black people become free.

CHAPTER 8

YOU MADE IT!

Welcome to 1827, the year historians tell us the actual US labor movement began.

It all starts in the city of brotherly love, Philadelphia, where organizations, guilds, and benevolent societies gave way to the actual use of the word *union* in the formation of the Philadelphia Mechanics' Union of Trade.

With the battle between the Federalists and Democratic Republicans mostly settled and the wishy-washy War of 1812 fought to a draw, workers were once again organizing to improve their working lives. This time they'd go big around a single issue that concerned them all: the ten-hour workday.

To be clear . . . the above "all" means "skilled white men." Unskilled men, white women, Black, Asian, Indigenous, Latine, and disabled workers were not included in this beginning organization. They would be included over time, but—and this is a really big but—sexism, racism, and ableism will exist inside unions until the day you're reading this.

The normal workday was twelve to sixteen hours long, and employers and merchant capitalists aimed to keep it this way. So they took these "trade unions" to court to stop them on the basis of conspiracy. They also went out to the newspapers they owned, to sway the court of public opinion using the usual nonsense that working fewer hours would *"exert a very unhappy influence"* on workers by *"seducing them from that course of industry and economy of time, to which we [the employers] are anxious to ensure them."*

But they also tried out something new—the language of false patriotism—where anything good for capitalism is labeled American and anything bad for capitalism is labeled un-American. Trade unions, they argued, were *"un-American,"* and had been brought over from Europe by *"foreigners"* who carried with them *"a spirit of discontent and insubordination to which our native Mechanics have hitherto been strangers."*

Un-American.

Foreigners.

Natives.

Capitalists had discovered the pyramid of oppression—dividing people up into categories, ranking those categories based on differences the capitalists themselves promote, and then turning the categories against each other to fight over the promoted differences. In other words, turning the struggle into one between "real" Americans and unpatriotic Americans, foreigners and native born, skilled and unskilled, etc., distracting from the true struggle between owners and workers for a ten-hour workday.

The pyramid was successful this first time in Philly . . . and the second, and a few more times. But each time it won, it also brought on more solidarity. Unions across the city eventually united, and the mechanics won their ten-hour workday.

Boston and New York immediately jumped into the ten-hour

fight. Boston failed to win ten hours but did win a bunch of wage increases. New York succeeded.

These victories were a boon for the new trade unions, and membership jumped from 25,000 to over 300,000! City unions spawned smaller organizations they called "locals," with the city unions acting as a federation or umbrella organization. The structure of a union as it exists today began to emerge.

Over fifty union newspapers cropped up, giving workers a place to express their ideas, needs, and desires, as well as competing with the powerful capitalist-owned papers consistently reporting that trade unions made workers "*lazy*" and were filled with "*foreigners*" exerting "*an unhappy influence*" on real Americans.

By 1834, workers had organized the first national union. It proposed that every working person be supported by all working people. Solidarity: the ultimate working-class superpower. The new National Trades' Union came up with a list of the demands of working people:

National minimum wages
National working hours
Public education
Free lending libraries

At this time in US history, there was no public education or public libraries, but there was forced military service and debtors' prison. Men needed to show up for military service three times a year, and if they missed any, they were fined $12—about three weeks' salary. Meanwhile, the rich paid their twelve bucks and stayed home.

If the penalty for a crime is a fine, it is only a crime for people who can't afford it.

Those who couldn't pay the fine were thrown in debtors' prison. Over 75,000 men sat in prison for debt in 1830. Convicts were then hired out by the government to work in industry—a practice that continues today. So: men worked for a pittance, and if they couldn't afford to stop work and serve in the military, they were imprisoned and forced to work for free.

The working-class people who stayed out of prison were taxed heavily, but there were many tax exemptions for wealthy property owners. Any person attempting to leave the working class to join the business class hit big barriers, as creating a corporation cost money and needed approval from a government run by the already successful.

Corporations, on the other hand, continued to enjoy the perks of being corporations, one of which was going bankrupt right before payday. Since the bankrupt corporation was no longer in existence, there was no one to sue, and the workers were out of their wages.

Working-class people needed to be represented in government— as was clear to the working people of New Castle, Delaware, who in 1829 announced in their newspaper, "*The laws are made by the rich and of course for the rich.*"

This was also clear to the city unions of Philadelphia, New York, and Boston. So they attempted to enter politics by supporting representatives who supported them or by putting up representatives of their own. This first real foray into politics by unions got them seriously schooled.

The major newspapers—all owned by capitalists—came down hard, saying these men were "*lost to society, to earth and to heaven*" due to "*engaging in incest, robbery and murder.*" It's no wonder Philadelphia and Boston unions lost their first elections. New York unions fared a little better, having a few of their representatives elected.

The unions might not have been totally successful at their first attempts to gain a shorter workday or representation in government, but they did make it known they were around. This first flexing of the labor movement's official muscles saw:

> *the beginning of public education*
> *the creation of public libraries*
> *an end to forced military service*
> *the closing of debtors' prisons*
> *the emergence of a fairer tax system*
> *a full stop to the notion that working people organizing was*
> *conspiracy, and*
> *the establishment of a ten-hour workday for federal*
> *employees.*

They were on a roll. Nothing could stop them now!

CHAPTER 9

HEAVEN AND HELL

Except a depression. This one in 1837.

Along with the economic collapse of the country came the collapse of the fledgling labor movement. Wages were cut. Jobs were lost. Food and roof-over-head worries replaced union organizing. The National Trades' Union vanished.

With the working class on its knees, employers and capitalists attacked through the commercial press (privately funded and for-profit newspapers): *"Employ no men who do not forever abjure the unions"* and *"The rules of the unions as to hours, pay, and everything else, ought to be thoroughly broken up."*

But there were other voices out there . . . and these voices were saying the future could be brighter for the suffering working class. Who were these folks?

The Utopian Socialists.

Yikes. Socialism. A big word in America. Let's chat about it, along with some other words often partnered with it: capitalism and communism. These three words have complex meanings and even more complex histories. At the most basic, they are economic systems.

Capitalism is when private property and private profits drive a country's economic system, with the "free market" determining what is produced, how much is produced, and who gets the stuff produced.

Socialism is when people drive the economic system for the benefit of people, with people deciding what is produced, how much is produced, and who gets the stuff produced.

Communism has collective/government ownership driving the economic system, with property collectively held by the state, which works to produce products for everybody.

Capitalism came over from Europe to the colonies in the form of corporations, companies, and royalty: wealthy people looking for more wealth. It was a first come, first served system, and the American colonies made corporations, companies, and royalty even more rich. In turn, this wealth made them even more powerful. And by using words like *individual* and *freedom*, they created a vision where everyone is free to individually make their own fortunes. But do we?

According to the National Academy of Sciences, we don't. For the last 150 years, each generation has made less than the generation before it. The long-term trend in US history for social mobility is downward, not upward.

But what about hard work paying off?

Sometimes it does, but more often—according to the National Academy of Sciences—it doesn't. The class you're born into, the sex you're born as, and the color of your skin still have more of an effect on you economically than hard work. Capitalism is historically a difficult system to get ahead in if you're not already ahead. But if you are already ahead, it's a good way to stay there.

Is capitalism democratic?

No, democracy is a system of government, not an economic system. Democracy gives everybody a say in the laws of the land. The United States is what is called a representative democracy. Everybody has a say by voting for people to represent us, like senators and presidents.

A democracy can have a capitalist economy. A democracy can have a socialist economy. A democracy can have a communist economy. Most democratic countries around the world today are a mix of these three economic systems—but the trend is toward capitalism.

Is this a good thing?

Not according to the Utopian Socialists in 1837.

These men believed the economy should be run for the benefit of all people. They spoke out, saying that capitalists had gained control of the economy and used the profits to benefit themselves and nobody else. Whenever these profits stopped, they simply shut down, and misery ensued for workers.

For working people, this was a truth they lived.

Next came the utopian part. The Utopian Socialists dreamed of a better world: one without slavery and oppression, based on the shared values of society, including universal freedom and peace. The only hitch was that capitalists would have to step aside. But working people weren't so focused on that hitch. Instead, they focused on the heavenly vision presented by two of the biggest Utopian Socialists.

Robert Owen came from Wales, where he owned factories in which he experimented with his utopian theories. He advocated for the creation of cooperative communities where private property was abolished. He supported some cool things, like working only eight hours a day, promoting public education, and stopping child labor.

Charles Fourier came from France and was also into cooperative communities, only without the "no private property" thing. Owen and Fourier also disagreed on where society should head, toward industry or farms. Owen said industry. Fourier said farms. But both were into remaking the world, which the working people of 1837 were totally into since their world stunk.

Many working folks joined in on cooperatives started by these men and ended up living better lives inside the pocket of these great ideals. But these cooperatives didn't catch on for a lot of reasons, maybe the first of which was that hitch: capitalists weren't about to step aside.

In fact, capitalists actively denounced socialism and communism, turning these economic systems into everything the United States was against. Over the centuries, this would help solidify capitalism as "American," keeping wealthy Americans in power. Since red is the color of revolution, and socialism and communism were seen as revolutionary horrors (unlike the American Revolution, which was portrayed as necessary and good), socialism and communism became synonymous with "red." A *red scare* meant the "American way of life" was in danger of being toppled by socialism or communism or both, and *red-baiting* meant harassing or persecuting folks whose ideas were known or suspected of being sympathetic to these two economic systems.

Despite capitalists making out socialism and communism to be the big bad, regular Americans kept coming up with socialist and communist ideas. George Henry Evans was one such American. He formed a group called the Agrarians. His suggestion was to divvy up public lands owned by the US government—lands stolen from Indigenous nations, remember—and hand them out to workers.

According to Agrarians, everyone would live on a farm and the industrial cities would fall to pieces. Evans painted a nice picture for the starving millions in cities dreaming of a way out of growing industrialization. But it was only a dream, and most of them knew it, as this factory worker makes clear: "*We could not travel to the West without money. And we cannot save money; it is as much as we can do to provide for our families with necessaries.*"

Working people might have been dreaming with Robert, Charles, and George, but they were also rebuilding their unions—believing that, as one worker said: "*Our salvation must, through the blessing of God, come from ourselves.*"

Back to work they went, this time on a dream they had more control over: bringing back the ten-hour workday, which the depression had wiped out along with their wages.

Back to work went the capitalists as well—who endlessly repeated that working fewer hours would "*increase crime, suffering, wickedness, and pauperism.*" And that it wasn't the hours that people worked in a day that broke people down, but the "*hours spent in dissipation,*" which is a throwback term for drinking a lot and getting into trouble.

On top of crushing hours and diminishing wages, employers began something new called a speedup. This was a part of the day when everyone had to work faster. For example, where normally women in factories had been in charge of two looms making about 270 picks a minute, they were now in charge of four looms at 480 picks a minute. What's a pick? It's a weaving thing, and let's just guess that having to do so many of them was exhausting.

For the employers, speedups meant more profit. For the women, speedups meant a lot more work for the exact same pay, plus exhaustion.

When the Massachusetts Corporation in Lowell decided to make the speedup the norm while also decreasing wages, the women were like, *hell no*. They'd been working the factory floor since 1790—about fifty years—and not much had changed. Led by a weaver named Sarah G. Bagley, they formed the Female Labor Reform Association and all signed a pledge stating they wouldn't speed up.

Every single woman stayed true to the pledge. The company was forced to stop the speedup.

Bagley became a big voice for labor. She was a writer as well as a fighter, and when the corporations threatened to blacklist any woman who joined these associations, Bagley shouted from the now-returning labor newspapers: *"Deprive us, after working thirteen hours, of saying our lot is a hard one! We will make the name of him who dares the act stink with every wind."*

Bagley's Female Labor Reform Association helped lead the second big fight for the ten-hour workday—engaging in both strikes and politics. Thousands of workers signed a petition begging the government to step in and save them from *"a premature grave."*

Some state governments listened and instituted committees to discuss the long workday. But—as this bit of hell on earth would have it—all the committees were made up of corporate men. Therefore, their findings went like this: *"The mills could not be improved by any suggestion of ours."*

Workers didn't give up, and some states agreed to make the ten-hour workday a law. But—more hell on earth—those that did also voted in a clause that allowed employers to draw up special contracts with workers for more than ten hours. Before the law was even passed, employers had already drawn up those special contracts, and the ten-hour fight was lost a second time.

Dealt this blow, the unions dialed back and tossed white women and unskilled workers out of their ranks.

But it's always a mistake to boot out people like Sarah G. Bagley.

FOREIGNERS AND FRIGHTFUL ATROCITIES

Into this mess sailed a whole lot more people. Utopian dreams weren't just for workers on the continent of North America. Europeans were also dreaming of a better life.

In 1840, there were about 17 million people living in the United States.

In 1860, there were over 21 million people living in the United States.

This big jump in immigration can be chalked up to something called the Springtime of the Peoples (or the Revolutions of 1848), which began in France in 1848 but wound up spreading across the European continent to include fifty countries. Working people revolted against what historians call absolutism—kings and queens holding absolute power. All over Europe, people fought for a democratic society—freedom of the press, a more equal economy, and a voice in government.

They didn't get it. And so they crossed the Atlantic to the United States, where supposedly, these ideals lived.

What else lived here?

Economic strife.

In 1857, yet another depression hit, bringing unemployment and hunger. For every boat pouring hopeful immigrants into the US, there was a crowd of disillusioned immigrants standing on the dock attempting to catch a ride back home. But without jobs or money, everybody was pretty much stuck.

Except the capitalists, who were jubilant.

Employers sent agents down to the docks to meet ships and engage the newcomers for half the money they were paying the people who were already employed by them—thereby forcing existing workers to accept lower wages or walk away jobless.

The working class watched the wave of immigrants hitting American shores with fear and anger. This made employers even happier—a new opportunity to apply the pyramid of oppression by declaring American workers "nativists" and immigrant workers "foreigners." The low wages and living standards, employers said, were the fault of the foreigners "*who feed upon the coarsest, cheapest and roughest fare—stalk about in rags and filth—and are neither fit associates for American laborers and mechanics nor reputable members of any society.*"

Some workers bought into the pyramid, where powerless people are directed to turn against each other based on cultural, racial, or religious differences in order to deflect awareness from the people actually oppressing them. Working-class groups like the Order of United Americans and the United Daughters of America cropped up—huffing about patriotism and the superiority of the native born. These groups fought to make it harder for immigrants to come to the United States and harder for them to become citizens if they did make it here.

Other workers saw behind the propaganda of scapegoating

immigrants. A leading labor newspaper, *America's Own*, wrote: *"The feeling of animosity which exists against foreign mechanics was originally started by employers to distract your attention from measures of importance and which would ultimately prove of real practical benefit to you."*

Opening their arms to immigrants would prove to be very practical for working people. These foreign folks had lived through the Springtime of the Peoples and were totally up for the fight against employers and capitalists.

The Irish came over almost entirely as unskilled workers and were at first unwanted by the unions. But these Emerald Islanders quickly became union assets. Centuries of butting up against English rule had made them experts in both struggle and at standing up for themselves. English immigrants arrived on US shores already knowing a ton about unions, and many of them headed into American coal mines carrying that knowledge with them. Germans just brought their unions right along with them. There were so many German unions that they rivaled the membership of the US-based unions. Another thing the Germans brought was their antislavery ideals, which helped kick the abolition movement up a few notches.

Of the 4 million immigrants who braved the crossing of the Atlantic at this time, barely any of them headed south, to what was called the Cotton Kingdom.

The reason?

Slavery.

Selling Black people into bondage in the United States had been so profitable that by 1860, enslaved people made up almost 20 percent of the entire country's population—that's approximately 4 million people living in complete misery.

As one British diplomat wrote in a letter home in 1854: "*The frightful atrocities of slave holding must be seen to be described.*"

By this time in history, these frightful atrocities had been the norm in America for 250 years. In all that time, little had changed for these workers—although not for lack of trying. Just as free white workers in the American north were fighting for a better life, Black enslaved workers in the American south also fought. But—and this is a super-important point—there is no comparison between being an oppressed white worker in the north and being an oppressed Black slave in the south, as this shoe worker in Massachusetts pointed out in 1860:

"*You know we are not a quarter as bad off as the slaves of the South though we are by our foolishness ten times as bad off as we ought to be. They can't vote, nor complain and we can. Then just think of it, the slaves can't hold mass meetings, nor 'strike' and we haven't lost that privilege yet, thank the Lord.*"

Enslaved people couldn't gather, vote, or even complain. However, for over two centuries they organized against their oppressors both individually and collectively.

There are hundreds of written accounts of Black people individually standing up against the practice of slavery. Most of these accounts come from white slave owners, because slaves were kept uneducated for the further protection of the white aristocracy. Education was (and is) dangerous to small groups of ruling people. The more educated people are, the easier it is for them to engage in their communities. The small group of slave owners didn't want the 20 percent of the nation's population they kept in chains engaged.

All these accounts are heartbreaking, and often end with the individual being beaten or murdered. Even more heartbreaking is when the individual died by suicide. Like the Lokono in the fifteenth century, without hope, some Black folks saw all-the-way-out as the only way out.

But many others took a different route and banded together in collective action by using work stoppages. As a group, they laid down their tools and refused to work until conditions were changed, though instead of asking for higher wages or shorter hours, these stoppages had more to do with not being lashed or whipped.

Black folks also ran. By the tens of thousands they headed north to Canada. Many did it alone. Some in groups. Others made use of the Underground Railroad with the help of heroic people like Harriet Tubman. No matter how they did it, every single one of them needed tremendous courage and strength. An abolitionist recalled the story of one Black man who had *"come 1,200 miles from the lower part of Alabama, traveling only at night, feeding on roots and wild berries. He swam every river from Tuscaloosa to Pennsylvania."*

The most explosive way the enslaved organized against their oppressors was through insurrection. Gabriel Prosser in 1800, Denmark Vesey in 1822, and Nat Turner in 1831—along with over 250 others—coordinated to attack the practice of slavery. They did it knowing that the law, private southern militias, and the US Army stood against them.

These uprisings did win some improvements. A handful of southern states reduced the working hours from sixteen to fifteen hours a day in the spring and summer, and from fifteen to fourteen hours in the fall and winter. Georgia instituted penalties on slave owners for overworking Black workers. And Louisiana gave more time for dinner.

The ridiculousness of these changes highlights the obscenity of slavery. However, it was slavocracy's harsh response to the uprisings—the torture and hanging of these courageous people—that fueled the growing abolitionist movement taking hold in the north.

Southern cotton lords understood that free white workers had more in common with enslaved people than they did with rich cotton owners, and so they did everything they could think of to obscure this fact. They succeeded for far too long, but the moment did come when free white workers realized that as working people, their fate was tied to Black enslaved workers. That moment was westward expansion.

Westward expansion was the use of violent force and genocide through the Mexican-American War and the Indian Removal Act combined with Manifest Destiny—the propaganda that it was destiny for white people to conquer a large swath of North America. Expansion had begun around 1810 and was hopping at this time in 1860.

This seized territory was now becoming states . . . but free states or slave states?

Working folks were beginning to see the writing on the wall. Sentiments like this were cropping up in labor newspapers across the north: "*In the South we hear the clanking chains and heart-rending pleadings of the sons of Africa that they may have freedom—while in the north the voice of our laboring classes ascends up to heaven in earnest prayer, that they too may be free from the galling yoke of aristocratic power. What a picture our country presents—then why add more of this corrupting evil to the already heart-sickening fact of slavery and bondage?"*

The southern powers did not take this sitting down, hitting back hard in their own newspapers: *"Slavery is the natural and normal condition of the laboring man. Master and slave is a relation in society as necessary as that of parent and child, and the Northern States will yet have to introduce it. The theory of free society is a delusion."* Basically, southern power was saying that northern power would come to realize the necessity of slave labor.

White workers were quick to rise up. In New York and New Jersey, 15,000 workers rallied against slavery. In New Hampshire and Pennsylvania, workers came together to write resolutions in opposition to slavery. Similar meetings were being held in Illinois, Ohio, Massachusetts, Michigan, Vermont, Connecticut, Indiana, and Wisconsin.

Out of this argument between slave state or free state, the two-party system of Democratic Republicans (now called just Democrats) and Whigs (who took over as the second party after the defunct Federalists) started to unravel.

Workers had been supporting the Democrats since the Revolutionary War. But the Democrats were the party of slavery. The Whigs, however, were the party of northern industry. Neither was a party that workers wanted in on. Out in Wisconsin, a worker and union man named Alvin E. Bovay began a third party, the Republican Party.

Tired of the Whigs and the Democrats, Bovay hoped to bring together liberals and reformers dedicated to stopping slavery (yay!) and supporting a "free" land program called the

Homestead Act (No! That land wasn't free!).

The workers went Republican.

The rich were split. Should they stay with the conservative Whigs, who more and more had been bowing to the southern power of the Democratic Party, or join the new Republican Party? Fear of the south seceding from the United States had many staying with the Whigs, as a top Boston newspaper noted: *"The truth is that Republicanism is neither more nor less than Radicalism."* When people fear something, they usually call it names. *Radical* is often one of those names.

Then John Brown happened.

Brown was a leading abolitionist—a white man who had been fighting against slavery for years. Frustrated by his inability to stop a disgusting practice using peaceful means, he moved to violence. His plan was to rouse a slave liberation movement in Virginia by raiding an armory with a small group of men and handing the weapons to enslaved people.

Abolitionist leaders Frederick Douglass and Harriet Tubman met with Brown about the plan. Douglass didn't think it could work. Harriet Tubman wanted in on it. Had she not fallen ill, she would have been fighting alongside him.

Brown was caught, tried, and hanged by the state of Virginia. As Eugene V. Debs—you'll meet him later—said, John Brown *"dared the whole world and gave up his life for freedom. What more can a man do?"*

Brown's attempt to end slavery was supported by the masses of working people. It was not supported by those wealthy conservatives who had joined the Republican Party, and they quickly tamped down their antislavery chitchat. But the election of 1860 was right around the corner, and the workers pushed back. It would be an antislavery candidate for president of the United States or no support for the candidate from the working class.

Along came Abraham Lincoln.

The lawyer from Illinois was well known to small farmers and laborers because he had come from a working-class family. Lincoln's father was a farmer and a carpenter. Immigrants also liked him because he supported a fast track to citizenship. Lincoln frequently spoke about the amazing contributions of these foreign-born Americans. And of course, he spoke glowingly of labor. *"Capital is the fruit of labor, and could never have existed if labor had not first existed; that labor can exist without capital, but that capital could never have existed without labor. Hence . . . labor is the superior . . . greatly superior to capital."*

Despite the Democrats shouting from the newspapers that Lincoln didn't care for working people and only *"had tenderness for the Ethiopian race,"* and that Republicans *"shut their eyes to the squalor around them, and shed crocodile tears over the imaginary ills of slavery,"* and that electing Lincoln would be a *"disastrous event"* and a *"blow to every working man,"* working white men voted Lincoln into office in 1860.

What happened next was out of working-class hands. Southern power saw Lincoln as their end, and seven southern states seceded from the Union. They not-so-politely asked their northern neighbors to give up their forts in the south.

The north did not.

Four more states seceded . . . and the war between the states was on.

CHAPTER 11

BUSTED DREAMS

The Civil War was a clash between northern and southern power, not a clash of the people. Northern power was looking to expand. Southern power was looking to continue their comfortable way of life.

Why did working folks fight?

In the words of a New York working-class newspaper, the *Iron Platform*: "*There is one truth which should be clearly understood by every workingman in the Union. The slavery of the [B]lack man leads to the slavery of the white man. If the doctrine of treason is true, that 'Capital should own labor,' then their logical conclusion is correct, and all laborers, white or [B]lack, are and ought to be slaves.*"

Working white men in the north were the first to volunteer for war. The Thirty-Fourth Regiment of New York was made up entirely of farmers and mechanics, the De Kalb Regiment all German clerks, and the Garibaldi Guard all Italian working men. The lumbermen of Wisconsin formed the "piney boys," the Polish working men created the Polish Legion, whole regiments were made up of Illinois miners, and the Brooklyn Painters' Union enlisted together.

Enslaved people also jumped into action. It was illegal for them to have weapons, so they helped the Union in other ways, like sabotaging Confederate troops, secreting information to Union commanders, and walking off plantations by the thousands. They also risked their lives carrying out heroic feats, like riding to Union troops to warn them of Confederate ambush or memorizing Confederate fortifications and then escaping north with the information. Robert Smalls, a Black twenty-three-year-old ship's pilot, even delivered an entire Confederate ship to the Union Army in a daring escape to freedom that included his wife, four-year-old daughter, and infant son.

After so many slaves risked their lives to make it north, the Union Army was forced to legalize arming them. Immediately, thousands joined the Union, dying in larger numbers than white Union soldiers and putting up with appalling discrimination: less pay, more work, and no ability to rise in the ranks.

But it wasn't just men who honored the Union Army with their service. Harriet Tubman served courageously, as was reported by the *Boston Commonwealth*: "*Col. Montgomery and his gallant band of 300 [B]lack soldiers, under the guidance of a [B]lack woman, dashed into the enemy's country, struck a bold and effective blow, destroying millions of dollars' worth of commissary stores, cotton and lordly dwellings, and striking terror to the heart of rebel don, brought off near 800 slaves and thousands of dollars' worth of property, without losing a man or receiving a scratch. It was a glorious consummation.*" The article later added that Tubman not only led the raid, but the whole thing had been her idea.

Meanwhile, capitalists would once again reap the rewards of

war while workers would die in it. The draft cost $300 to avoid. The rich paid. The workers served.

Since they weren't fighting in the war, capitalists spent their time amassing fortunes by selling goods to the war effort. The stuff they sold was often defective, and the Civil War was one of the worst eras of corruption in American history. Guns exploded in the hands of soldiers. Sugar showed up as bags of sand and coffee as bags of rye. Shoes were made with paper soles, while uniforms disintegrated in the rain. On top of this, millions of dollars were being made trading illegally with the enemy. At the same time, workers' living standards dropped and the price of food and clothing soared.

Meanwhile, the Homestead Act had passed, but workers were too busy fighting a war to apply for land grants. The Indigenous land they had so hoped might be theirs to farm was instead snapped up on the cheap by wealthy speculators.

If this weren't bad enough, Congress handed over (for free) more than 70 million acres of public land to the railroads, and another 140 million acres to the states, both of which turned around and sold what they didn't need or want . . . to land speculators. Massive fortunes were being made through fraud and corruption, not hard work.

The war, however, was fought through the hard work of coal miners, steelworkers, shipbuilders, tracklayers, and the constant clicking of the looms run by women and children in the textile factories. Without labor—both Black and white—the war could not have been won. Even in the south, the rich paid their way out of fighting and dying, while poor whites fought and died.

By the time the Union Army had triumphed and the country

was restored, the United States was well on its way to changing from an agrarian economy to an industrial economy. With this change came the broken hopes of the working class who had been dreaming of farming their own land or working their own shop for almost 200 years, but who would now spend their lives locked in a wage system inside a factory or mine.

Even the newly freed slaves—who had been promised forty acres and a mule by the United States government for past payment of wages—had their dreams dashed when southern whites pressured the government to rescind those reparations, sending Black Americans back into the fields as sharecroppers or into the factories as unskilled labor.

In less than 400 years, a continent was invaded, populated by invaders, and taken from an agrarian society that had existed since the last Ice Age to an industrial society. Workers' heads were spinning. American labor was definitely disappointed and down . . . but it was far from out.

SECTION TWO

The Industrial Revolution to the Gilded Age
1873–1900

CHAPTER 12

WELCOME TO THE NEW HOT MESS

With the war over, workers took a breath and looked around to discover that capitalists had been quite busy while they'd been off fighting to keep the country together. Besides selling sand as coffee, trading with the enemy, and grabbing up millions of free acres, they . . .

> *Passed the Act to Encourage Immigration of 1864, allowing corporations to sign contracts with foreign workers— the same foreign workers they said were not "reputable members of any society"—and paying their passage to the United States in exchange for a year's worth of labor (Indentured Servants 2.0). This made wages drop for US workers and made striking impossible because there were boatloads of people coming for the jobs.*
>
> *Adopted hundreds of local and state laws benefiting landlords and merchants, and not a single one benefiting workers.*
>
> *Gave railroads eminent domain, which is the right of the government to take private land.*

Moved damages against businessmen from a jury system to
judges. Easier to pay those fellas off.

On top of all this, the Civil War that workers had fought to free enslaved people . . . didn't. With Lincoln murdered and Andrew Johnson now president, Reconstruction of the south—a period in US history that could have changed so very much for the better— took a serious U-turn for the absolute worst. The US government enabled southern power to void freedom for Black Americans by allowing the enactment of Jim Crow laws (state and local laws enforcing segregation) and opening the door wide for violence through the rise of the Ku Klux Klan and other terrorist groups.

But workers had just returned from fighting a war to keep the states together, and they now began organizing across those state lines. For the first time in US history, strong national unions cropped up. Two of the biggest were the National Labor Union (NLU) and the Knights of Labor (KoL).

Both unions wanted nothing more than to increase membership, yet both set limits on who could join. The NLU accepted white working women into their membership but denied Black workers. The KoL happily welcomed the newly freed Black men into their fold but denied all women. At the local level, most trade unions shut out Black workers completely, and so, like white women before them, they organized on their own. Some even saw early success. The Longshoremen's Protective Union Association struck in Charleston, South Carolina, in 1867 and won higher wages.

Workers were just getting things rolling when another depression hit. And it was a big one.

On September 18, 1873, Jay Cooke woke up early and quietly left his mansion in Philadelphia while his bestie, Ulysses S. Grant—who also happened to be the president of the United States—slept upstairs. He traveled downtown and locked his bank. Cooke, who had made many millions of dollars selling government bonds during the Civil War, had overinvested (not just his money, but lots of other people's money) and was now bankrupt. With that single click of the lock, 5,000 businesses came tumbling down. Panic ensued. And the entire credit structure of the United States fell.

If you're worried about Cooke, don't be. Not too many years later, he came back and created another fortune. In fact, the fortunes of the very rich actually grew during these economic depressions. For example, in this particular depression, a man named Andrew Carnegie was buying up the steel industry on the cheap, while another man named John D. (J. D.) Rockefeller was using the economic downturn to wipe out his competition in oil.

If you're worried about the people who weren't best friends with the president of the United States—the workers—you should be. In the first six months alone, 90,000 workers lost their jobs, with 3 million unemployed by the depression's end.

Half these workers were women. With no money and nowhere to go, many were forced to sleep on the floors of police stations across the country, becoming known as "revolvers" because they weren't allowed to stay in the same police station more than two nights in a row. Newspapers condemned this charity, thinking the cold floors of police stations might "*sap the foundation of that independence of character, and that reliance on one's own resources,*" summing the whole practice up as "*thoroughly communistic.*"

The no-longer-working class was left to gather in shacks and pick over city dumps for food. With survival the only thing on people's minds, unions—once again—fell apart. Of the thirty national unions that had leapt onto the scene following the Civil War, only about eight were left by the end of the crisis.

Employers helped unions out the door using lots of tricks: lock-outs (locking workers out until they agreed to terms of employers), blacklists (listing workers not to be hired and sharing those lists across business associations), and yellow-dog contracts (forcing workers to sign a contract saying they will not join a union). Wages were cut. Hours were extended. Company militaries were built. Corporate spy rings were developed and deployed. As one European visitor noted, union members "*were hunted like mad dogs.*"

This was not an exaggeration. Railroad baron Franklin B. Gowen literally hunted union leaders by planting spies inside the Ancient Order of Hibernians—a group of Irish workers nick-named the Molly Maguires. Accusing them of murders that historical study has now determined were committed by the spies themselves, Gowen, who also happened to be the prosecutor in these cases, had the Mollies executed on testimony he knew was false.

By the summer of 1877, after four years of economic depression, things were desperate.

The overcrowding, the hunger, and the heat led to disease, especially among the very young. The *New York Times* reported, "*already the cry of the dying children begins to be heard.*" In the first week of July, the city of Baltimore alone saw the deaths of 139 infants.

The second week, all hell broke loose.

CHAPTER 13

ALL HELL BREAKS LOOSE

What happened next became known as the Great Upheaval—basically, the shit hit the fan.

It all started in the small town of Martinsburg, West Virginia, at the Baltimore and Ohio Railroad (or B&O Railroad). With the Mollies executed and the unions all but crushed, the railroad announced yet another wage cut. The workers immediately uncoupled the engines from the trains and drove them into the roundhouse.

Local police showed up, but so did a crowd of supporters.

B&O called the governor. A thing corporations can do. Workers don't get to alert the governor when their wages have been cut for the third time in a year.

The governor sent the militia, who attempted to get a train through to the station. A striking worker derailed it. Gunfire was exchanged. The train didn't make it, but unfortunately neither did the striker, who was shot twice and died nine days later.

With trains coming in and no trains leaving, over 600 freight trains piled up in Martinsburg. (The workers continued to allow passenger trains and mail trains through the station but no freight.)

After the initial attempt to retake the station, the militiamen disappeared into the crowd—they were mostly railroad workers who served part-time and therefore were a lot more supportive of the strikers than they were of the B&O Railroad corporation or the US government. As one militiaman told the local newspaper, *"Many of us have reason to know what long hours and low pay mean."*

The governor now called the new president of the United States—Rutherford B. Hayes—and asked him to send the army.

Unfortunately, the army was busy out west at war with Indigenous nations over their land, and without enough money for more troops, Hayes was stuck. Lucky for him, a group of bankers got together and loaned the government money so they could send troops.

So, for the first time in United States history, the army marched on its own citizens, and the trains in Martinsburg began to run.

But B&O was not out of hot water, because workers were still pissed.

Down the line in Cumberland, Maryland, rail workers picked up where their coworkers in Martinsburg left off and began stopping trains.

Troops and strikebreakers were sent to Baltimore, from where they were supposed to head up to Cumberland. But by this time, workers everywhere had heard about Martinsburg, and thousands of people sympathetic to the strikers surrounded the troops on their way to Cumberland and began hurling rocks. The guard turned and fired on the crowd, killing twelve men and wounding eighteen. *"All the men killed were shot through the head or heart,"* reported the *New York Times*.

The army marched on Cumberland. All strikers were arrested.

Anyone who got in the way of the army was fired on. Cumberland was placed under military control.

The depression had begun in 1873 and it was now 1877—four long years of workers begging their government for help. Four long years of silence from that government. But the moment corporations reached out for help, the government sent troops, and workers were killed.

People were desperate, so the trouble spread.

Pittsburgh was the scene of the next bloody mess. The railroad workers on the Pennsylvania line not only had their wages cut—all the railroads colluded on those cuts—but the company announced half the workers would be fired and the other half would be responsible for making up all the work. The saddest part came when the train workers met with the CEO of the Pennsylvania Railroad Company and said they'd accept the cuts and firings and extra work, if only the company would agree to rehiring the fired workers and a return to the old wages once business improved.

The company refused—so all freight trains stopped leaving Pittsburgh.

The CEO called the governor, bragging that he would *"settle this business with Philadelphia troops."*

When the troops arrived, they were met by a hissing crowd. Someone threw a rock. The troops turned and opened fire, killing twenty people. This time, the dead included children.

Thousands of angry people poured in from the surrounding area . . . coal miners, factory workers, mill workers. The railroad station went up in flames.

Who set the fire? The company said the crowd set it. The crowd said the company set it. No matter who set the fire, Pittsburgh was now burning, and the president of the United States surrounded it with troops while the country's newspapers fanned the flames.

The crowd "*is a wild beast who needs to be shot down.*"

"*The ignorant rabble with hungry mouths needs to be fed a diet of lead.*"

"*The only way to deal with a mob is to exterminate it.*"

The trouble spread from Pittsburgh along the Erie tracks to New York, then headed north to Canada and west through Chicago and out to San Francisco. Six days after it all began, the strike hit St. Louis, and the papers were calling it a "*Labor Revolution.*"

It was no longer just a railroad strike. It was a general strike, which means lots more workers from lots more industries walked off their jobs. The working class of St. Louis put out a statement: "*We are asking the public to condemn the government for its action in sending troops to protect capitalists and their property against the just demands of railway men.*" Using fife and drum, workers marched through the streets of St. Louis. Men and women, Black and white.

They put out a second statement, calling for an eight-hour workday, wage increases, and a law prohibiting any child under the age of fourteen from working. St. Louis companies responded with wage increases but ignored the other demands. So the strike continued.

The governor of Missouri called for martial law. The strikers sent him a message asking him to support them in the eight-hour workday and the ending of child labor.

He responded with militiamen, police, calvary, armed vigilantes, and the US Army. They marched on St. Louis, raided the strikers' homes and meeting places, and arrested anyone who had a leading role in the strike. What began on July 16 was over by August 2—not just in St. Louis, but everywhere.

Strikers were fired.

Wages were cut.

Hours were extended.

And children continued to work.

1877 was when workers learned just how powerful the combination of capital and government was. But according to the newspaper the *Labor Standard*, they also learned what solidarity could look like: *"white and colored men standing together, men of all nationalities in one supreme contest for the rights of workingmen."*

Capitalists also did some learning. They now understood the need to be tightly knit into the government, with a hand in the militia, National Guard, and the US Army. In the next few years, state militias were centralized, more armories were built, and conspiracy laws were strengthened.

The heat of the summer of 1877 would not burn them so easily again.

EAT THE RICH

"*When the people shall have nothing to eat, they will eat the rich*," Swiss philosopher Jean-Jacques Rousseau supposedly said at a time of great inequality in Europe.

The United States was now experiencing some pretty incredible inequality. The working class was suffering while the very rich lived the life. Giant mansions. Diamond tiaras. Suits lined in gold. Extravagant events worth millions of dollars; at one such gala a young lady wore a taxidermy cat head on her own head while wearing a skirt made of the tails of actual cats.

How do you make enough money to wear dead domesticated animals to a party?

The first thing you do is gather power tightly around you.

With the Great Upheaval's lessons still fresh, the northern industrial powers took the hands of both the southern powers and the political elite and organized what historian Howard Zinn called "*the greatest march of economic growth in human history.*"

They did this on the backs of white, Black, Chinese, and European workers. By paying each of these peoples differently depending on their race, sex, national origin, and social class, they strengthened the pyramid of oppression on top of which they sat.

The Industrial Revolution had ushered in the Gilded Age. Steam and electricity replaced human muscle. Iron replaced wood. Steel replaced iron. Machines ruled. In pre–Civil War times, it had taken sixty-one hours to work an acre of wheat. By 1900, it took three hours. But throughout all the progress, human hands were still needed to dig coal and mine copper, to lay train tracks, to run the massive machines in textile mills. And for this reason, immigration was welcomed by both the northern and southern power structures. An overabundance of people drove down wages, which increased their profits. In ten years:

The population of Philadelphia jumped from 650,000 to 1.5 million.

Chicago from 110,000 to 2 million.

New York from 850,000 to 4 million.

So many people, all of them looking for the American Dream. But they'd have to go through American industry to get it.

Unfortunately, what we call the "rags to riches" story is just that, a story. These millions of people working the life out of themselves would mostly die in rags. Ninety percent of all industry executives during the Industrial Revolution came from the high-middle to upper classes. This didn't leave a lot of room for folks working their way to the top.

But this story of making it rich through hard work and perseverance is a convenient one for capitalism. It keeps people hoping, and therefore, it keeps people working.

Not only did corporations profit off the labor of workers, they also profited from both government gifts and outright theft. The railroads received some of the biggest presents and were some of the biggest thieves.

The Union Pacific Railroad was given 12 million free acres from the US government, while the Central Pacific Railroad was handed 9 million acres. Not content with this, Union Pacific created a shell company (a company in name only, with no actual business attached) and then charged the US government $50 million in tax dollars of fake work done by this pretend company. Central Pacific did the same, charging the US government $36 million for false work. Shares were sold cheaply to congressmen to prevent an investigation.

The faces behind this wealth have names that still hang around on buildings and organizations today.

J. P. Morgan was a banker. He made his money selling defective guns during the Civil War. These guns shot off the thumbs of soldiers when they fired. There was an investigation, but Congress decided to pay him anyway. He also sold war bonds for the US government. A war bond is issued by a government to fund a war. Any person can buy them. A war bond may cost $25 in the present, for example, but then be worth $100 in the future. The government could have sold these bonds directly to people, but they chose to sell them through bankers like J. P. Morgan— making millions of dollars in commissions for the banker.

One thing Morgan didn't do during the war was fight in it. He paid his $300 to get out, along with men like J. D. Rockefeller and Andrew Carnegie.

This power structure of bankers and industrialists and politicians knew each other, ate dinner with each other, and held secret meetings with each other. This was how they were given bonds to sell, or free land on which to build factories and railroads. This is how they were reelected to office year after year. They weren't born in rags. They didn't work hard for their riches. Morgan's fortune was worth $200 million after the Civil War. Twenty years later, it was worth $2 billion. Not billions as in today's billions. Billions as in 1890 billions.

J. D. Rockefeller began in oil refineries. He made secret deals with the railroads so they'd only move his oil . . . thereby squeezing out the other companies and then buying them as they went bankrupt. One memo from his company, Standard Oil, said: *"Wilkerson & Company received car of oil Monday 13th . . . Please turn another screw."*

Other times he wasn't that patient and just blew up the other refineries—crimes he was never prosecuted for.

Andrew Carnegie began in steel. First, he bought up all the steel companies. Then he had his contacts in the government create laws keeping foreign steel out of the United States. With its monopoly on steel, the company made him $40 million dollars a year. In today's dollars, that's $1.2 billion.

But weren't monopolies against the law? Wasn't blowing up competitors against the law? Wasn't paying off congressmen against the law?

This was how it worked: The president of the United States at that moment in time, Grover Cleveland, appointed William Whitney, a millionaire and corporate lawyer, as his secretary of the navy. Whitney was invested in steel. He decided to redo all navy ships in steel, and then he bought that steel (using US tax dollars) at ridiculously high prices. He made himself a fortune. No one stopped him.

Meanwhile, Texas farmers were struggling due to a drought. When they asked for federal relief, President Cleveland said: *"Federal aid in such cases encourages the expectation of paternal care on the part of the government and weakens the sturdiness of our national character."*

And so it went. A democracy?

Not really.

CHAPTER 15

HOPE BETWEEN THE PAGES

Workers and their labor movement had taken two huge hits from the depression of 1873 and the Great Upheaval of 1877. In the years that followed, they searched for answers to their many problems: Pitiful wages. Long hours. Subpar living standards. Child labor. The government's use of police and armed forces against them. Even more laws being passed that didn't help them . . . or worse, put them in jail.

In their despair, they turned to books.

The working class picked up, and then couldn't put down, Henry George's book *Progress and Poverty*. It was about ending poverty using a tax on land . . . and no other taxes. Since the rich owned land, they would pay the taxes, and the money would be used to help the poor. You can imagine that poor readers loved it.

They were also reading *Looking Backward* by Edward Bellamy, a novel where a man falls asleep in 1880 and wakes up in the year 2000 to meet a socialist America where workers are living good lives. Like the Utopian Socialists before them, these two books showed an optimistic future for working folks, and they sold millions and millions of copies.

The working class also turned to each other. They formed clubs. The most popular were socialist labor clubs where they could actively work toward Bellamy's vision of a world with equal rights for all, without the distinction of sex, race, class, or nationality. This view was especially welcome since high immigration combined with low wages was forever heating up the tensions between those already here and those coming over.

But there were other clubs. Clubs that bought into those above tensions. The Workingmen's Trade and Labor Union of San Francisco was a club focused on the "yellow menace," a racist term for Chinese workers. Groups like this attacked and killed Chinese workers throughout the west, murdering innocent people while avoiding the real problem: huge profits being made by corporations while those corporations paid below subsistence wages to workers.

Twisting in the capitalist wind, workers searched for hope and change. Out of this searching environment the anarchist was born: people who had once believed in the hope of democracy and were now frustrated by what they'd ended up with. One of American history's most famous anarchists, Emma Goldman, defined anarchism like this: *"The philosophy of a new social order based on liberty unrestricted by man-made law; the theory that all forms of government rest on violence, and are therefore wrong and harmful, as well as unnecessary."*

In the early decade of the 1880s, workers were in need of a new social order. Wages were lower than they had been in 1870. Working hours remained anywhere from ten to sixteen hours per day. Good working conditions—safe spaces, breathable air, drinkable water—were hardly thought to be important for folks in the working class. The poverty line was approximately $750 a year for a family, and your average worker was only pulling in $550.

The unions that had crawled their way through the depression of 1873 and the Great Upheaval slowly returned. Two grew faster than the others: the International Labor Union (ILU) and the Knights of Labor (KoL). A third, the American Federation of Labor (AFL), was gathering speed in the background as a cigar maker's union.

The International Labor Union came from a socialist background. Calling for labor solidarity, it welcomed everyone, regardless of skill, nationality, sex, race, or religion. Because of this, it grew fast. Their goal was to build a massive working-class organization where eventually the wage system would be abolished. The ILU focused on Black workers: *"The Negro population of the South deserves our kindest and most careful attention."* However, its greatest numbers came from white women, along with its greatest triumphs. During the textile strikes of 1878–80, the working women with the ILU in New Jersey, New York, and Massachusetts won a wage increase and fifty minutes for dinner (which back then meant lunch). More money *and* they had just invented the lunch hour.

The ILU's rallying cry, "less work and more pay," led union members into multiple strike situations. But most of them didn't turn out like they had for the women in the textile mills, and the endless striking eventually depleted its membership.

The Knights of Labor had been founded as a secret society following the Civil War, but it didn't pick up real membership until it dropped the secrecy stuff and, like the ILU, opened its membership doors to a wide swath of workers. The KoL stood for the eight-hour day, no child labor, health and safety laws for workplaces, education of the working class, and equal pay for equal work for women, immigrants, and Black workers. With a platform like this, they went from 10,000 members in 1878 to 600,000 members in 1885. Their rallying cry was *"an injury to one is the concern of all."*

The American Federation of Labor would burst onto the scene in the following year, 1886 . . . a turning point in labor history.

CHAPTER 16

1886

The year began with anti-Chinese violence in Seattle, as a mob attacked Chinese Americans in their homes and attempted to run them out of town.

The year would end with the dedication of the Statue of Liberty—a gift from the French. The statue's actual name is "Liberty Enlightening the World," but the light of liberty in the United States in 1886 was barely brighter than a firefly.

What happened during this year would change the lives of the working class.

In 1886, the Gilded Age was in full swing. Certain folks were making gobs of money. And those gobs were empowering them with the ability to manipulate laws while downplaying the alarming increase in monopolies.

This was happening in tandem with a growing gap between rich and poor, record-shattering immigration, and industrial jobs being replaced by machines. All this turned up and turned out the labor movement.

In 1886, membership in the Knights of Labor was on a meteoric rise after the union won a strike against Jay Gould and his Southwest Railroad the year before. Gould was one of the richest men in the United States, and once openly admitted to the pyramid of oppression, saying, *"I can hire one-half of the working class to kill the other half."*

It was a gigantic win. And capitalists desperately attempted to stir the pot in the usual ways—harassment, targeted firings, etc.—to put a stop to the growing solidarity and successes of the working class.

But this wasn't 1877. It was 1886. This moment had more thinking, planning, organizing, and most of all, more solidarity on the part of labor . . . making it much more revolutionary.

Workers should have felt beaten, because they had been beaten. In over a hundred years of fighting—ending with the heartbreaking loss of the Great Upheaval—they were still working incredibly long hours, for sad wages, and under dangerous conditions.

But they *weren't* beaten.

In 1886, they were hoping, organizing, and listening—to socialists, communists, and anarchists who told them life didn't have to be this way. Whether or not the mass of workers saw *themselves* as communists, socialists, or anarchists is up for debate—but what workers did see was that democracy was heading in the wrong direction. Freedom did not ring.

Was this the toppling of everything America stood for? Only if what the country stood for was inequality and anti-democratic ideals.

Today, most Americans may have come to see capitalism as synonymous with America, but in 1886, they didn't. Capitalism did not (and still doesn't) promote liberty, opportunity, or equality, the main ingredients of the American Dream. Their hope in

1886 was for a more cooperative society, where people came before profit.

Backing up a moment. In 1884, the soon-to-become American Federation of Labor (AFL)—at present the Federation of Organized Trades and Labor Unions—declared May 1, 1886, to be the day everything would change for the working class. They named it May Day and asked all workers in the United States to join in on a massive strike for an eight-hour workday. No one had much cared about or noticed the announcement, or the AFL, in 1884.

But it was now 1886, and everything *had* changed. Workers across the United States signed on for the world's first May Day. It was to be celebrated with parades, picnics, and songs.

> *"We mean to make things over;*
> *we're tired of toil for naught*
> *But bare enough to live on: never*
> *an hour for thought.*
> *We want to feel the sunshine; we*
> *want to smell the flowers;*
> *We're sure that God has willed it,*
> *and we mean to have eight hours.*
> *We're summoning our forces from*
> *shipyard, shop, and mill:*
> *Eight hours for work, eight hours*
> *for rest, eight hours for what we will!"*

On May 1, 1886, 350,000 workers walked off the job at over 13,000 businesses across the country. Solidarity on this scale was an American first. Black, white, and all nationalities of workers marched together down main streets in hopes of securing an eight-hour workday, a first step to changing their lives.

It was a Saturday.

It was spring.

It was jaw-dropping to the capitalists.

On May 2, the party continued. Workers marched, waved flags, picnicked, and paraded. And on May 3, even more folks joined the strike.

New York, Baltimore, Pittsburgh, Grand Rapids, Detroit, Indianapolis, Louisville, Fort Worth, Wilkes-Barre . . . the list went on. The parades continued. The bands played. The weather held. It was a good time to be out and feeling that sunshine.

The party first came to an end in Milwaukee, when the governor called out the militia and ordered the marching workers fired upon, killing six people—and then next in Chicago, where the heart of the eight-hour campaign beat strongest.

Chicago started May Day with a bang when 30,000 Chicago workers walked off the job, meeting up with another 30,000 in the streets ready to party. On that first day, Chicago brewers and bakers won reduced hours, and striking furniture makers won the big one: an eight-hour workday. Those who didn't secure shorter hours remained on strike—bricklayers, stonemasons, butchers, carpenters, shoemakers, etc.

While workers celebrated, the police and militia prepped behind the scenes by signing on a horde of special deputies—basically, vigilantes. The business community also prepared. They had banded together to purchase a machine gun for the occasion. Local and national newspapers helped grease the wheels for future violence, with one Chicago paper calling out the International

Working People's Association, along with its leaders Albert Parsons and August Spies: *"Hold them personally responsible for any trouble that occurs,"* and *"make an example of them"* if it did.

On May 3, the good times in Chicago came to an end. The McCormick Harvester Works brought in strikebreakers. The company's striking workers attacked them, trying to keep them out of the factory. The police were called. The strikers took off running. The police fired on their backs.

Four more dead. It was an old story. A tired story. Four here. Six there. Over the years, those numbers kept adding up. They were about to get even higher.

On May 4, with permission granted by the city of Chicago, 3,000 people met in Haymarket Square. It was a quiet group— there to mourn the four people killed the day before. The mayor attended. It rained. It got late. The crowd wandered off.

Only about 200 people remained when, to their surprise, the police—in full force—marched into the square, ordering everyone to disperse. Before anyone could, a bomb flew into the air and exploded in the middle of the crowd of police.

The police opened fire. Many more died.

Anger and hate followed—again egged on by the press. *"Hang them first and try them afterwards!"*

But hang who? No one knew who threw the bomb. To this day, no one knows who threw the bomb.

Since the bomb was thrown at the police, people assumed it had come from the ranks of the workers. This was a bad assumption. Many times before this (and many times after), employers and private military had blown up their own equipment, their own men, and even the police in an effort to blame workers.

Law enforcement began to "find" bombs all over the city, but it was quickly discovered that many of these bombs did not exist, and the ones that did had been planted by the police themselves. Evidence emerged that an agent of the police had thrown the bomb, and absolutely no evidence emerged pointing to anyone else having thrown it. And yet—they arrested eight leaders of the labor movement, all of whom were anarchists: Albert Parsons, August Spies, Samuel Fielden, Michael Schwab, George Engel, Adolph Fischer, Louis Lingg, and Oscar Neebe.

With nothing linking these men to the bomb and seven of them not even in Haymarket Square when it exploded, the *New York Times* had this to say: *"No disturbance of the peace has occurred in the United States since the war of the rebellion has excited public sentiment through the Union as it is excited by the Anarchists' murder of policemen in Chicago on Tuesday night. We say murder with the fullest consciousness of what that word means. It is silly to speak of the crime as a riot. All the evidence goes to show that it was concerted, deliberately planned, and cooly executed murder."*

All eight were charged with murder.

The Haymarket eight were put on trial because they believed in worker rights, that capitalism and authority might not be all that great, and that violence was necessary as a means of defense. These were ideas, not bombs.

Four were hanged.

One died by suicide.

Three sat in jail for years under threat of execution.

Later, the judge who presided over the case would be quoted as saying: *"If I had a little strained the law, I was to be commended for so doing."*

CHAPTER 17

SUGAR, SPIES, AND SUPPRESSION

1886 shocked everybody. Workers had gone from solidarity in the May sunshine to watching men hang. Capitalists had experienced a close call, when a country full of workers experiencing a few spring days might have changed the world. The hangman's noose had brought them back into power, and they planned to stay there.

Their plan wasn't rocket science. It only had three steps:

1. Red-baiting. Red-baiting is the persecution of people for known or suspected political leanings toward socialism or communism. Using the American press in a campaign of propaganda, red-baiting was effective in imprisoning and/or murdering anyone capitalists suspected of not being in their corner. It was used so widely that even today, words like *socialism* or *communism* have the connotations of being wrong, bad, undemocratic, or un-American.

2. Violence. Haymarket solidified that the "order" part of "law and order" was super useful. Not only was it paid

for by the government (not capitalists) and helpful in breaking up meetings and making organizing difficult, but enforcing order—aka committing lawful violence—scares the crap out of people.

3. Spies. Solidarity between workers was a very real problem. Red-baiting helped to suppress it. Violence helped to suppress it. But having eyes and ears inside the organizations of the working class was also a good idea.

Corporate spies were having a moment, and the Pinkerton National Detective Agency was born. The organization, which still exists today, was more of a private police force than a ring of spies. Ironically, its founder, Allan Pinkerton, began his life as a radical for worker rights in Scotland. His political beliefs landed him on the wrong side of Scottish law, and he quickly emigrated to the United States. Over the years, it seems, monetary success overshadowed democratic rights in Allan's heart, and he signed on with the very type of people he had fought against in Scotland: the corporate rich.

Employing more armed men than the US Army, Pinkerton built a force of vicious and violent strikebreakers, jurors on stacked courts, star witnesses in many perjured testimonies, and outright murderers. In between these activities, they would be used by corporations to infiltrate unions, identify leaders, and blacklist workers—stealing workers' ability to support themselves and their families.

They often advertised in newspapers, *"We break strikes,"* adding, *"We help eliminate the agitator and organizer quietly and with little or no friction."* Eliminate. Quietly. No friction. This is called suppression, and the Pinkerton agency was extremely successful at it.

But the shock of Haymarket and the suppression that followed had not succeeded in slowing the labor movement. It had only sent it underground—where it was busy growing.

First to break back into the sunshine were Black sugar workers in Louisiana. On the one-year anniversary of the hanging of the men who had now become known as the Haymarket Martyrs, the sugar workers walked out of the fields on strike.

It was much more frightening for Black workers in the south to strike than it was for the white men who organized the May Day strikes leading to Haymarket. And those white men had been convicted and executed without evidence.

Nevertheless, the sugar workers struck, and the sugar corporation promptly evicted them from their company-owned shacks. The workers took refuge in the town of Thibodaux, arriving, as one historian described, *"penniless, ragged, and carrying their bed clothing and babies."*

The governor was disgusted by the mix of Black and white sugar workers striking together—90 percent of sugar workers were Black and 10 percent were white—saying: *"God Almighty has himself drawn the color line."* He sent the militia to Thibodaux.

The first thing the militia did was arrest the leaders of the sugar strike—two brothers, Henry and George Cox. These men were not charged with anything, yet they were led away in handcuffs.

The order part of law and order is scary and intimidating, but the strikers refused to head back into the fields. Sugar comes from plants. Plants need to be harvested at a certain time. With no one to harvest, the entire crop was threatened. This was the whole point of the strike, to (1) show the corporation how necessary workers were to the process of making sugar, and (2) show how necessary workers were to the process of the corporation making money . . . and that perhaps, the workers should share in that money.

The second time the militia showed up in Thibodaux was the last time. On the night of November 22, 1887, the militia attacked the unarmed Black community. They murdered men, women, and children. How many? If you research the Thibodaux Massacre, there are different numbers of dead.

Thirty people? Fifty people? No one really knows. But how many people shot in the night by the government does it take to make it outrageous?

Later that night, Henry and George were pulled from their prison cells by a white crowd and lynched.

A Black journalist writing about the event a few days afterward said everything that needs to be said: *"At such times and upon such occasions, words of condemnation fall like snow-flakes upon molten lead. The [B]lacks should defend their lives, and if needs must die, die with their faces toward their persecutors fighting for their homes, their children and their lawful rights."*

CHAPTER 18

OH, FRICK

Workers rang in the next few years with strikes, strikes, and more strikes. By 1892 it seemed like everybody was walking off the job.

Coal miners in Tennessee.

Railroad switchmen in New York.

Copper miners in Idaho.

Scalesmen, packers, and teamsters all together in New Orleans.

Corporate and government pushback was swift and violent. Workers were denounced as socialists and communists in the press, then they were fired, arrested, and brutalized using spies, police, the National Guard, the state militia, and the US Army. Next came hiring strikebreakers and moving on with the business of profit.

The Homestead Strike in Homestead, Pennsylvania, seemed to be on this same horrendous path . . . until it took a turn.

The Carnegie Steel plant, owned by Andrew Carnegie, was located in Homestead—a town outside Pittsburgh. It was managed by a real butthole named Henry Clay Frick. Frick hated unions and decided, not for the first time, to attempt to bust the plant's union.

Carnegie, who was busy traveling around Europe, told Frick to go for it. Steel was doing great and profits were up, but this dynamic duo went ahead with their plan.

Frick built a three-mile-long, twelve-foot-high fence around the plant, topped with barbed wire and peepholes for rifles. Then he cut wages from $180 a month down to $84.

The workers were shocked. They knew that both production and profits were up. Of course they said no to the cut and walked out—playing right into Frick's hands.

He quickly shut down the mill and locked them out. Then he got busy hiring strikebreakers from Boston, St. Louis, and Philadelphia.

The workers now understood what had happened. They set up a picket line outside the plant—in essence, guarding it against strikebreakers.

Frick called on the local police to clear his front gate. But the police sympathized with the workers. It must have been hard not to when you lived in the same small town as all these people who had just been fired for no reason.

No big deal, though. Frick had hired the Pinkertons to break through the picket line and usher in his strikebreakers.

The private army came by night, on a special train with the windows darkened. It then transferred to barges, which silently proceeded up the river while the 300 men on board changed into the blue uniforms of the Pinkertons and armed themselves with Winchester rifles.

The workers knew they were coming. They'd been watching.

When the barges were spotted, a steam whistle called out everyone in town.

It was four in the morning.

The mill had its own boat landing, and the Pinkertons headed for it. The workers tore down the fence and met them at the dock. The hired army announced they were there to take over the mill and that the crowd should disperse. The workers shouted them down.

A shot rang out. Then several. Then an all-out battle ensued.

No one knows who fired first. What is known is that the Pinkertons fired into a crowd that included children. The battle lasted thirteen hours. Twelve people were killed and hundreds wounded before the Pinkertons surrendered.

Reporters poured in from across the country, and a new song became an overnight hit: "Father Was Killed by the Pinkerton Men." It wasn't the only song to come out of the strike, but it was the one with the most on point title.

Frick called the governor.

At first, the governor wavered. All was now peaceful in Homestead. The union was working with the local government to keep residents calm.

But then the governor worried that a union and a local government working together might give other towns and cities dangerous ideas . . . so he sent in 8,000 troops.

With the militia on the way, Frick did something that other capitalists were also learning to do: he moved a lot of the work being done in Homestead to other Carnegie factories that weren't on strike, thereby keeping the company profits flowing. (Later capitalists would move production to other countries when workers struck.)

The governor's troops arrived, took over the town, and arrested sixteen strike leaders, charging them with murder.

Newspapers across the country were busy headlining the workers as "*savage beasts who deserve no pity.*" But the American public wasn't so sure this time. The plant had been profiting. Frick had fired an entire town. Regular folks were struggling to side with Carnegie Steel.

With the military on-site, the mill reopened staffed with strikebreakers, but public opinion was slowly building against Frick, and his new workers couldn't keep up with production. He desperately needed the workers he'd fired to come back to work. Instead of breaking a union, that union might end up breaking Frick.

Then things got weird.

Emma Goldman, now twenty-three years old, and her twenty-two-year-old partner, Alexander Berkman, were working in an ice cream shop in upstate New York and watching the events at Homestead unfold.

Haymarket had brought them both to New York City, where they'd met and fallen in love—while also falling in love with a man named Johann Most as mentor and hero. Most was a famous German anarchist who taught the idea of something called an attentat, or "propaganda of the deed." This deed was a brief, violent act that would inspire working people to overthrow capitalism.

The young ice cream scoopers truly believed in Most and in his "attentat." Now Homestead had them thinking it was time for that deed. They decided to murder Henry Clay Frick.

The plan was simple. Alex would go to Homestead and stab

him to death, and Emma would go to New York City, where she would write about the event, thereby turning it into the inspiration the people needed to free themselves.

The plan didn't work.

Alex had bad aim. Frick didn't die. Instead, his brush with death turned him into a national hero. The Homestead workers, once the object of the public's sympathy, now lost that sympathy—even though they had absolutely nothing to do with the stabbing. The newspapers flocked to the story, tying the sixteen strike leaders sitting in jail to Alexander Berkman's stabbing. The Pittsburgh police stepped in and investigated, finding the region "*full of men with Anarchist principles.*"

With public opinion back on their side, Carnegie and Frick charged the sixteen tired strike leaders with treason. Though in the end, none were convicted, all sixteen spent years defending themselves, exhausting them financially and emotionally.

The Homestead workers returned to work at the reduced wages, and Frick wrote to Carnegie: "*Our victory is now complete and most gratifying.*"

Same old story. Same old ending.

Frick had broken the steel union, and it would stay broken for twenty years. Alex went straight to jail. Emma stayed down in New York City, stunned that things hadn't followed the plan. Both these young people learned lessons.

Sitting in jail, Alex would change his mind about Most's single violent event, although he would remain a dedicated revolutionary. Emma's goals for change amid the anger and injustice of the times would only grow, although she too would give up the way of the attentat.

When the state or powerful individuals used violence—Haymarket, the Great Upheaval, Thibodaux—it was deemed necessary, unfortunate, or both. When a powerless individual or individuals used violence, the full force of law and order rained down on them, cementing them in the public consciousness as a cautionary tale, memorialized to condemn a wide circle of ideas, organizations, and people for years to come.

Alex and Emma weren't the only ones with a takeaway from Homestead.

Samuel Gompers—a one-time cigar worker who was now the president of the growing American Federation of Labor—watched the combination of powerlessness and violence at Homestead and came to the conclusion that if you can't beat 'em, join 'em. The AFL moved toward what was being called new unionism, or trade (craft) unionism—unionizing men who had learned a craft to perform their jobs. So basically returning to a focus on skilled white men. This backward move would win the AFL early success, and they'd quickly build to 140,000 members in twenty-five national unions.

Another man watched what happened in Homestead and went in the opposite direction.

His name was Eugene V. Debs.

CHAPTER 19

DEATH BY DEVIL FISH

As a young teen, Eugene V. Debs cleaned railroad cars for a living. He was good at it and was quickly promoted to fireman, shoveling coal into a firebox that heated water into steam to run the train. Debs shoveled two tons of coal a day, for sixteen hours, six days a week. Not only was it exhausting and dirty, it was dangerous. Thirty-five thousand people died at work each year, and hundreds of thousands were injured. Debs's best friend was crushed to death when he slipped and fell under a moving train.

After the accident, Debs took a desk job working for the Brotherhood of Locomotive Firemen, a union for skilled white railroad workers. In 1892, he watched the sugar workers of Thibodaux lose their lives, the coal miners of Tennessee fight off cheap convict labor (only to become it themselves), and of course, the steel workers in Homestead meet their sad end. He made his thoughts on this year pretty clear.

"If the year 1892 taught the workingman any lesson worthy of heed, it was that the capitalist class, like the devil fish, had grasped them with its tentacles and was dragging them down to fathomless depths of degradation."

By devil fish, Debs meant the kraken, the giant sea monster that had the ability to telepathically possess humans, grant eternal life, and control the weather.

If a sea monster wasn't enough, 1893 hit, and with it, yet another depression.

Seven hundred banks went under. Sixteen thousand businesses closed. Three million people were thrown out of work. There was so much homelessness that once again, the police station floors and stairways were flooded with sleeping bodies.

Folks cried out for relief.

Newspapers proposed the homeless be fed a "*leaden*" diet—actually suggesting that the government shoot people. When the government offered small jobs for small pay instead of murdering folks, the business associations went bananas: "*It is a waste of taxpayers money. It is communistic in principle. It is demoralizing to those who receive it.*"

All this is still shouted today when people in need receive government help—not because it's demoralizing or a waste of taxpayer money, but because capitalists like hungry workers. Hungry workers need to take any job at any pay.

Emma Goldman stood up in New York's Union Square and told poor people to go into stores and take food to feed their children. She was promptly arrested and spent the year in jail.

Things got so bad that even the now-powerful head of the AFL, Samuel Gompers—usually a friend to business—spoke out against all the depressions and recessions: "*In a society where such abnormal conditions prevail there must of necessity be something wrong at the basic foundations, and it requires but little study to come to the conclusion that the ownership and control of the means of production by private corporations which have no human sympathy or apparent responsibility, is the cause of the ills and wrongs borne by the human family."*

Adding to the wrongs, the railroads began firing workers and doubling shifts to keep profits flowing during the depression, leading to more injury and death on the job.

Workers cried, "Unsafe working conditions!"

Corporations shrugged them off as *"acts of God."*

In 1893, God was super busy killing and maiming railroad men by the thousands—2,727 killed and 31,729 injured, to be exact. Most of these men were unskilled workers, and without a union. They had no way to survive once they were hurt, or for their families to survive if they were killed.

The depression of 1893 drove Eugene V. Debs into action, into industrial unionism, and into the fight of his life: the Pullman Strike.

George Mortimer Pullman owned the Pullman Palace Car Company, which built fancy railway cars for fancy people to travel in. With the depression raging, he did what his fellow capitalists in rail, coal, and iron were doing: he cut worker pay by 50 percent.

Workers at the Pullman Palace Car Company lived in the town of Pullman—a company town built around Pullman's factory south of Chicago. Everything in the town of Pullman was owned by Pullman. And everything in the town needed to be approved by him:

> *the books in the library,*
> *the performances at the theater,*
> *the sermon in the church,*
> *the products on the shelves in the store,*

the curriculum taught in the school, and
the flowers planted in the window boxes.

The town of Pullman had no bars or taverns because Pullman didn't approve of his workers drinking. (Of course, he drank.)

There was also no town hall—he didn't want his workers gathering together for anything but church.

Pullman workers worked six days a week, but rarely saw a paycheck. The company subtracted rent and any bills at the company store, and if a worker's aunt or cousin got sick and they couldn't pay what they owed, the company took this amount out as well. At the end of the month, instead of Pullman paying his worker a wage, the worker often received a paper containing the sum they owed him.

Life in Pullman's town was pretty much crap, and it was about to get 50 percent worse.

But then along came Debs. Tired of all the above, he formed the American Railway Union (ARU), an industrial union bringing workers together across an entire industry, both skilled and unskilled. His goal was "*to eliminate the aristocracy of labor*," or trade (craft) unions . . . the very thing Gompers and the AFL were busy embracing, and as a consequence, prospering from.

Pullman workers—a hotbed of unskilled labor—joined the ARU in droves. So too did 150,000 other railway workers. Opening its arms to the unskilled proved wildly successful. The ARU quickly rivaled the AFL in membership.

(Note: This number could have been even higher. Debs had envisioned—and voted for—total inclusivity for the ARU; however, a democratic vote of the rest of the union leadership denied membership to Black railroad workers by a vote of 110 to 112. Ditching solidarity is never the answer.)

White Pullman workers—now all union members of the ARU—attempted to talk to their boss through arbitration, where union workers and Pullman would sit in a room with a third neutral person to help bring the two parties into an agreement.

Pullman refused.

So in May of 1894, his workers did the only thing they could—walk off the job. Feeling quite desperate, they announced, *"We do not expect the company to concede our demands. We do not know what the outcome will be, and in fact we do not care much. We do know we are working for less wages than will maintain ourselves and our families in the necessaries of life, and on that proposition we absolutely refuse to work any longer."*

A month later, the Pullman workers were still out on strike. They met with Debs to float a risky idea: a boycott of Pullman cars.

This meant all railroad workers would uncouple those fancy Pullman cars, recouple the train without them, and then send the train on its way. This meant a lot of rich people stranded in train stations and a lot of workers across the railroad industry involved in the Pullman Strike. This meant Debs was about to step right in it . . . and he knew it.

He tried one last time to arbitrate. Pullman refused. The ARU voted unanimously for the boycott. This included 150,000 rail workers from across the country.

The unanimous vote was part solidarity with Pullman workers, but also part frustration with the industry-wide wage cuts all railroad workers had recently experienced. Because the railroad brotherhoods—those trade (craft) unions—hadn't stopped the cuts, railway workers were now turning to Debs and his ARU.

What Debs and the ARU did not know was that all the managers of all the railroad companies in the United States had met the year before in Chicago and formed an illegal plan. They called themselves the General Managers' Association (GMA) and they called the plan the Chicago Plan. They wanted to cut all wages across the industry together in an attempt to—in their own words—*"add to our treasuries thousands upon thousands of dollars."*

The Chicago Plan depended on the pyramid of oppression— skilled workers fighting against unskilled workers, and no one fighting against the GMA. The ARU was not following the plan.

The boycott began on June 26, 1894.

The first switchmen to refuse to hitch up a Pullman car were in Chicago, and they were instantly fired. Eighteen thousand men walked off the job with them.

The boycott was now a strike. Within two days, all tracks running out of Chicago were paralyzed. Within three days, the strike included twenty-seven states and over half a million workers.

At this time in history, cars and highways didn't exist. What existed were trains and tracks. It was how things and people moved from one place to another. Now . . . nothing was moving.

The *New York Times* claimed it was *"the greatest battle between labor and capital that has ever been inaugurated in the United States."*

While Debs struggled to direct the enthusiasm of workers across the country, the General Managers' Association was busy pooling their enormous fortunes, staff, and political power toward, in the words of Pullman Strike scholar Almont Lindsey, *"the complete annihilation of the American Railway Union."* They announced that anyone refusing to do their duty (run those Pullman cars) was officially fired and blacklisted for life.

The few folks still on the job, walked.

The entire US rail system was shut down, and 750,000 workers were now on strike.

From coast to coast, the working class donned white ribbons in solidarity and camped out on tracks to keep trains from running. It was truly a national strike, and one without strikebreakers or violence, rendering the US Army powerless.

Behind the scenes, the GMA admitted that the ARU had them. There was only one way out . . . negotiate with their workers.

JK. There was another way—they could engage the power of the US government. They chose the second way.

The GMA and the United States government hatched a plan that neither Debs, the union, nor the workers would ever see coming because it was so terribly evil. Corporations and the government would turn this battle that was obviously between American corporations and their workers into one between citizens and the government . . . because if citizens are in a battle with the *government*, those citizens are called criminals.

It was a beautiful plan—if you owned a corporation.

The GMA and the government used the US Postal Service as an excuse. The strikers were allowing the mail through, as it was against the law not to, but sometimes if a mail car was attached to a Pullman car, it was stopped. The US Postal Service could have easily ordered mail cars not be attached to Pullman cars until the strike was over. But then the corporate-government plan wouldn't have worked.

As per the General Managers: *"It is the government's duty to take this business in hand, restore law, suppress the riots, and restore to the public the service it is now deprived of by conspirators and lawless men."*

The *"service it is now deprived of"* were those few mail cars not getting through. There had been no riots.

President Grover Cleveland and his attorney general—a long-time lawyer for the railroad companies—un-shockingly agreed. The attorney general ordered a blanket injunction—a court order making a person or group either stop or start doing something. In this case, the injunction was for the strikers to stop striking. The word *blanket* meant it applied to all strikers across the country.

Fun fact: 1,845 injunctions against labor would follow this one, until they were deemed illegal in 1930.

If the strikers did not listen to the injunction, they would be charged with criminal conspiracy to block the mail—a serious offense with a long jail sentence. The federal government could call out the US troops and arrest them all.

The workers didn't listen to the injunction.

Due to the astonishing nature of what the federal government was doing, the governor of Illinois sided with the workers. He said, do not send the US Army into my state.

The US Army marched into his state.

Until the army arrived, the strike had been almost entirely peaceful. With the army on the scene, everything changed. The railroad companies paid members of the crowd to start fires, over-turn train cars, block tracks, throw train switches, and wreak general havoc. This was followed with headlines in national papers like:

"From a Strike to a Revolution"

"Mob Bent on Ruin"

"Anarchists and Socialists said to be Planning the Destruction and Looting of the Treasury."

In the next few days, "order" followed the law, and 14,000 soldiers would kill 13 people, seriously wound 53, and arrest 700.

Unions across the country converged on Chicago.

What should they do?

This new injunction thing was happening, and the army was on the move. They didn't have much time. Many called for a general strike of all workers. But Samuel Gompers and his AFL—and it was now *his* AFL—wanted nothing to do with industrial unionism and unskilled labor. Believing that he, the AFL, and skilled white workers were the future of the labor movement, he walked away from the Pullman workers. The rest followed his lead.

Debs was arrested for conspiracy. All documents of the ARU were confiscated. Their offices were destroyed. Pullman rehired workers at half their wages.

And just like that—it was over. The capitalist class, like the devil fish, had grasped him in its tentacles and dragged him down.

The Great Upheaval, Haymarket, and the Pullman Strike revealed the extreme exploitation of American workers. It also exposed the American government as the partner of capitalists in that exploitation.

Labor was once again down, but as Debs saw it: *"They might as well try to stop Niagara with a feather as to crush the spirit of organization in this country."*

BLOWING THAT SHIT UP

Sitting in his jail cell, Debs wrote: *"The issue is Socialism versus Capitalism. I am for Socialism because I am for humanity. Money constitutes no proper basis for civilization."* Farmers in the Midwest wholeheartedly agreed, since that same devil fish had these farmers in its tentacles.

Like industry, farming was becoming heavily reliant on machines—mowers, reapers, harvesters. Machines cost money, and so did transporting farm goods to markets on railroads. Both banks and railroads were held in monopolies and set high prices that small farmers couldn't afford.

Companies called furnishing merchants cropped up to loan small farmers the money for machines and to pay the rail fees. When folks couldn't pay the loans, the furnishing merchants (who worked for the banks) got the farms. In 1880 there were close to 6 million independent farms being operated by individual farm families. By 1900, 75 percent of these families were reduced to tenants, working their old farms for the banks.

The rise in radical farmers began in Texas. They called themselves the Farmers' Alliance (FA) and were at first formed like a cooperative—buying and selling seed and equipment together to get a better price and be able to compete with larger farms and the growing number of corporate farms.

It was a simple idea, and a way for the farmers to bypass banks.

But less like a cooperative and more like a political movement, the Farmers' Alliance kept going—attempting to change the system that was slowly killing them off. In a few short years, it grew from a single alliance in Texas to over 3,000 groups across forty-three states.

The Farmers' Alliance petitioned the government for help, but the government told them to stand on their own two feet.

Hmm. The railroads were given free land and tax subsidies, and the banks were given tax money to loan back to Americans. Neither the railroads nor the banks—the two industries busy hosing farmers—were standing on their own two feet.

The Farmers' Alliance and industrial workers came together for a national conference where they called on government to change the laws in order to *"secure to our people freedom from the onerous and shameful abuses that the industrial classes are now suffering at the hands of arrogant capitalists and powerful corporations."* The farmers and workers demanded that the railroads be regulated, that land bought for speculation be taxed at a higher rate, and that predatory banks be removed as the middlemen between farmers and loans.

The US government didn't bother to respond. So the Farmers' Alliance started their own political party—the People's Party, or the Populists.

At first, they were successful. Thirty-eight People's Party farmers were elected to Congress, along with a few gaining the governorships of states. These farmers were no joke, as can be seen in the fiery speech of Kansas FA member and Populist Mary Elizabeth Lease.

"Wall Street owns the country. It is no longer a government of the people, by the people, and for the people, but a government of Wall Street, by Wall Street and for Wall Street. There are thirty men in the United States whose aggregate wealth is over one and one-half billion dollars. There are half a million looking for work. We want money, land and transportation. We want the abolition of the National Banks, and we want the power to make loans direct from the government. We want the accursed foreclosure system wiped out. We will stand by our homes and stay by our firesides by force if necessary, and we will not pay our debts to the loan-shark companies until the Government pays its debts to us. The people are at bay, let the bloodhounds of money who have dogged us thus far beware."

The Populist movement grew so large and so fast that it began worrying the Republicans and the Democrats.

Republican Theodore Roosevelt was pretty up-front with his feelings on the People's Party: *"The sentiments now animating a large proportion of our people can only be suppressed, by taking ten or a dozen of their leaders out, standing them against a wall and shooting them dead."*

A pretty undemocratic thing for a future president of the United States to say. But real democracy can be scary to people in power. Voters had the power to remove them, and they knew it.

Instead of murder, however, the two parties would bury the People's Party using the same tactics regularly used against labor.

Division. Laws. Intimidation. Money. And the adoption of a few of the Populists' ideas into their own platform.

The Democrats stepped in first with division—the old pyramid of oppression. The Farmers' Alliance and the Populist Party were open racially. A leading Black Alliance farmer from Florida said: *"We are aware of the fact that the laboring colored man's interests and the laboring white man's interest are one and the same."* A white FA leader responded: *"They are in the ditch just like we are."*

It was known even then that racism was a useful tool in dividing the powerless. And the Democrats used it.

They encouraged the firing of white tenants from their land, and then replaced them with Black tenants. This was a double whammy: Black labor could be paid less, and it turned white farmers against Black farmers.

Next, they used the law.

The Democratic Party instituted voting restrictions against folks they knew would vote for the Populists: Black men and poor white men (women couldn't vote yet).

Finally, the Democrats made political promises to the Populists, who knew they would struggle as a third party in a country with a strong two-party system.

The Republicans took the intimidation and money front. They had employers shut down mills and factories, telling workers that unless they voted Republican, their jobs would be gone. They also promised raises to anyone who voted Republican.

In the end, it would be the above combination of race, laws, and dealmaking that brought down the Farmers' Alliance and People's Party, along with their own failure to create a stronger alliance between industrial labor and farmers. Its end would come with the election of 1896, two years after the Pullman Strike.

The People's Party would back the Democrat, William Jennings Bryan, for president against the Republican, William McKinley. Corporations came out in full force for McKinley, who would go on to win the presidency, stating: *"This year is going to be a year of patriotism and devotion to country. I am glad to know that the people in every part of the country mean to be devoted to one flag, the glorious Stars and Stripes; that the people of this country mean to maintain the financial honor of the country as sacredly as they maintain the honor of the flag."*

The financial honor of the country?

Farmers, railroad workers, factory workers, miners, and all who labored at the end of the nineteenth century would totally disagree that there was much honor in how the country was being run financially. Anger and disillusionment ran rampant—which was evidenced when a small group of coal workers sent the country into the twentieth century with a bang.

Coal mining in 1899 was pretty damn scary. There were so many ways to die:

fire,
explosion,
asphyxiation,
electrocution,
being crushed to death,
and more!

After the Western Federation of Miners lost a decade-long struggle for safer working conditions to the Bunker Hill Mining Company, the miners were over it. Stealing a train, they piled on as much dynamite as they could find and took off down the tracks. Along the way, they picked up more miners . . . and more dynamite.

Local police attempted to stop the train. They failed.

Everyone knew exactly where those men were headed, and so everyone got the hell out of their way as it got closer to its destination.

The train arrived at the Bunker Hill Mining Company's headquarters with over 1,000 angry miners and 4,000 pounds of dynamite, which they promptly lit and sent down the track into the abandoned mine offices, popping that building like a pimple.

Violence from the working class brings on the full force of law and order.

The US Army was called in. The miners were arrested. And the state of Idaho endorsed a permit system allowing mining companies to never hire a union member.

SECTION THREE

The Progressive Era
1900–1916

CHAPTER 21

GOD AND SCIENCE PREFER
THE RICH

Ah, the Progressive Era. A shiny new century. The US had won another war—this time against Spain over Cuba. Territories like Puerto Rico, Guam, and the Philippines were being added to the country. The economy was chugging. And educated men were bettering society.

But the working class missed out on the shine. They were busy dying in the war with Spain for the benefit of American sugar corporations in Cuba. Or worrying that those new territories were cheaper places for corporations to set up shop, thereby reducing jobs in their country. As for that growing economy? It never did include growing wages.

In the end, the progressives and the shine won out in the history books.

The progressives were a group of liberal, white, and (mostly) wealthy men who took a look at American society and didn't like what they saw.

Poverty.

Uneducated masses.

Farmers and unskilled workers "causing trouble."

Progressives accepted capitalism's abuses as unchangeable, but wanted those abuses checked for two reasons: to help people, and to ease the longing of working folks for a changed system.

The progressives harnessed the power of state and federal governments to lessen inequality and corruption, as well as to build schools, hospitals, and housing for the poor. All good things.

But who were they helping?

Unfortunately, the enlightened progressives weren't totally enlightened. They set a standard for who got help and who didn't. As they saw it, not everyone deserved it. This is the crucial crossroads of gender, class, and race. Unmarried white women with children, the extremely poor, Black and brown folks . . . all tended to fall outside the realm of deserving help. Using something called social Darwinism (a budding "science" that Darwin had nothing to do with), the progressives embraced a belief called eugenics. This is a pseudoscience that uses physical and intellectual traits to separate those who "matter" in society from those who don't, and so those who receive help from those who don't.

Corporations loved eugenics because it took the responsibility of abuse out of their hands. It allowed them the argument that if people were poor and miserable, it was due to their bad biology, not their salaries and working conditions.

Mixed in with this false science was religion. If God rewarded the virtuous and punished the wicked, then the wealthy must be blessed. The flip side of this lie turned a poor worker into someone with a questionable character and bad genes. Or as the US secretary of state under presidents McKinley and Roosevelt put it: *"That you have property is proof of industry and foresight on your part or your father's; that you have nothing is a judgement on your laziness and vices."*

But the working class was far from lazy. They had been clocking ten to sixteen hours a day, six to seven days a week, from childhood until their deaths for close to four centuries . . . with little time for "vices." If they had a few vices, who cared? They had long ago realized that hard work was not the key to success the wealthy claimed it was.

The now-powerful Samuel Gompers had his American Federation of Labor join the progressives in focusing on people they felt were worthy of being helped—skilled white male workers. The past twenty years had taught the AFL that attempting to uplift all workers was tough. Playing the middle meant success for that middle. But it also meant leaving poor white people, Black folks, and immigrants behind.

Capitalists now witnessed two teams forming under them.

The progressives and the AFL who only wanted to help "deserving" people

versus

farmers, socialists, anarchists, and unskilled workers who wanted to change the rigged system.

Understanding that the collapse of the pyramid of oppression meant their downfall, capitalists quickly chose the former, and then fanned the flames of division.

CHAPTER 22

LEFT OUT IN THE COLD AND TRAPPED IN THE HEAT

Samuel Gompers's new team was a winner—for him, for business, and for skilled white workers. The most successful union of all time achieved its initial success from the decision to choose business interests over the interests of the rising number of unskilled workers.

And that number was seriously taking off.

Black people, white women, and immigrants were pouring into the workforce by the millions. Pretty much all of them were unskilled, so pretty much all of them were left out of the AFL. But these folks desperately needed to be organized against the strength of capital, because that strength was also increasing by the year.

Monopolies were on a meteoric rise. The 4,000 corporations that had existed in the last decade of the nineteenth century had combined to become only 256 corporations by 1904. Frederick Taylor introduced Taylorism into factories and mills—a system of dividing jobs into tiny tasks so that any worker could do any job. This made people interchangeable and therefore easily replaceable.

The open shop was introduced. This was a factory or business where no unions were allowed, and workers (mostly unskilled) were made to sign agreements stating they would never join one.

The new century also saw a growing number and strength of business associations, those groups of rich men who owned, ran, and invested in corporations. They in turn boycotted union-made goods, built armies of strikebreakers, hired scores of spies, and outfitted arsenals and corporate armies. They also boycotted newspapers that said anything bad about business, while financially supporting newspapers friendly to them. On top of this, the associations paid for propaganda in those friendly newspapers with articles overstating union corruption and repeating that unions were un-American.

Corporations weren't done yet. Along with the growth of business associations and the usual engagement of the country's law enforcement, armed forces, and court system injunctions against workers, they now began organizing powerful lobbies. These were groups of people paid to chat to politicians on the day-to-day about things capitalists wanted those politicians to do, like vote against safe working conditions or a national minimum wage.

If all the above weren't enough to bury unions, corporations replaced worker-led unions with company unions where management was in charge. Workers were "given a voice" in these corporate organizations as long as it wasn't about their jobs, their wages, or safe working conditions.

"Respectable" workers had allies in the progressives and the AFL. But the unskilled and unorganized had a harder time ignoring the hunger and homelessness capitalism produced. Hundreds of thousands of men, women, and children were trapped in sweatshops where they worked all day, every day, in filth, heat, and cold. The long hours and horrible conditions took their toll. In a single year in New York City (1904), 27,000 workers died on the job.

In one factory where chalk was used to help transfer designs from paper to cloth, it had been found that another powder was cheaper. The women who worked with the new powder lost their appetites, couldn't remember things, had their hands and feet swell, their gums turn blue, their teeth fall out . . . and then they died. The new powder was lead.

Out of the mounting failures of the progressives and the AFL stepped a new union: the Industrial Workers of the World.

CHAPTER 23

WHAT JUSTICE IS

Everyone who was anyone in the labor movement in 1905 was in Chicago for the first meeting of the Industrial Workers of the World (IWW), or, as they later became known, the Wobblies.

Eugene V. Debs was there, now the leader of the Socialist Party of America. "Mother" Mary Jones was there, a seventy-five-year-old dressmaker from Ireland who was a top organizer for the United Mine Workers. "Big" Bill Haywood was there, a miner since the age of fifteen and now the head of the Western Federation of Miners. So were representatives from unions spanning industries across the country—bakers, brewers, railroaders, metalworkers, and musicians.

They were there to form One Big Union. All workers were to be organized into a single union undivided by skill, industry, sex, race, or national origin: the most inclusive industrial union yet attempted. According to Big Bill: *"There is no color line in the furnace hells of the steel trust and there will be none in the One Big Union."*

The IWW quickly became a symbol of the struggle going on between labor and capital—not just in the United States but around the world. They made no apologies for their beliefs or for their goals. They were an organization of the working class, for the working class. The first sentence of their constitution set the labor movement on its head: "*The working class and the employing class have nothing in common.*"

Who were these folks?

Miners, lumberjacks, blacklisted railway men. They were the unemployed longshoremen from New England, laborers in the fruit orchards in California, and cornhuskers in Utah. They were often young, usually on the move, and creating solidarity and songs wherever they went. Their bard was a man named Joe Hill, who wrote his heart out until he was convicted of murder during a strike despite serious lack of evidence, and then executed by firing squad.

> "*Tie 'em up! Tie 'em up! That's the way to win.*
> *Don't notify the bosses til hostilities begin.*
> *Don't furnish chance for gunmen, scabs and all their like.*
> *What you need is One Big Union and the One Big Strike.*"

The IWW were serious labor organizers. They took to the road to bring workers into that One Big Union, standing up on actual soapboxes to invite folks to join them. In cities and towns, on street corners and outside factories and mills, they stood and spoke about bad wages, long hours, and unsafe conditions . . . and about changing all their lives by sticking together.

In this new century, union organizing had become something done behind the scenes by men who were mostly controlled by corporations and capitalists, and for men who were skilled workers.

Now suddenly miners and farmers were shouting about industrial unionism, singing songs about solidarity across industries, and inviting everyone—Japanese Americans, Filipino Americans, Mexican Americans, white women, Black women—to join them. They published their desire to break down the pyramid of oppression in over ninety newspapers in nineteen different languages.

None of this was going over well with the AFL or with employers.

Samuel Gompers attacked the IWW, accusing them of being socialists (which they were and professed to be). Capitalists were more blunt: *"Hanging is none too good for them. They would be much better dead."*

The Wobblies were jailed wherever they went. They responded by showing up in groups. When one IWW member was pulled from the soapbox and thrown in jail, another would hop up and keep talking. Sometimes they would just recite the Declaration of Independence instead of giving a speech, and even then, they were arrested.

What began as an organizing campaign turned into a campaign for free speech. From San Francisco to New Bedford, Massachusetts, the Wobblies stood up, spoke up, and were locked up. They started to scatter, making the police chase them around each new city. As soon as one group was arrested, another group in another part of town hopped on their soapbox. In Spokane, they didn't stop speaking until 600 of them were sent to jail in a single day. As one Wobbly song went:

> *"There is one thing I can tell you,*
> *And it makes the bosses sore.*

As fast as they can pinch us,
We can always get some more."

Jail was brutal, and some folks died. But that didn't stop the Wobblies. One reporter documented the free-speechers on the inside: *"They took turns lecturing about the class struggle and leading the singing of Wobbly songs. When they refused to stop, the jailor sent for fire department trucks and ordered the fire hoses turned full force on the prisoners. The men used their mattresses as shields, and quiet was only restored when the icy water reached knee-high in the cells."*

Their membership grew, and with it came more soapboxing. Their cases clogged the courts. Towns and cities complained that they were housing and feeding armies of Wobblies in their jails. The fight became one of endurance. Who would last the longest . . . the batons and jail cells of law and order or the voices of the IWW?

The winner would be the Wobblies. A Wobbly named Jack who was sentenced to six months in jail on a bread and water diet was asked if he had anything to say before he was hauled away. Jack did.

"The prosecuting attorney, in his plea to the jury, accused me of saying on a public platform at a public meeting, 'To hell with the courts, we know what justice is.' He told a great truth when he lied, for if he had searched the innermost recesses of my mind he could have found that thought, never expressed by me before, but which I express now, 'To hell with your courts, I know what justice is,' for I have sat in your court room day after day and have seen members of my class pass before this, the so-called bar of justice. I have seen you, Judge Sloane, and others of your kind, send them to prison because they

dared to infringe upon the sacred rights of property. You have become blind and deaf to the rights of man to pursue life and happiness, and you have crushed those rights so that the sacred right of property shall be preserved. Then you tell me to respect the law. I do not. I did violate the law, as I will violate every one of your laws and still come before you and say 'To hell with the courts.' The prosecutor lied, but I will accept his lie as a truth and say again so that you, Judge Sloane, may not be mistaken as to my attitude, 'To hell with your courts, I know what justice is.'"

CHAPTER 24

BROKEN NOSES AND BUSTED RIBS

The spirit of the IWW was catching on. The International Ladies' Garment Workers' Union (ILGWU) operated under the umbrella of the AFL. The AFL, however, barely paid attention to them due to the "ladies" portion of the name. Sparked by the actions of the IWW and led by an aggressive young woman named Clara Lemlich, the ILGWU seriously turned up the noise.

Lemlich had come over from Ukraine when she was seventeen years old to escape a wave of Russian violence against Jewish people. Within days of landing in the United States, Lemlich found herself inside a factory, hunched over a sewing machine from seven a.m. until seven p.m., seven days a week. Dark, dirty, either freezing or sweating, stuck with gross bathrooms and groping managers, the first English word she learned was *forbidden*, from the signs on the walls:

"Laughing is Forbidden."
"Singing is Forbidden."
"Talking is Forbidden."

Lemlich learned lots more English words. She joined the Women's Trade Union League (WTUL), the first national organization dedicated to organizing women, and started working for change. Then she got fired . . . over and over.

She was back at work at Leiserson's shirtwaist factory making shirtwaists—loose and frilly blouses made for women—and organizing when she helped convince the women at Leiserson's to strike for better wages and working conditions. Out to the picket line they went.

Targeted for her leadership role in the strike, Lemlich was followed home by a man hired by Leiserson. This man—an actual boxer—beat the crap out of Lemlich in an alley, breaking six of her ribs and leaving her a bloody mess. Labor organizing was not for the fainthearted.

Inspired by the women at Leiserson's, the women at Triangle Shirtwaist factory met to talk about joining the strike. Triangle immediately locked the women out of their jobs and hired strikebreakers.

The picket line now included both Leiserson and Triangle factory workers. It would also include Lemlich once she had recovered. They struck for weeks, asking for a fifty-two-hour workweek, a 20 percent raise, an end to paying for their own needles and thread, and recognition of their union. But with no work, no money, and strikebreakers in the factory, things looked grim.

The ILGWU needed help. They needed an industry-wide shirtwaist strike.

The AFL called a meeting. Three thousand women showed up. Gompers himself came to speak. He hemmed and hawed onstage about being patient. He wasn't about to call a general strike for a bunch of women in 1909.

More men followed Gompers. All of them talked about chilling out. It was not what the women wanted to hear. It wasn't what Lemlich wanted to hear. She sat and listened until she couldn't listen anymore, and then she jumped onstage.

"I have listened to all the speakers, and I have no further patience for talk."

Every woman in that room knew Clara Lemlich, and every woman in that room was hoping she'd do exactly what she did next—call for a general strike.

The crowd went coconuts.

They screamed. They stamped their feet. They waved their hats. And the next morning, they went on strike. Fifteen thousand of them. Within days, that number would rise to 30,000.

The owners of all the shirtwaist factories signed a "never surrender" pledge.

The police were brought in. More beatings and lots of arrests.

While one young woman—Lemlich—was having the crap kicked out of her a second and third and fourth time, another young woman—Frances Perkins, an investigator for an anti-sweatshop group—was standing across the street watching. *"The brutality of the police was terrible. They would take these young Jewish girls and bang them over the head with a nightclub. Pictures were taken of them bleeding with their noses broken open."*

Once again, things looked bad for the women. Then J. P. Morgan's daughter showed up. She wanted in on the fight.

Being an ally can be tough. You're not in the shoes of the people you want to help. Often you're wearing shoes that have been standing on the necks of people you want to help. But Morgan's daughter gathered her friends and, using both her money and her voice, brought public pressure down on the factory owners. She was extremely effective.

The shirtwaist companies held out another month, but they were screwed. The women had won.

Factory owners across the industry increased wages and recognized the union, except for Triangle. They were notorious jerks in 1910, and would end up becoming notorious murderers a year later.

Inspired by the militancy of the IWW, Lemlich and the women of the shirtwaist factories would go on to do their own inspiring. A few months following their stunning victory, the men of the cloak-making factories walked out on strike.

CHAPTER 25

BETTER WORKING CONDITIONS, OR NOT HAVING TO JUMP TO YOUR DEATH

It's easy to understand fighting for more money or fewer hours. But better working conditions? What does this even mean?

For the working class of the early twentieth century, it meant not dying in a horrifying way, because unfortunately, that happened a lot—like Debs's friend getting run over by a train, the young women who died of lead poisoning, or the many, *many* mine disasters. The workplace was an incredibly dangerous place.

There were almost no rules, regulations, or laws stating that workplaces had to be safe places. Even if some regulations existed, they were not often followed or checked up on. And if people like Frances Perkins found violations, the fines were cheap and frequently left unpaid.

Regulations only work when they are enforced by hefty fines. If parking tickets only cost a dollar, everyone would just illegally park and pay the buck. Mills, factories, and mines let people *die* and paid the buck.

But things were beginning to change.

The IWW was tramping about the country singing songs and leading strikes.

The ILGWU brought 30,000 seamstresses into the streets of New York, which then brought 60,000 cloak makers into the streets of New York.

The daughter of one of the richest men in the United States had stepped in to help.

Things were definitely changing. But they wouldn't change fast enough for the women at the Triangle Shirtwaist factory.

It was the end of a Saturday shift just one year after the end of the big strike. The buttonhole makers and sleeve setters on the eighth floor—most of whom were in their late teens or early twenties—were gathering their things to leave when someone shouted that awful word.

Fire.

It started in a scrap bin, a garbage can filled with pieces of cloth. There were a lot of these bins, and since it was the end of the day, they were all full. Now, in a matter of seconds, they went up in flames.

One of the workmen grabbed the fire hose, which was fed by a water tank on the roof. But that water tank was empty. (Later, Triangle would pay its buck for that violation.)

Amid smoke and screaming, 180 women ran for two doors, one of which was locked. Someone from the eighth floor called up to the ninth floor, where 200 more women had no idea what was happening. Neither did the workers on the tenth floor. But they would all find out within a few minutes, as the heat of the fire blew out the windows in the entire building.

Workers from the tenth floor ran to the roof, where students from New York University's law school quickly erected ladders crossing from the roof of the factory to the roof of the law school.

This saved the lives of dozens of workers. But the doomed young women on the ninth floor were stuck.

The fire was all around them, and many of the doors were locked. Attempting to find an open one in the heat and smoke was difficult. Those who made it off the ninth floor later described the horror of trampling over the bodies of women who had died of smoke inhalation.

Two elevator operators named Joseph and Gasper ran the elevator up and down—knowing the risk—and ended up saving hundreds of women. On its last trip down, women jumped onto the top of it, trying to save themselves.

Those who couldn't find the doors ran for the fire escape. Untested and unsecured (another dollar fine to be paid another day), the fire escape collapsed, and dozens of women fell to their deaths.

Those still alive on the ninth floor stood in the broken windows looking down at the street, grappling with an awful choice. People on the street, one of whom was Frances Perkins, screamed up at the young women not to jump.

But would they rather burn?

They jumped.

Some held hands. Some hugged one another. All of them died.

A reporter standing below wrote: *"I learned a new sound—a more horrible sound than description can picture. It was the thud of a speeding, living body on a stone sidewalk. Thud-dead, thud-dead, thud-dead, thud-dead. Sixty-two thud, deads."*

The fire department arrived. Their ladders didn't reach high enough. More women jumped.

By the time the firefighters had put out the flames, 146

people were dead. Piled up by locked doors. In broken heaps on the street. Tangled beneath the twisted iron of a failed fire escape. The youngest was a child of fourteen years old, who died along with her mother and sister.

The two owners of the Triangle Shirtwaist factory got themselves the best lawyer in town. They were found not guilty. On top of this, the insurance company paid them thousands of dollars for the burned factory (none of which went to the dead workers' families). Two years later, their new factory was fined for locking doors again.

They paid $20.

STOP THE CHANGE

While Lemlich and Perkins were attempting to change the world, there were others who were attempting to hold it back. The AFL had entered the twentieth century as *the* union. But it had a few problems. First, it represented less than 20 percent of the country's workforce. Second, it didn't care about organizing the other 80 percent.

For these reasons, the powerful team of government and corporations liked the AFL best of all. Was this helping workers? No. But it was helping the men who ran the AFL.

Let's talk about corruption.

Whenever unions come up in conversation, corruption frequently comes up too. This is because media owned by corporations makes sure to overreport union corruption. Most unions are not corrupt. But at this time in history, the AFL did have a problem with corruption. Why?

Power. Gompers and his AFL had become the only game in town—with the help of workers, yes, but more with the help of corporations and the government. Corporations and the government worked with the AFL under groups like the National Civic

Federation—which married the interests of capitalists with the labor-elite, but not with labor itself.

It must have been difficult to be a cigar maker, a shoemaker, or a pipe fitter, and suddenly find yourself being literally wined and dined by rich folks. This is where the leaders of the AFL found themselves. When workers questioned these fancy lifestyles, leadership said it was necessary to hang out with the enemy so they could bargain with them. But maybe also because the food was good and the perks even better?

One story in the Atlantic City newspapers went: *"Engaged in a game of bathing suit baseball with President Sam Gompers, Secretary Frank Morrison and other leaders of the A.F. Of L., on the beach this morning, John Mitchell, former head of the mine workers' union, lost a $1000 diamond ring presented to him by his admirers after the settlement of the big Pennsylvania coal strike. Capt. George Berkeley, a veteran life guard found the ring, whereupon Mitchell peeled a hundred dollar bill from a roll he carried in his pocket and handed it to the captain as a reward for his find."*

Baseball on the beach. Diamond rings. Rolls of hundreds. These folks weren't living the lives of workers any longer. The AFL had developed a corruption problem, with lots of union officials on the take in lots of different ways. So why wouldn't workers just vote them out?

That was harder than it sounded.

Over the years, the union leaders had developed something called bureaucratic control (vs. democratic unionism). Gompers had gathered loyal people around himself and then created a hierarchy of voting that kept them all in office.

Gompers was never accused of stealing funds, but many of the folks who supported him were. However, he needed them to stick around and vote him into the presidency each new term. Big business joined in with the corruption by handing out gifts like those diamond rings when the AFL took their side instead of having the backs of their workers. Business also gifted the AFL an oversized voice in their mass-market newspapers while shutting out competing unions like the IWW.

Corruption didn't begin and end in the Gompers era—like any large organization, labor has experienced bouts of corruption throughout its history. The most notorious example was the Teamsters' alliance with organized crime in the 1950s and 1960s, and even today, a group of UAW senior officials sit in jail after pleading guilty to stealing union money.

But it's important to note that the bulk of the unions that made up the AFL were not corrupt. And corruption wasn't invented by unions, as journalists of the era—called muckrakers—pointed out over and over again. The muckrakers called it "the system": *The United States as government of the corporations and privileged interests, under political machines and their tools and their beneficiaries, for the enormous enrichment of the privileged few and for the perpetuation of machine-rule.*

Let's talk about other machines—the kind that grind and turn, which were a growing problem for the AFL.

Machines were taking over industry, but the 20 percent of the workforce that the AFL organized were craft union men. Handcrafted goods were on the way out, and craft unionism was on the way out along with them. Did they start organizing the growing group of unskilled workers in the quickly expanding technological industry or did they double down on the past? You can probably guess.

A typical example was that of the National Window Glass Union (AFL-NWGU) with their fantastic motto, "Never Surrender." The NWGU began in 1880, and by 1910 it controlled every shop in its trade. But by 1926 it *had* surrendered. Glass had been a hand industry, meaning it took skill and knowledge of chemistry to make it. But the introduction of the cylinder blowing machine in 1902 replaced skill and knowledge, and without the organizing of unskilled workers as a part of its union, the union died.

Just as American business had transformed from small shops into corporations, trusts, and monopolies, the American worker was shifting from skilled to unskilled.

Corruption, mechanization, automation . . . there was no shortage of problems for labor during the Progressive Era, and along came another—the ballot box.

Political action came up again and again. Should unions pick sides in politics? Should unions create their own political party? Both the IWW and the AFL chose a no-politics route. Neither made a good decision.

Although the AFL's policy was to stay out of politics, it did attempt to lobby Congress to put an end to injunctions like the court order that had stopped the Pullman railway strikers in their tracks. Injunctions were now being used by corporations on a regular basis. They essentially made it illegal for unions to fight the abuses of their employers.

In the famous case of the Danbury Hatters, the owner of the

company ordered an injunction, the workers continued to strike, and the judge ruled that the strikers be individually held financially responsible for any money lost by the company while they were on strike. Individually responsible! Unlike corporate owners, who were never held individually responsible for anything their companies did.

The AFL saw little success lobbying the government against injunctions, as was summed up by *New Time*, a Spokane newspaper: "*Mr. Gompers betrays his ignorance of the class character of our government when he hopes that candidates of parties whose campaign expenses are paid by corporations, who owe their whole power to the fact that they are backed by corporate wealth, are going to vote for any bills which will interfere with their benefactors, the corporations.*"

But when unions did jump into political action, especially on a local level, they saw tremendous success.

After years of being clubbed and shot by company mercenaries, the police, and the army, workers in San Francisco fought back in 1901 by forming their own political party called the Union Labor Party of San Francisco. They put up a candidate for mayor and voted him in. The next time a corporation called on the mayor for police protection during a strike, the mayor said no.

Deprived of their personal army, business was forced to talk with the workers and hammer out an agreement. That agreement meant higher wages and shorter working hours for everyone in the city. The strikers won. San Francisco became the most "unionist" town in the United States overnight.

Of course, corporations fought back. They ran their own people in the next election, calling for a mayor that was for "*all the people*" who wasn't "*a classist.*" This was code for saying *their* class should be in power and wielding that power for *their* class. It's the same as saying All Lives Matter in response to Black Lives Matter today; since Black lives (and Indigenous, immigrant, brown, Muslim, etc. lives) historically have not mattered, All Lives Matter becomes code for white supremacy.

The corporate-backed candidate lost a second time.

The mayorship of San Francisco having the backs of the working class is one thing—but the presidency of the United States is quite another. President Theodore Roosevelt, whose support of labor was erratic at best, came down hard against workers: "*The greatest and most dangerous rock in the course of any republic is the rock of class hatred.*" His speech continued by saying that the city, state, and federal government would protect strikebreakers using law and order. Much like the corporations' argument for electing a mayor from the upper class, Roosevelt's comment shamed the working class for rising to his level. The words *law and order* have always been code for "our" law and "our" order.

A MAGICAL COMBINATION

In the second decade of the 1900s, the American public looked around their country and didn't like what they saw.

Massive political and economic corruption was being uncovered by muckrakers. A novel called *The Jungle* by Upton Sinclair detailed the horrific lives of the working class inside the meatpacking plants of Chicago. Young women were having their heads cracked open by police clubs and jumping to their deaths out of factory windows.

The city of Lawrence, Massachusetts, wasn't Boston, it wasn't San Francisco, and it certainly wasn't New York—but soon, the entire country would be focused on it.

The American Woolen Company in Lawrence was owned by J. P. Morgan. It was the richest and most powerful textile corporation in America. How did it get that way?

By hanging signs all over southern Europe with fake pictures of textile workers in the US holding bags of gold and standing next to pretty houses. The ads worked. Thirty-two thousand immigrants flooded into Lawrence to work in Morgan's mills.

When they arrived, though, they were packed into four-story

slums with a single bathroom per building and spent their lives breathing in lint that later manifested as pneumonia, killing them in their forties.

During those years, they'd be exposed to verbal abuse, work speedups, accidents, poor air quality, sexual intimidation and assault, hunger, and disease. Far from bringing home bags of gold, they instead found themselves having to pay for a drink of water at work.

Meanwhile, company profits were increasing by the millions every year—$212 million in 1905 alone.

On January 11, 1912, workers walked off their jobs at the American Woolen Company. "Bread and roses," they shouted. They wanted a decent living, but also, they wanted to live lives that had joy and beauty in them:

> *"Our lives shall not be sweated from birth until life closes; Hearts starve as well as bodies; give us bread, but give us roses."*

At the time of the strike, almost all the workers were unskilled and therefore un-unionized by the AFL. The IWW had started a small local in Lawrence—Local 20—made up of low-paid, unskilled, foreign, and mostly women workers: a magical combination, as it turned out, for revolt. What was the spark that lit their strike fire?

Pay cuts.

The owners and managers of the mills made the decision to cut wages, believing the workers were not a threat. They believed this because managers had divided workers based on homeland

and language inside the mill, and knew workers were divided by homeland and language outside it. Workers came from twenty-five different countries and spoke forty-five different languages in Lawrence.

The owners and managers of the mills would turn out to be wrong.

When the workers were handed their reduced paychecks, the indignity tipped the scales already weighed down by years of work and starvation. They turned off their machines, ripped the cloth, busted the lights, and walked out. Within thirty minutes of receiving their reduced pay, the mill was effectively shut down. *"Better to starve fighting than to starve working,"* they shouted.

A week later, 23,000 people were on strike and the militia and police were camped in Lawrence.

Joseph Ettor, an organizer for the IWW, ran to Lawrence to lead the strike. Nicknamed "Smiling Joe," he was only twenty-seven years old, but had been busy in those years organizing mine, migrant, steel, and shoe workers. After the local police arrested Ettor (because they always did), Big Bill Haywood, head of the Western Federation of Miners, and the "Rebel Girl" Elizabeth Gurley Flynn, one of the top organizers for the IWW, came to town.

The workers—with the help of the Rebel Girl and Big Bill—began an epic nine-week battle. A battle they would win.

How?

Democracy!

The IWW gave each nationality equal say in the strike, with all mills and all crafts represented on an executive committee. Also, every striker had a vote—men, women, and children. If you were old enough to work, you were old enough to vote. Subcommittees were formed for food, finance, publicity, etc.

They don't call them organizers for nothing.

Each committee and subcommittee member had an alternate who they trained to take their place if anything happened to them. Interpreters were elected, and all decisions made by committees were relayed to the strikers in their own languages.

Meetings grouped by nationality were held every day, with a mass meeting of everyone on the weekends, followed by dancing, singing, and speeches.

Democracy wasn't given lip service; it was given full service.

The IWW might be organizing the workers, but it was the workers who were driving the strike. As was the IWW way, leaders were chosen by the workers from the workers, giving rise to strength and solidarity by shining a light on the existing strength and solidarity found in those who worked the jobs. Today this is called being run by the rank and file.

Reporters from across the country hightailed it to Massachusetts, where at first they ran the regular stories of violent strikers. But once encamped in Lawrence alongside those "violent strikers," different reports began to surface: *Never before has a strike of such magnitude succeeded in uniting in one unflinching, unyielding, determined and united army so large and diverse a number of human beings.*

Every day this diverse group of 23,000 workers would picket outside the mills. Every. Day.

The world had never seen a picket line this big. It was mesmerizing.

The mill owners fought back, and the police broke up the

picketing—it was against the law to gather in front of the mills. So the picketers didn't "gather," they walked. Day after day, the 23,000 strikers formed a marching and singing chain around the mills. After this first "moving" picket line, all picket lines began to move—and still do today.

Strikebreakers had to pass through this moving mass of people with police escorts to get into the factory. Each time they tried, hundreds of workers would fall to the sidewalk and dare the strikebreakers to walk over them or the police to arrest them—both often happened.

The business association of mill owners fought back again. They wrote in their newspapers that the workers were rich and had stowed millions in the bank in Lawrence.

The bank in Lawrence offered evidence that the workers had nothing in their bank.

The business association then sent in Pinkerton spies posing as strikers to gather information, but also to cause division in striker ranks.

It didn't work.

They had strikers beaten up. Police were instructed to club the women strikers on the hips and arms to keep bloody female heads out of the press, and to arrest anyone walking down the street on charges of intimidation and disturbing the peace.

The strike continued.

Once again, the US government was called on. It quickly came to the aid of J. P. Morgan and the other mill owners by sending in the US Army with its infantry and cavalry. Sharpshooting soldiers were positioned on the roofs of the mills with orders to shoot to kill if the strikers tried to break in.

With 23,000 people on the street, Pinkerton spies in place, sharpshooters on buildings, and the army and infantry marching and riding around town, bad things were bound to happen, and they did. A young man who had been playing his drum for the strikers was bayoneted in the back by the military. No investigation took place, and the soldier was let off. During that same incident, hundreds of other strikers were wounded by tear gas and bayonets.

The strikers kept cool. They understood that any trouble at all would be an opening for the police, armed Pinkertons, and the military to attack. A standstill formed, but the owners weren't done.

They lashed out at the IWW through the papers, saying it was the organizers, not the *"poor, ignorant"* workers, who started the strike, Lawrence was under *"a reign of terror,"* and that the IWW was working for *"the destruction of the present social order."*

That last one was true, because the present social order sucked for working-class people.

But this didn't move the needle on public opinion, and their mills stayed closed, so the owners used another reliable method—the frame-up.

Their newspapers printed a rumor that dynamite had been brought in by the strikers. The next day, the headlines screamed that state police had found three bundles of dynamite in the homes of people friendly to the strikers. The police detectives said the strikers' plan was to blow up bridges leading to the mills. Eight people were arrested.

But before they could be tried, it was discovered that a prominent citizen of Lawrence had purchased and placed the dynamite.

In turn, this citizen confessed that the president of the mill had paid him to plant it. The rich guy was fined $500 and the mill president went free.

On went the strike . . . until the next dead striker, Anna LoPizzo.

According to nineteen witnesses, police officer Oscar Benoit shot and killed LoPizzo. Instead of seeing a dead human, the mill owners saw an opportunity to use "law and order" to end the strike. Martial law was instituted, meaning no meetings or marching. Smiling Joe (who had been let out of jail because he had not broken any laws) and his fellow organizer, Arturo Giovannitti, were arrested for LoPizzo's murder, even though they were not present when she was shot.

It was Haymarket all over again.

With Joe and Arturo sitting in jail, the IWW did all they could to keep the strike going, part of which was feeding hungry strikers.

Big Bill Haywood reached out to the working class across the United States and that working class responded to the tune of $75,000. This was a lot of money at the time, but 23,000 people is a lot to feed. The Rebel Girl Gurley Flynn decided that strikers should send their children out of Lawrence. This would mean fewer people to feed, but also would remove the children from the very real dangers of striking. The word was put out through worker-friendly newspapers in New York City: "*Take the Children.*"

The response: "*Send us Your Children.*"

Hundreds of children boarded a train down to New York. These pale, sick, and underfed little kids were not a good look for the mill owners, who tried to convince the American people to see it from their point of view. In their newspapers, they said that the parents were inhuman to give away their children, that people like this were a threat to the American family, and that the children *"would become in time veritable breeders of anarchy."*

On top of this, they had the police try to stop more of these starving kids from leaving on trains so as not to be seen by people in other cities. On February 24, thirty police officers ordered mothers not to put their children on the train. When the mothers refused, both mothers and children were beaten with clubs and arrested.

The American public lost it—pictures of emaciated children, reports of women and children being clubbed by police, a dynamite plot by the owners, and two men sitting in jail charged with a murder they weren't present for. What the hell was happening in Lawrence?

The public outcry over police brutality forced the US government to send an investigative team to Lawrence. The governor of Massachusetts, not wanting to be part of the mess, informed the mill owners he would soon be removing the militia, as he didn't want the state's troops used *"for the purpose of tiring out or starving strikers."*

Mill owners immediately granted raises.

Victory.

The workers went back to work, but they did not celebrate. Instead, they threw themselves into the defense of Smiling Joe Ettor and Arturo Giovannitti, who were still in jail for murder.

They were joined by the working class across America, and then by the working class across Europe. Workers in Germany and Sweden called for a worldwide boycott of American goods.

The labor leaders of eight nations joined together to demand Ettor's and Giovannitti's release. Three days before the trial, the 23,000 walked out once again, this time in mass protest.

The trial lasted fifty-eight days. The men were locked in metal cages inside the courtroom. The prosecution called the men "*labor buzzards*" and "*social vultures*." There was no evidence.

Ettor asked the jury that if he and Giovannitti should die, that the verdict find them guilty of their real offense: their ideas, not the crime of murder.

On November 25, the jury returned with a verdict of not guilty.

CHAPTER 28

ONE STEP FORWARD IS
NOT ENOUGH STEPS

The IWW, the muckrakers, Eugene V. Debs with his Socialist Party of America, and even the AFL were improving things for American workers. They may not have always been working together as a team, but their separate efforts were paying off.

As one journalist wrote of Debs: "*That old man with the burning eyes actually believes that there can be such a thing as a brotherhood of man. And that's not the funniest part of it. As long as he's around I believe it myself.*"

Besides waging and winning strikes, raising paychecks, reducing hours, and bettering working conditions, these organizations were changing laws.

In 1912, thirty-eight states restricted the age and hours of child workers.

In 1913, the Department of Labor was separated from the US Commerce Department.

In 1914, the Clayton Act recognized that unions were not illegal organizations.

In 1916, the Adamson Act finally granted railroad workers their federally protected eight-hour day, with twenty-five states also passing laws limiting the hours in a workday for all workers.

These, along with a host of others—the Meat Inspection Act, the Pure Food and Drug Act, and the Federal Trade Commission (formed to control the growth of monopolies)—would begin to transform the landscape of the working class.

The response of business? More violence and repression.

In January 1913, one year after Lawrence, 25,000 silk workers walked off the job in Paterson, New Jersey, with the help of the IWW. Authorities arrested IWW leaders on fake charges, closed every meeting hall in town, and then arrested over 2,000 strikers. The Socialist Party of America stepped in to help, and every single one of them was arrested. When a newspaper editor protested the abuse of civil liberties, he was arrested. When the mayor of the neighboring town allowed strikers to meet there, he was arrested.

The strike failed. Years later, during a US government investigation, it was found that police authority had been turned over to the silk mill owners and the fundamental rights of strikers had been completely violated. They also found that all violence—including the killing of two striking workers—was the fault of the police and the hired mill military.

A month after Paterson, 15,000 rubber plant workers walked out in Akron, Ohio. The IWW stepped in to organize, and along with the workers, were attacked, beaten, and arrested. This strike also failed.

Loggers in Oregon struck three months after the rubber workers. The IWW headed west, and again they were attacked, beaten, and arrested. On top of this, many of the immigrant loggers were deported.

Yes, this strike failed too.

Behind the gains in laws and wages and hours was the very real pushback of propaganda, money, guns, spies, police, and the nation's military and legal structure, which sat solidly in the hands of corporate America. They used all these tactics to prevent, interrupt, deflate, inhibit, and confuse the labor movement through beatings, shootings, stalling, jail, and poverty.

What kind of money was buying the guns and influence? The Commission on Industrial Relations report of 1915 put the difference between rich and poor in pretty stark terms. The richest 2 percent owned 35 percent of the wealth. The poorest 65 percent owned 5 percent of the wealth. The numbers are worse today.

The robber barons who had accumulated the above big bucks were now old men and had been replaced by their sons. J. P. Morgan spent his days wandering through his collection of worldly treasures—Chinese vases and medieval armor. He died on a trip to Rome. Andrew Carnegie moved to a castle in Scotland, where he built a waterfall outside his bedroom window and ate his meals to the music of a private organist. He died in that castle. J. D. Rockefeller shriveled into a tiny man who handed out dimes to everyone he met. His son, John D. Junior, was still hard at work, though. Bragging to another corporate executive about the latest campaign he was leading against his workers, he said, *"I know that my father has followed the events of the last few months in connection with the fuel company with unusual interest and satisfaction."*

The events that he was sure his dad was following *"with unusual interest and satisfaction"* are what today we call the Ludlow Massacre.

Leading up to the Ludlow, Colorado, strike was yet another

recession. It started in 1913 and turned into a depression by 1914. President Woodrow Wilson took office with unemployment, hunger, and homelessness on the rise.

In sync with the economic downturn, the Ludlow strike began in late 1913 and dragged into 1914. Following the murder of one of their labor organizers, 11,000 miners who worked for J. D. Junior's company walked off the job.

The miners were immediately evicted from their homes— homes owned by J. D. Junior, since Ludlow was a company town. The miners and their families set up tents in nearby hills to live. This was not unusual. Across the country, striking workers were often evicted from their company-owned homes, with a tent becoming their only option.

The United Mine Workers sent in Mother Jones. The eighty-three-year-old veteran organizer, who had just been released from prison after helping the miners in West Virginia, was promptly tossed back into jail in Colorado. The miners continued to strike.

The company hired men to raid the tent colony with machine guns. The miners continued to strike.

The company called the governor, who, it will not surprise you, sent in the National Guard—financed by the Rockefellers.

The strikers and their families greeted the National Guard with flags, believing they had arrived to help them.

They had not.

The National Guard beat and arrested workers by the hundreds, and then brought in strikebreakers to work the mine— although not enough to replace all the miners.

The miners still didn't give in. When their determination lasted through the cold winter, it became clear to the company that more was needed to get them back to work . . . more violence, that is.

On Easter evening, the National Guard and hired company men drenched tents with gasoline while the strikers and their families slept. Then they lit the camp on fire. When the people awoke and ran from their tents, they were machine-gunned down. Many people died that night, including thirteen children and a pregnant woman.

While one son—J. D. Junior—gleefully pictured his father following these events *"with unusual interest and satisfaction,"* another father was to stand and testify for a judicial inquest about the events of that fateful Easter. Striking miner William Snyder's eleven-year-old son was killed by a bullet to the head that night. He remembered his wife screaming, *"For God's sake, save my children."* He led his family to safety carrying his dead child.

Thus ended the Progressive Era.

SECTION FOUR

World War I and
the First Red Scare

1917–1920

CHAPTER 29

SUBMARINES, A LUXURY LINER, AND SOME REALLY BIG LOANS

World War I broke out in the summer of 1914 between the Central Powers (Germany, Austria-Hungary, Bulgaria, and the Ottoman Empire) and the Allied powers (Great Britain, France, Russia, Italy, Romania, and Japan). What started this war? Scholars have a long list of ideas, but it always seems to come down to imperialism—numb-headed world leaders itching for other countries' land. Or as our own president Woodrow Wilson put it, *"Britain has the earth, and Germany wants it."*

Initially the US remained neutral, which generally meant we were busy selling ammunition, food, and other materials of war to both the Central and Allied powers. In the first two years of the war alone, US exports to Europe rose from $1.5 billion to over $4 billion. Not only was the US fueling a war overseas, that war was fueling the American economy at home. Profits were rising and the unemployment of 1914 was fast becoming a distant memory.

But there was a hiccup.

Supplying the Allied powers with war goodies was easy. The Allies controlled the Atlantic Ocean, and so the United States just shipped those supplies straight to their front door. The Central

Powers had no front door on the Atlantic, but the US needed to cross that ocean to get the Central Powers their stuff. When the US shipped supplies to the Central Powers, those supplies often got jacked by the Allies. It was a pretty big hiccup for the Central Powers, but it wasn't so bad for the US because the Allies still paid us for the stuff they stole.

To sum up: the Allied powers got double the goods, the Americans got paid, and the Central Powers got nothing. Officially pissed, the Central Powers came into the Atlantic with their submarine torpedoes blazing.

The war had been going hot and heavy for almost three years when the United States entered it in 1917. There are a lot of reasons listed in textbooks as to why Congress and President Wilson took the US into war. The one you hear about most is the sinking of a luxury ship named the *Lusitania* by a German submarine.

The *Lusitania* was secretly carrying weapons for the Allied troops. Some military person had the terrible idea to transport a large amount of ammunition on a ship filled with rich passengers because no way would the Germans bomb it out of the water.

The Germans bombed it out of the water.

Is it worse to place people's lives at risk to secretly transport weapons or is it worse to blow people up because you know those weapons will be used on your own people when they hit their destination? Tough question. War sucks. And World War I was definitely one of the suckiest.

The sinking of the *Lusitania* was a pretty horrific event, and for this reason it was an easy excuse for the US to enter the war. Why did Wilson and Congress need an excuse? Because most Americans did not want to enter the war, especially the working class.

There was a small group of Americans who did want to join the war: rich investors on Wall Street.

With the knowledge of a chosen few in the US government and in industry, American banks began financing the Allied powers, which was not very neutral of them. The first loan was for half a billion dollars, the largest loan ever to come out of the United States and on which the commission alone made bankers $22 million. By 1917, those loans had risen to over two and a half billion dollars. If the Allied powers lost, Wall Street would lose the money they'd loaned. They needed the Allies to win.

An old-timey email called a cable was sent to Wilson from the American ambassador in London describing the bleak situation of the Allied forces: they were losing. The ambassador wrote: *"Perhaps our going to war is the only way in which our present prominent trade position can be maintained and a panic averted."*

Less than a month later, President Wilson declared war.

CHAPTER 30

PARADES AND PROPAGANDA

For Wilson and Congress, going to war meant added stress. For US business, going to war meant money. For working folks, going to war meant dying.

The Socialist Party of America gained 12,000 new members and the IWW 30,000 new members after each announced their opposition to the war. Antiwar organizations like the People's Council of America for Peace and Democracy formed almost overnight and began traipsing about the country holding rallies with ever-increasing crowds.

These groups were met by organizations who were for the war, of which the National Security League was the most powerful. The league was a group of men from industry, banking, government, and universities, but mostly from industries benefiting from the war. It began supporting programs aimed at preparing the nation's citizens to fight. It pushed for "patriotic education" in schools while eliminating the teaching of the German language, which at this time was the US's most spoken second language. It also funded physical education of boys to give them a head start on manhood (read: becoming soldiers).

Investing in this super-patriotism (the worship of the Constitution, the flag, and America), the league financially backed a number of programs it felt were doing the most good for the country: opposing suffrage for women because they believed women voting made the nation look wimpy, weeding out sexual deviants (anyone not heterosexual) from the military, and holding lots of parades.

They loved parades. The league called them preparedness parades, and they were designed to get people excited about the war. These parades took place all over the country and in almost every major city, but today we mostly just remember one of them—the preparedness parade in San Francisco, where a bomb killed nine people and wounded many others.

Thirty-five-year-old Tom Mooney was arrested for the bombing before the bodies were cold. Mooney was an energetic union organizer who had just led a strike of San Francisco streetcar workers against a streetcar tycoon named Patrick Calhoun.

Charles Fickert was the district attorney of San Francisco. Fickert had recently won the election for district attorney using a secret fund of over $100,000 given to him by a streetcar tycoon named Patrick Calhoun.

There was no evidence that Mooney had bombed the parade, but once he was in custody, all other investigations into the bombing were stopped. Fickert quickly went forward with the case, promising the judge and jury *"new and startling disclosures"* on a daily basis.

None ever came. In the courtroom, Mooney was denounced by Fickert as a dynamiter, a dangerous man, and a German agent. The San Francisco newspapers agreed, creating the image of a vast pro-German conspiracy. Using perjured testimony, paid witnesses, and a jury working directly with Fickert, Mooney was convicted and sentenced to be executed.

Working people across the United States and from as far away as Europe filled the streets in protest. It was so widespread that President Wilson stepped in to stop the execution, commuting Mooney's sentence to life in jail and ordering an investigation.

Even after that government investigation had proved conclusively that Mooney had been framed, he still wasn't released. He would remain incarcerated for twenty-five years for a crime he didn't commit.

Despite super-patriot parades and indoctrinating children in the classroom, anti-war feelings remained strong. Wilson's top military brass estimated they would need a million men to volunteer, but only 70,000 did. Since the people who needed to fight the war didn't want to join it, Wilson enacted a draft.

How did people react? They evaded it to the tune of 350,000 draft dodgers. Of those who didn't dodge, 60 percent asked to be exempted.

Wilson had a big problem. The rich and powerful wanted war. The poor and powerless didn't. He had to change someone's mind, and it wasn't going to be the rich.

The government put together a publicity team, much like the National Security League. It was called the Committee on Public Information and was basically a propaganda agency assembled by the government and paid for by American tax dollars. Its single goal: sell working-class Americans on war. George Creel, a former journalist and now chairman of this committee, had a big job ahead of him. But he had tools—fear and nationalism—and he wasn't alone.

Standing before Congress, Wilson announced that Germany had "*filled our unsuspecting communities and even our offices of government with spies, and set criminal intrigues everywhere.*" Not even two months later he gave a speech saying "*the masters of Germany*" were using "*liberals,*" "*socialists,*" and "*the leaders of labor*" to "*carry out their designs.*" Powerful words like these gave the government reason to arrest whoever they pleased and neighbors an excuse to accuse other neighbors of all sorts of unpatriotic feelings.

The war was not only making the rich richer. Now the government was going to help those rich folks round up all the *liberals, socialists,* and *leaders of labor*—basically, anyone attempting to help the working class.

George Creel would also have the aid of Samuel Gompers. Gompers was pro-war, and he dragged the AFL in this direction without a vote from either member unions or from the rank and file. Together, Creel and Gompers formed the American Alliance for Labor and Democracy, with Gompers in charge. This organization pushed working-class Americans to sign up to fight the war, supported working them harder at their jobs to make stuff for it, and promoted putting off their own needs in support of it.

In return, President Wilson endorsed the AFL, spoke glowingly of Gompers, and talked up the "rewards" that would be heaped on workers once the war ended. (Spoiler alert: those rewards never came.)

To further tamp down protest against the war, the US government enacted the Espionage Act and the Sedition Act, laws that criminalized any "disloyal, profane, scurrilous, or abusive language" about the US government or military. It also criminalized any speech intended to "incite insubordination, disloyalty, mutiny, or refusal of duty."

Profane language? Disloyal speech? These are pretty broad terms, and they ended up getting a pretty broad group of people thrown in jail, from Eugene V. Debs, the head of the Socialist Party of America, who said in a speech in Canton, Ohio, in front of a thousand people: *Wars throughout history have been waged for conquest and plunder. And that is war in a nutshell. The master class has always declared the wars; the subject class has always fought the battles,"* to a plumber from upstate New York who had the misfortune to drunkenly rant in a bar, *"I wish Wilson was in hell, and if I had the power, I'd put him there."*

These two men weren't alone. More than 2,000 Americans were jailed, some for up to twenty years, many of them for doing as little as that poor plumber. Meanwhile, a federal judge in Texas suggested that six allegedly anti-war senators should be shot. He did not go to jail.

As regular Americans were learning to keep their mouths shut, the Committee on Public Information was busy running theirs. Creel was promoting the war in more than 20,000 newspaper columns each week. At the same time, another government division monitored hundreds of newspapers across all languages to be sure none of them were putting out words the government didn't like. Any newspapers not cooperating were shut down, and the editors arrested. Some papers were forced to remain closed for up to two years following the war's end.

Creel, big on opening up divisions, next created the Division of Civic and Educational Publications, publishing more than a hundred books that defined American ideals (as per Wilson's government), shouted down German militarism, promoted expanding Wilson's power, and endorsed censorship.

For the visual learners, another division was born, the Division of Pictorial Publicity. Its job was to generate vivid posters designed to demonize Germany. One of its most famous depicted Germany as a giant ape like King Kong swinging a helpless, half-naked white woman around. It read: *Destroy this mad brute: Enlist.* Soon, there was to be no such thing as German culture left in the United States.

What effect did all these departments and divisions have on the American people? Unsurprisingly, it increased fear and nationalism, as was the plan. And Americans began to see traitors everywhere.

CHAPTER 31

COLLINSVILLE, TULSA, BISBEE, AND BUTTE

One of these "traitors" was a thirty-year-old coal miner named Robert Prager who was arrested for "disloyal utterances" in his small town of Collinsville, Illinois.

Not content to let the law handle it, a mob of over 200 Collinsville citizens high on the fearmongering the Committee on Public Information had created, overpowered the police and dragged Robert from jail. They wrapped him in an American flag and beat him with fists and clubs, after which they hanged him to death outside town.

Eleven men were tried for Robert's murder. All were acquitted.

Like the citizens of Collinsville, the captains of industry were quick to wrap their extreme moneymaking tactics in the American flag. Any talk by working people about higher wages, slowing the speedups, safer workplaces, or more reasonable hours was either outlawed or decried as socialism or communism . . . code words for un-American.

War had people working harder and longer for less pay. Public opinion was to put up and shut up for the war effort. If anyone mentioned unions, attempted to organize, or even complained, things did not go well for them. For seventeen oil workers in Tulsa, it went worse.

As jobs go, oil workers had it pretty rough—in fact, they were called roughnecks. They lived in corrugated iron shanties where they paid half a day's salary to rent a shared cot. They were fed watery beans on a daily basis and breathed in gas that caused blindness and death. Safe drinking water did not exist, but dysentery did—an awful intestinal infection that caused severe diarrhea and frequently led to death.

Whether there was a war going on or not, oil workers desperately needed a union.

In Tulsa, Oklahoma, twelve oil workers attempting to organize their industry were arrested for vagrancy, a fancy way of saying hanging out and doing nothing. Five other roughnecks took the stand as witnesses for their fellow oilmen. They were also thrown in jail.

That evening, a robed group of men calling themselves the Knights of Liberty showed up at the jail. They dragged the seventeen men from their cells, tortured them, and then released them naked into the night, saying they would be killed if they ever returned.

Though the Knights of Liberty took responsibility for the attack, no investigation ever took place.

Copper miners in Bisbee, Arizona, were not faring much better than the oilmen. Copper mining was also a dangerous job: low oxygen, toxic dust, and temperatures reaching 125 degrees Fahrenheit, not to mention the long and dangerous crawl from the surface to the rock face and back again. Since the war had begun, the tunnels had become crowded with men, making the conditions even more treacherous.

The miners in Bisbee walked off the job, protesting a host of bad stuff, including unsafe working conditions. The company, Phelps Dodge, blasted the workers, saying the strike was pro-German.

In the middle of the night, the 1,300 striking coal miners were roused from their beds at gunpoint by company men, loaded into cattle cars, and driven by train into the desert, where they were incarcerated for two months by the US Army. Unlike Tulsa, an investigation took place. Those responsible from Phelps Dodge were put before a jury in Bisbee, who acquitted them all, stating the deportation "*had been a good thing.*"

Espionage and sedition laws arresting people out of bars.

Neighbors lynching neighbors.

Kidnapping condoned and aided by the US government— a precedent that would later lead to deportations of millions of Mexican Americans in the 1930s and the internment of 120,000 Japanese Americans in 1942.

And still most American workers were not convinced to support the war. It wasn't like capitalists and the government weren't giving it their all, but they were obviously going to have to work a bit harder. Especially with people like Frank Little walking around.

Frank Little was a legend in his own time. Born in Oklahoma, he worked the copper mines until he joined the IWW and began to organize. He was funny, talkative, and sincere about changing the lives of working folks, and because of this, working folks really dug him.

There was no industry Frank wouldn't try to organize—lumber, agriculture, and of course, mining. He crisscrossed the country, speaking on street corners in tiny towns and major cities. There was a fearlessness to Frank, and in his chosen line of work, he needed it. Employers despised him. Newspapers denounced him. Police jailed him. And hired thugs beat the crap out of him pretty much wherever he went.

Within months of Wilson declaring war, Frank openly called it a capitalist slaughter-fest for which no worker should die. In the end, he would die for that belief.

Following the Bisbee deportations, Frank immediately headed to the copper mines of Butte, Montana. Why Butte? It was the location of the richest copper mine in the United States and was run by the richest copper company in the United States—the Anaconda Copper Company. Anaconda didn't just own the mine, it owned Butte: employment, newspapers, politicians, and the local police.

After what had happened in Bisbee, you'd think Frank would have thought twice about heading to Butte. But Frank felt he had a good reason to go.

Butte had just experienced a horrific mining fire. It had happened in the early summer of 1917 at the Speculator Mine—a 3,000-foot-deep copper mine with over 40 miles of tunnels. During the war, production was everything, and everything required copper: phones, cars, electric lights. The morning of the disaster, 400 men went into the mine, but 168 of them never came out.

The fire was massive. Most men suffocated. Some burned. Others lived long enough to scratch goodbye notes to their loved ones on the tunnel walls. Going to work in 1917 was dangerous, and approximately 35,000 people were still dying on the job each year, but 168 dying together in such a heinous way reminded folks of the Triangle Shirtwaist fire. They felt for the men and their families, just as they had felt for the young women dying in lower Manhattan. They wanted to know what had happened. They wanted it not to happen again.

So Frank went to Butte.

For two weeks straight, Frank spoke to the miners about fighting for their rights instead of fighting the Germans. This gave the pro-company newspapers lots to write about—headlining each news day with how *"the authorities"* should crack down *"without gloves"* on such *"sedition"* and *"treasonable tirades."* A few days later, six men in masks calling themselves *the authorities* did just that. In the dead of night, Frank was pulled from his bed, tortured, beaten, and hanged from a train trestle. The investigation never found his murderers. The vice president of the United States joked about Frank Little's death: *"A Little hanging goes a long way toward labor peace."*

Instead of sending Frank's body back to Oklahoma, he was buried in Butte. It was the largest funeral the town had ever seen—3,500 people marched past 10,000 others lining the streets. Frank had been a top organizer for the IWW. He'd been brazenly tortured and murdered. Industry or police or both may have been in on his death. The US Army was now patrolling Butte. All this was diverting public sympathy to the IWW and the plight of working people.

Not a good thing for either the men in government or the men of industry.

CHAPTER 32

THE "RIGHT" KIND

The murder of Frank Little was a turning point in the United States. For almost a hundred years, corporations had been teaming up with the US government against the working class. In all that time, corporations had taken the lead in the clubbing, shooting, and arresting of workers, with the federal government marching in with an army or an injunction when needed. But now the federal government was about to step into the limelight of working-class repression by taking on—and crushing—labor's radical thinkers.

How would they do it?

Using something much less bloody than bayonets and bullets, but so much more effective: lawyers.

The United States' Department of Justice (DOJ) got its start in 1870. It was a scattered and unorganized beginning. The job of the attorney general was a part-time gig for decades. And until the injunction was introduced during the Pullman Strike, the legal fight against unions and its organizers had always been an afterthought. It was about to become a pretty big forethought.

And it all began with letters.

Six giant boxes in 1917 alone, to be exact. Capitalists began a coordinated and planned pen pal campaign with the DOJ—an avalanche of correspondence all demanding the same thing: the end of the IWW. They enlisted state and local governments as well as religious leaders to join in.

What did these letters say?

The IWW was dangerous. The IWW was violent. The IWW leadership needed to be arrested, jailed, and deported.

Using false patriotism and red-baiting in a time of war, capitalists saw their chance to label the labor organization as un-American "*fiends*" working for the Germans. One such writer to the president of the United States put it bluntly: "*I can shoot quickly and straight. Can I do anything for you? I would rather begin in Washington.*"

They began in Washington. A government commission called the Presidential Mediation Commission was formed. The unstated but completely understood goal was to eliminate the IWW. They immediately sent in spies.

In Minnesota, a business commission was formed called the Commission on Public Safety, run by the former governor of that state, John Lind. This commission's goal was also to eliminate the IWW, and it too sent in spies. Lind hoped to connect the labor organization to German money, and if that didn't work, to just make it *sound* like it was connected to German money. He met with the DOJ's Bureau of Investigation (eventually to become the FBI) to present his plan to use legal-sounding action to take out the IWW under the new Espionage Act.

Lind wasn't alone in his scheming. Concerned (and connected) citizen George Lewis Bell began yet another commission—no yawning—the California Commission on Immigration and Housing. Bell *also* sent spies into the IWW and *also* had a plan to ruin the organization. Bell's plan was to quietly arrest and detain IWW leaders across the country, and then infiltrate the organization and smother it from within.

Bell's plan was better than Lind's because it didn't mess with pesky legalities. As he saw it, the world was at war, and this was enough reason to arrest anyone those in power wished to. He met with President Wilson and admitted that the IWW hadn't done anything yet to hurt the war effort, but urged the president not to wait until they did.

When Wilson didn't listen, more letters were sent. A lot more.

Why was business and government so intent on destroying the IWW?

The Industrial Workers of the World was an industrial union organizing across entire industries. They signed up anyone and everyone who wished to join them. With America now at war, and the first draft calling 1.3 million men overseas, lots more anyones and everyones were taking the places of these draftees inside the mines, mills, and lumber camps. Namely, white women and Black men.

White women had been working in US industry since it began. But with the draft calling so many men to war, they were now entering the workforce in higher numbers and taking jobs that had previously been worked by white men. (BTW: women from every background also worked the necessary and unpaid labor of home and children, supplying all the workers for all the jobs.)

Black Americans had been enduring horrible working conditions in the south since . . . forever. But with Europe at war and

American industry in the north booming with war business, tons of low-paying jobs opened up. Previously, immigrant workers had been given these jobs over Black men due to racism and the pyramid of oppression, but now these would-be immigrants were busy fighting and dying in a war on another continent. Black people moved north en masse to fill these positions in a movement history calls the Great Migration.

With so many anyones and everyones now working in industry, sexism and racism ran rampant. White women were paid less than white men. Black men were paid less than white men and were worked harder. Black women were shut out altogether. These folks desperately needed a union. Since the AFL wasn't exactly reaching out and the IWW was . . . they began signing up with the One Big Union.

The working class was (and is) large and diverse, and because of these two things, it has the potential to wield some serious economic power. White men in business and the government needed to keep a check on that power, which meant keeping the pyramid of oppression between workers intact. Business and government continued to divide the working class by suppressing the IWW, while at the same time crowing over the AFL. As one attorney general of the United States put it: *In a great industrial nation such as ours, labor organizations are necessary, but they must be the right kind of unions under the right kind of leadership.*

The "right kind" of labor organizations were the kind that business and government controlled. Why? Because the "right kind" needed to support capitalism. Business favors capitalism because it is the economic system that supports it. Labor is more open to socialism and communism because these economic systems tend toward a more equitable world. The "wrong kind" were organizations supporting this more equitable world . . . which brings us to folks attempting to do just this.

Enter Russia.

Right before the United States entered the war, the Russian Revolution happened, and the Russian czar was overthrown. At first, President Wilson was thrilled. In about a month, he would be declaring war on Germany alongside Russia, and he'd often shouted that this war was all about making the world safe for democracy. The only problem with this line, which he himself would later call cow dung, was that Russia wasn't a democracy. It was a monarchy. With the czar now gone, that problem was totally solved. He announced war in April, because *the world must be made safe for democracy.*

But when, a few months later, the working-class Bolshevik party took power in Russia, quit the war, and made a dramatic call for world peace, Wilson became a lot less happy. It was one thing for a monarchy to fall. It was another to have the economic and political institutions of a government run by the working class instead of by the business class.

The United States attacked the new Soviet government in the press, sent money and American troops to help the old czar's army, and blocked all trade with the new government . . . basically throwing Russian democracy under the bus. (Even with so much US aid, though, the Imperial Army lost.)

Along with this attack on the socialist Soviet state came an attack on socialism at home. This included all socialist societies and groups, as well as the IWW. Best to get these folks out of the way to make room for a more democratic world.

THE "WRONG" KIND

The pen pal campaign began to have an effect. When an Arizona senator nicknamed the IWW "Imperial Wilhelm's Warriors" it was immediately picked up in the business-owned commercial press. This gave Lind's idea, that the IWW was connected with Germany, the traction it needed. (The IWW was never connected to Germany.) And though Lind and Bell were really protecting rich businessmen from labor's demands, they were about to convince the public that crushing the IWW was protecting the US from foreign threats.

The DOJ agreed to help, and using the Bureau of Investigation, they too spied on the IWW. After a short while, the DOJ decided to go with Lind's plan. The federal government would coordinate a legal attack on the IWW all at once, coast to coast.

They didn't have a legal basis for this attack. As they themselves put it, it would "*look lawful*" and that was enough. The case they would argue (once they collected the "evidence" and arrested the people) would be that the IWW may not have committed any crimes, but that "*someday, some of them would commit substantive crimes.*"

This would be the BOI/FBI's first act on the national stage. They would take down the IWW by *using* the law but not by following the law. In other words, by committing a crime.

Step one: open an investigation into the IWW publicly.

The IWW welcomed the federal government into their offices, but the government didn't take the Wobblies up on that. They'd already collected the information they wanted, taken in by hundreds of spies hired by businesses and local, state, and federal governments. They had also already met with a corporate lawyer who said yes to taking on the case, as well as chosen a judge to oversee the case. (Picking your judge is against the law.)

Next, the BOI obtained search warrants on a grand scale, allowing them to enter all forty-eight IWW offices across the country at the exact same time.

The Fourth Amendment to the Constitution states that a search warrant must have a good reason and be limited in respect to that reason. But the Espionage Act threw that out the window. These search warrants had no limits. Their plan was to take every scrap of paper, even the blank typewriter paper, and destroy everything left behind. This kind of tactic is meant to "*dispirit, disorient, and disable*" the people being attacked, and for this reason, it is illegal.

At two p.m. on September 5, 1917, just thirty-six days after Frank Little's murder, agents moved in and ransacked IWW offices across the country.

More warrants and searches followed in the next few months, until the budding FBI and the DOJ had collected five literal tons of IWW documents, furniture, and equipment, disabling the union, which was their goal.

Using these documents, the DOJ would bury the court under 15,000 pages of testimony against the IWW. It was easy to get things started because the DOJ had written the indictment before they seized a single piece of paper from the IWW. The charges included 166 defendants—the largest mass trial in US history to this day. The case, held in Chicago, was just one of four that would happen.

Who were the 166? They were the executive board, the organizers, the soapbox speakers. They were the workers of words: the writers, the editors, the poets, and the songwriters. They were American-born and immigrants from many countries, including Ireland, Poland, and Mexico. Some were older, most were young. One was a Black man, Ben Fletcher, head of Philadelphia's Marine Transport Union's Local 8. One was a white woman, Elizabeth Gurley Flynn, the "Rebel Girl." They were all from the working class except for one. A Harvard college student had written a letter to the IWW saying he opposed war—his only connection to the One Big Union. Lastly, it also included Frank Little, a dead man.

What was the charge?

Conspiracy.

The defendants were never charged with an actual crime but instead with a possible one—a whispered crime, a future crime, or a crime of thought or idea. Like the Haymarket Martyrs and Smiling Joe and Arturo Giovannitti, the 166 would go on trial not for any actions they were a part of but for the opinions they held. The indictment was forty-three single-spaced typed pages, legally dense, and totally confusing on purpose.

With the Wobblies sitting in jail, it was time to set up the trial. The attorney general, Thomas Watt Gregory, wrote a stunning telegram referring to the judge as the prosecution's *"main man."* He knew the "Honorable" Judge Landis was in the DOJ's pocket. Not a good look for someone who ran a government department with the word *justice* in it, but of course, justice was not what Gregory, Wilson, Lind, Bell, or any of the businessmen were after.

Helping these men suppress justice was Samuel Gompers of the AFL. Gompers would receive copies of court documents, notes, and questions about the case, and he would allow himself to be used by the prosecution for propaganda as the "respectable" voice of labor. A congressman who had questions about the difference between other organized labor and the IWW was told by the prosecution to speak with Gompers, because: *"No one understands the distinction better or states it more forcibly."*

The US government had given Gompers a choice: join the team about to hammer the IWW or get hammered along with them. Gompers had long been heading toward this choice, and he gladly signed on with the government, thus cementing the fate of the IWW.

The trial went on for almost five months. Most court cases have one defendant, a few might have two, but 166? Who could keep track? The judge, for one, could not. He eventually allowed every piece of paper into evidence because it was just easier that way.

Much of the prosecution's time in the case was given to reading these thousands of collected documents out loud to the jury. At one point, snoring was heard from the rows of defendants. Often the prosecution read Frank Little's letters—his were the most fiery, and so caused the most stir in the jury box. But of course, they were not the words of anyone actually sitting in the courtroom.

The defense attorney's closing remarks focused on patriotism: *"Patriotism may be the inspiration of many a heroic deed, but it is often used as a cloak by many a scoundrel as well, and you cannot always judge a man by the amount of noise,—patriotic noise he makes, and I do not want you to judge the I.W.W. that way. If patriotism means that one must believe in war as the best way of settling things, that one must believe that the wholesale slaughter of innocent people is right, then again I say the I.W.W. for years, has been in that sense unpatriotic, because the I.W.W. has not believed and does not believe in war."*

The prosecution's closing remarks basically asked the jury to convict the defendants for *not* making enough patriotic noise. *"Take this same organization, put it in the hands of honest, patriotic American citizens."* And *"then let them, if you please, be patriotic, work for their country, love their country, revere their flag, not desecrate it, not revile it, not go out to undermine the institutions of the country that has taken thousands of years to build up, because the struggle for liberty did not begin one hundred years ago."*

The prosecution's main man, Judge Landis, instructed the jury to convict . . . and in less than half an hour, all 166 were found guilty.

World War I went on for another year. The convicted IWW sat in jail, along with Eugene V. Debs, that poor plumber, Emma Goldman and Alexander Berkman (arrested for their opposition to the draft), and so many others.

After dying in the trenches, spending years fighting a foreign war, bending over looms, and digging in mines at dangerous and exhausting speeds, a new era did not dawn for workers. Instead, workers helped create 20,000 new American multimillionaires while they returned to the low wages, lockouts, police beatings, and bullets they'd known before the war.

A tired President Wilson, no longer shouting about "*making the world safe for democracy*," was now saying things like: "*War in the modern world is industrial and commercial rivalry. This was a commercial and industrial war. This was not a political war.*"

Which sounds quite a bit like what Frank Little had been shouting before he was tortured and hanged.

DON'T ROCK THE BOAT

The US government, business, and the AFL had all asked workers to chill out, work hard, be patriotic, and once the war was over, all things would be made right.

They weren't. Or at least they weren't made right for the working class.

The year after World War I ended, business was busy organizing around the doctrine of the open shop, an old idea that would eventually become what we know today as the "right to work." An open shop is defined as a workplace where workers don't have to join a union even if one exists at their workplace. Of course, what business knows it means is that workers don't have to pay union dues, which in the end strangles the union financially. The language business used when it declared their desire for the open shop says it all: *"The right of the employer and his men to continue their relations on the principle of the 'open shop' should not be denied or questioned."*

Should not be denied or questioned? That's a lot.

On top of this, Samuel Gompers—now labor's sole leader since most of the IWW was jailed—had some advice for workers: *"It is not good now to rock the industrial boat."*

How did workers respond?

They rocked the boat.

One in every five people walked off the job. Four million workers. 3,630 strikes.

The striking began in Seattle in February 1919 with 35,000 shipyard workers. They were joined by another 100,000 Seattle workers striking in sympathy. It quickly turned into a general strike, and except for essential workers like firefighters, who stayed on the job for obvious reasons, the city came to a screeching halt.

Strikers also set up food distribution, laundry stations, and a (weaponless) patrol to keep the peace. When the US Army was sent in—as they always are—the commander had to admit that he'd never seen such order.

The strike ended the way it started—peacefully. The strikers won. But once it was over, there was hell to pay.

Corporate and militia guns came out. Socialists, labor organizers, and strikers in other states and cities were attacked, jailed, and killed under newspaper headings like *"ringleaders of anarchy."* Why such a reaction to a peaceful and successful strike? Perhaps the answer can be found in the words of Seattle's mayor: *"The general strike, as practiced in Seattle, is of itself the weapon of revolution, all the more dangerous because quiet."*

Workers were tired. They'd just finished fighting a terrible war. They didn't want to return to the drudgery of inequality that had been their lives. They wanted fundamental change.

Unfortunately, the US government and business were not interested in change. They needed someone to ensure their rights would not be *"denied"* or *"questioned."* They needed someone willing to jump into the deep end of the villain pool.

CHAPTER 35

A VILLAIN ORIGIN STORY

J. Edgar Hoover was twenty-two years old when he started at the Department of Justice and only twenty-nine years old when he became the director of the entire FBI. He would go on to lead the FBI for forty-eight long years.

In that time, he would accumulate immense power, using it to carry out a long list of heinous acts in his pursuit of "law and order." Often these acts caused pain, disruption, and death for people who wanted to make life better for working-class Americans—people like Dr. Martin Luther King Jr., the Black Panther Party, Pete Seeger, Paul Robeson, and Eleanor Roosevelt.

But first, he'd cut his villain baby teeth on "*liberals, socialists,*" and "*the leaders of labor*" in the post–World War I era. And he'd have gobs of help.

His number one helper was Attorney General A. Mitchell Palmer. Palmer was on the short list to become the next president of the United States. Looking for a public image bump, he invented a new division of the BOI/FBI called the Radical Division, and then placed J. Edgar Hoover in charge of it. Together, Palmer and Hoover would direct what history would later name the first Red Scare.

His number two helper was the law. The government had kept many of its war policies on the books, just in case it needed them. J. Edgar Hoover would need them. A few of these "necessary" holdovers were:

> The Immigration Act of 1918, permitting the deportation of any immigrant holding radical ideas or membership in a radical organization. The US government had free rein to decide what they considered to be a radical idea or radical organization.

> The Alien Act of 1918, allowing the deportation of any immigrant considered an anarchist, even if said immigrant didn't identify as one.

> The Espionage Act and the Sedition Act, making any complaint against the war or government a crime. These acts were used to jail those people who the Immigration Act couldn't deport.

> State syndicalism and sedition laws, preventing individuals or groups from advocating for radical political or economic change by criminal or violent means, with the words criminal and violent being stretched to include noncriminal and nonviolent actions such as handing out leaflets objecting to US interventions in the Soviet Union. (Five young people who handed out these leaflets were found guilty and received sentences of up to twenty years.)

> The Trading with the Enemy Act, requiring all foreign-language newspapers to be approved by the post office. The postmaster general denied mailing privileges to twenty-two socialist newspapers during the war, and

then continued to use this law to censor journalists in
peacetime, effectively destroying the left-wing press.

The law might have been a helper to Hoover, but he actually didn't need it since he broke it quite often. Illegal raids. Secret testimony from undercover agents and informants. Seizing documents without warrants. Interrogating those arrested without the presence of defense attorneys. Detaining people in isolation, and with excessive or no bail.

His number three helper was the commercial press. Hoover sent out a letter signed by Attorney General Palmer to all major newspapers and periodicals beginning: "*My one desire is to acquaint people like you with the real menace of evil-thinking, which is the foundation of the Red Movement.*"

This was great news for the newspapers. With the war over, profits had dropped. But here was fresh drama. People had something new to fear: the immigrant radical.

The governor of Arizona would report to newspapers: "*The surest way to preserve the public against those disciples of destruction is to send them back forthwith to lands from which they came.*"

The president of Columbia University would warn: "*Today, we hear the hiss of a snake in the grass, and the hiss is directed at the things Americans hold most dear.*"

An American general stated: "*We should place them all on ships of stone, with sails of lead and that their first stopping place should be hell.*"

Disciples of destruction. Snakes in the grass. First stop, hell. Talk about sensational!

The truly sensational thing was that an "immigrant radical" didn't even have to be an immigrant. A senator from Tennessee suggested that anyone born in the United States who was acting up "*be deported permanently to the Island of Guam*."

The newspapers were doing a great job helping out our villain when the biggest helper of all showed up, number four: violence.

Bombs.

Thirty-six of them.

Mailed to a list of men against labor.

One of the bombs detonated, blowing off the hands of a maid. The others were intercepted before they exploded. Whoever sent the bombs—the culprit or culprits were never caught—had planned for them to arrive on May Day, the holiday created by the AFL back in 1886 as part of the fight for an eight-hour workday.

Why would violence help Hoover? Because it justified more violence against the very people Hoover and his pals wished to silence. And this was exactly what happened.

All across America, May Day parades were attacked by police, soldiers, and vigilantes in response to the mail bombs. During the May Day parade in Cleveland, police, military, and vigilantes killed one parade goer, wounded fifty others, and arrested one hundred and six marchers who were then held responsible for "the riots."

The *New York Times* reported that the May Day demonstrators were "*foreign agitators acting on behalf of the Bolsheviks in Russia.*"

They weren't. They were Americans. Acting on behalf of themselves in a May Day parade . . . an American-born labor tradition.

Instead of reporting that parades across the country were attacked by overly patriotic American citizens who claimed to love law and order, the Cleveland newspapers reported the "hero" of the day was an ex-marine who had lost an arm in the war yet was still able to *"use the other so well that five radicals required treatment by ambulance surgeons."*

The Red Scare was officially in full swing.

Five weeks later, nine more bombs were left on front porches. This time more of them exploded—one killing a night watchman walking by, another blowing off the front door of Attorney General A. Mitchell Palmer.

An anarchist pamphlet and a note about bloodshed, murder, and killing were found at the scene, both having miraculously survived the blast. The body of the supposed bomber—an Italian immigrant from Philadelphia—was also found at the scene. He did not survive. It was suggested he stumbled, and thus the bomb went off. Suspiciously, the medical examiner noted he had two left legs.

The commercial newspapers went bananas over the content of the pamphlet, crying Bolshevism and the overthrow of the American government. They ignored the evidence of a possible setup with the strange survival of the pamphlet and the examiner's discovery of two left legs. However, there were voices pointing out these other possibilities, like the *Liberator*, a socialist newspaper: *"The capitalist papers may shout 'Bolshevism' whenever an explosion occurs, but their shouting only strengthens the always plausible hypothesis that it was for the purpose of the shouting that the explosion occurred."*

It was a plausible hypothesis. Remember, for example, in Lawrence, where the boss had planted the bomb. Or in Haymarket, where the police had planted bombs. Even in this very case, the US attorney in Philadelphia wrote to Palmer and Hoover saying many of the most extreme agitators were their own undercover operatives, *"actively stirring up trouble because they know on which side their bread is buttered."* In fact, Hoover's own Department of

Justice caught private detectives planting bombs in Los Angeles to create more business.

After weeks of investigation by all crime-hunting agencies of the United States, they failed to find who was behind the May Day bombs. This mirrored the case of the bomb thrower at Haymarket back in 1886. The socialist newspaper the *Liberator* again pointed out one obvious possibility: "*We believe that the reason the perpetrators of these extensive and elaborate dynamiting have not been discovered is that some important person does not want to discover them.*" In other words, these bombs and this plot might have originated with Palmer and/or Hoover.

Meanwhile, both Hoover and Palmer were experiencing an increase in their personal profiles—and Hoover's budget from Congress was experiencing an increase of half a million dollars. Who cared that all they had was one dead immigrant with two left legs and a "somehow surviving the blast" pocket full of anarchist pamphlets. Attorney General Palmer had already pronounced: "*Ninety per cent of communist and anarchist agitation is traceable to aliens.*"

Misinformation and exaggeration were rising, newspapers were selling, fear was growing, law and order was gathering: it was now time to throw that law and order out the window, break the Constitution of the United States, trample civil liberties, and arrest and deport some folks. In the words of one famous preacher of the day: "*If I had my way, I'd fill the jails so full of them that their feet would stick out the windows. Let them rule? We'll swim our horses in blood up to the bridles first.*"

The preacher would get his bodies and blood. Hoover would see to it.

BODIES AND BLOOD

Hoover and Palmer hyped the fear of socialism and communism to serve their political careers. Capitalists hyped the fear of socialism and communism because these were ways of organizing economies that didn't put them first. Gompers hyped the fear of socialism and communism because he saw them trumping business unionism, which was fueling his comfortable life.

But what about workers?

US workers sympathized with the Soviet Union, which was attempting a worker-run government. US workers had been fighting for over 200 years for more control over their own lives with little success. They wanted their tax dollars to stop supporting the failed army of the now-dead czar. They wanted the blockade against trade with the new country lifted, because it was causing widespread suffering among the Russian people. They wanted their country to recognize the new government, just as it had previously recognized the monarchy of that country.

It was easy for business and the government to link American labor to the "red" of communism, because American labor openly sympathized with those "reds." This made labor vulnerable to the lies and terror being spread by Hoover, Palmer, and everyone else whose careers and pocketbooks it benefited.

Remember those 3,630 strikes? In this newest climate of fear and nationalism, all striking became a plot to overthrow the US government.

What would this do to the only real power workers had? It would kill it.

Sharecroppers in Arkansas would be one of the first groups to strike as the country waded deeper into the Red Scare. Phillips County, Arkansas, was known as the Black Belt due to both its fertile soil and the fact that a large number of Black folks farmed in the area. The land was mostly owned by white people, but the labor of farming was performed by Black people. According to the rules of sharecropping, the white owners and Black farmers would share the profit from the sale of the crop—that's why they called it "share" cropping.

How it really worked was: Black farmers farmed, white owners kept a list of all the money spent on food and equipment used by the farmer and his family, the owner sold the crops at the price he felt like, and then he deducted the year's list of money used by the farmer.

Unsurprisingly, Black farmers remained in constant debt to white owners. So Black sharecroppers unionized, and as a union, they went on strike: refusing to pick the crops until white owners agreed to enter into equitable contracts.

During a union meeting, a group of white men drove by and shot at the sharecroppers, killing one man and wounding another. The sharecroppers alerted the police. Instead of showing up to help the sharecroppers, the police showed up with a force of white people from a neighboring town who attacked the sharecroppers in their homes. In turn, the sharecroppers defended themselves.

Now white men from Tennessee and Mississippi poured into Phillips County. The Black sharecroppers fought for their lives. The governor of Arkansas sent in 500 soldiers with twelve machine guns.

Every Black person in Phillips County was arrested.

No white people were arrested.

It was announced that the governor had stopped a conspiracy.

It goes without saying that the sharecroppers' union was done. In the end, eleven Black sharecroppers were set to be executed and fifty-four others were sentenced to an average of twenty years in jail. Only the tireless efforts of journalist Ida B. Wells saw the men finally released after six years in prison.

Next, 365,000 steel workers walked off the job in six states. The steel workers were not only up against the Red Scare—now in full bloom—but also Mr. Elbert H. Gary, the chairman of J. P. Morgan's US Steel, the largest steel trust in the United States. Both Gary, Indiana, and Gary, West Virginia, are named in his honor.

Instead of heading to the negotiating table with his workers, Gary, with the help of the US Army, declared martial law— banning all meetings, restricting free speech, evicting steelworker families, kidnapping and deporting union organizers, and beating, arresting, and murdering people.

Twenty-two steelworkers were killed, along with an organizer for the United Mine Workers named Fannie Sellins, who had her head bashed in with a club by the vicious corporate-run Coal and Iron Police. Mother Jones would arrive—now eighty-nine years old and still organizing—only to be thrown into jail.

That woman was always getting thrown into jail.

None of this would be reported by the press. What would be? That the strikers were operating under a "*foreign element*," the strike had "*no good American reason*" and was "*not between workers and employers, but between revolutionists and America.*"

Alongside the above reporting came full-page reports from US Steel that highly paid steelworkers were vacationing in luxury hotels during the strike (a lie), American-born workers were returning to work while foreign-born were not (a lie), and that conditions were back to normal in steel plants (a lie).

These outrageous reports would end with "*Stand by America, Go Back to Work,*" insinuating that the US Steel Corporation was actually part of the government and that a strike against it was a rebellion against the country.

US Steel didn't need to work so hard. The US government was more than happy to help. Colonel W. S. Mapes, second-in-command of the troops imposing martial law, announced: "*We have conclusive evidence that the strike is in the hands of the Reds and we can prove it.*"

They couldn't, and they didn't.

The steelworkers put out a statement that ended with this question: "*Who owns this nation, one hundred and ten million people or one Gary?*"

The answer was "one Gary."

By November, the steelworkers were on the ropes. By Christmas, the strike was over, and the workers were back on the job with the same horrible wages, horrible hours, and horrible conditions.

J. Edgar Hoover and A. Mitchell Palmer rang in the New Year in a big way—with a massive raid across the United States, targeting socialists and communists.

Police, informants, undercover agents, and soldiers busted into homes, restaurants, bars, dance halls, and offices, leaving disaster in their wake. They seized personal letters, membership rolls, and random documents. They arrested 10,000 Americans, many without warrants. They interrogated and held them in terrible conditions for weeks without counsel and often without the knowledge of their families.

Palmer announced that information collected during these raids proved beyond a doubt that America's national security was at stake, revealing his open and eugenics-tinged bias against immigrants: *"Out of the sly and crafty eyes of many of them leap cupidity, cruelty, insanity, and crime; from their lopsided faces, sloping brows, and misshapen features may be recognized the unmistakable criminal type."*

In Boston, Palmer's *"unmistakable criminal types"* were ferried out to islands in the harbor, where they were held for days without heat. Several died of pneumonia. In Detroit, 800 people were kept in a single hallway for six days with one toilet and a single water fountain. Then they were marched in chains through the street for local press to take pictures of the *"dirty Bolshevik terrorists."* Some were children.

In the end, over 2,000 people were deported. Many were put on ships without proper clothing or shoes or any personal items. Most never got to say goodbye to family and friends they would never see again. Emma Goldman and Alexander Berkman were two of these people. Others just happened to be dancing at a club with a Russian name, eating at a vegetarian restaurant named after a Russian author, or singing in a Lithuanian choir. Today we call what happened the Palmer Raids—the culmination of the first Red Scare.

While the Red Scare launched the career of J. Edgar Hoover, it destroyed many others. People lost their livelihoods and, in many cases, their lives, as once again law and order was used for anything but law and order. Unions were decimated; membership dropped by almost 2 million.

By August 1922, World War I and the Red Scare were both over. Most of the actual German spies captured in the US had been freed from jail, and Attorney General A. Mitchell Palmer—who had once been praised as "*a lion-hearted man*" creating "*order out of chaos*"—was now being called "*Little Red Riding Hood with a cry of 'Wolf'*" by a tired country more interested in baseball than politics. But those 166 IWW members were still sitting in jail when they wrote to the president of the United States.

> *We believe in and uphold civil liberties because we are convinced that only through open and free discussion can the right idea prevail. Ideals are matters which cannot be altered by force. We claim that the honest convictions of the human mind cannot be caged by iron bars; we claim that the stream of human progress cannot be dammed with prison walls.*
>
> *Our bitterness does not count; it is to be expected. But the thing which does count is that for years the*

incidents of our persecution will be remembered with
growing exasperation by our friends outside of these
walls. These things will be recalled by the workers
of America every time the injunction, the bayonet,
and the anti-labor laws are used against them when
they strike to better their conditions. It will serve as
an example of class discrimination in a republic that
pretends to treat rich and poor alike.

Fear of socialism or communism is really the fear of corporations and rich people losing their dominant position to the
collective bargaining of unions and working-class folks. The writers of the letter were right about the United States not treating rich
and poor the same. It didn't. And doesn't. They may have lived (as
we do) in a democracy. It just wasn't a very egalitarian one.

The Great Depression
and the New Deal
1929–1938

CHAPTER 37

RAGS TO RAGS

The public was so over the Red Scare.

J. Edgar Hoover quietly stepped out of the limelight and focused on building up his spy network and helping individual states suppress pro labor thinkers and organizers. By the mid-1920s, the abuses of his Radical Division were so extreme that the newly elected President Coolidge ordered it closed, along with a total reconstruction of the Bureau of Investigation. Thankfully, Coolidge put someone in charge who would help shape a more just Justice Department.

Kidding. He kept Hoover.

Hoover hopped right on the new party line: that spying on people because you don't like their ideas is a violation of the law.

Kidding. He spewed the party line but kept on spying.

Hold on a minute . . . wasn't this period known as the Roaring Twenties?

The 1920s did roar . . . for those folks with the money to party. The new Mellon Plan (named by and for the secretary of the treasury and one of the richest men in America, Andrew Mellon) cut taxes on the rich by 50 percent—helping them buy all those cool flapper dresses and cigarette holders.

The working class received a 1 percent tax break while existing on below poverty-level wages, living in tenements, and still dying and becoming disabled on the job. Many of these poor were Black and brown folks who continued to be last hired and first fired, and who therefore were experiencing rising unemployment throughout the decade.

None of this inequality, however, was being reported in the commercial press. As one historian observed: *"All the chief avenues to mass opinion were now controlled by large-scale publishing industries."* Because the rich and powerful owned the national narrative, the "roaring" was reported and the struggle wasn't.

Some of the folks struggling were coal miners. Coal miners were just about the poorest paid workers in the United States. During one government investigation of coal miners' lives, the wife of a miner told of a single summer where thirty-seven babies died in her arms, *"their little stomachs busted open"* from hunger.

And if poverty didn't get them, the actual mining did. Deep holes, explosives, and lack of light and air all created deadly problems. Add in the fact that almost no regulations for worker safety existed, and it's a miracle anyone survived. Early in the decade, the American Association for Labor Legislation reported that the fatality rates in American coal mines were three times higher than those in England and four times higher than coal mines in Austria or Belgium—countries where safety regulations existed.

Hunger and accidents were only two of the ways in which coal miners met their demises—the third was being murdered by company militias like the Coal and Iron Police or by the US Army.

In 1921, West Virginian coal miners found this third way out of their very difficult lives at what became known as the Battle of Blair Mountain—the bloodiest strike in American history.

The US Steel Corporation and the Pennsylvania Railroad, two of the richest corporations in the US at this time, controlled the coal mines of West Virginia. Miners lived in company towns run by company and law enforcement thugs. They evicted, beat, jailed, and murdered workers, all without consequences. In the words of the vice president of the United Mine Workers about West Virginia coal miners: "*The individual is hopeless.*"

But two famous coal-mining families were determined to change their lives—the infamous Hatfields and McCoys. For over a hundred years, they had been shooting at each other. Then a bigger foe showed up to kill them both: US Steel.

Together, the Hatfields and McCoys joined the United Mine Workers and went on strike. Company men immediately moved in with their guns. But the Hatfields and McCoys knew how to use guns too. By the end of the summer of 1921, forty people were dead.

The miners were charged with murder, including Sid Hatfield, a young and popular member of the Hatfield family. The company men were not charged. The jury—made up of local people—acquitted the miners for lack of evidence, but on being released from jail, Sid was promptly murdered by US Steel men.

Now things went all hair, teeth, and eyes.

Miners from West Virginia, Pennsylvania, and Ohio grabbed their guns. Ten thousand of them marched on Logan City, the highly militarized center of U.S Steel. Instead of deescalating anything, the president of the United States, Warren G. Harding, sent in the US Army.

Mother Jones—now in her nineties—ran down to coal country. She lied to the miners, telling them that Harding had given her a message that he was on their side and had sent the army to take out the men in Logan City. She was trying to buy time, hoping the anger of the miners would cool, and they wouldn't march into town and die.

But they knew she was lying. The miners marched into town and died.

The company militia, US troops, and the fledgling US Army Air Force attacked the miners, dropping bombs and spraying poisonous gas. One reporter was amazed that *"airplane bombings of miners' villages could happen in America."*

Standing nearby, Mother Jones responded: *"Don't you know where you are? This is the place where they have been murdering men and women since labor first began taking coal out of the ground in West Virginia."*

CHAPTER 38

PROFIT OVER PEOPLE

The 1920s continued.

Women finally won the right to vote—though it remained a mostly wealthy white woman's right for the moment. The American Civil Liberties Union (ACLU) formed to legally battle the abuses of J. Edgar Hoover. Labor organizer and socialist William Z. Foster founded the Trade Union Educational League, attempting to build a labor political party. Labor organizer and budding civil rights leader A. Philip Randolph spent half the decade struggling to start the Brotherhood of Sleeping Car Porters, a union by and for Black railway workers. And Samuel Gompers died.

Commercial newspapers announced Gompers's death with headlines anointing him the savior of American labor. The decimated IWW's newspaper headline would scoff: "*Samuel Gompers Dead Since 1917.*"

All this and the decade hadn't seen its biggest event. On Tuesday, October 29, 1929, the stock market crashed—wiping out billions of dollars in a single day and leading to the loss of 13 million jobs. The commercial press ignored the impending doom as well as its aftermath.

"Brokers Believe Worst Is Over," reported the *New York Herald Tribune* two days before the crash.

It wasn't.

"Stocks up in Strong Rally," reported the *New York Herald Tribune* two days after the crash.

They weren't.

"Very Prosperous Year Is Forecast," reported *The World* a month and a half after the crash.

It definitely wasn't.

Perhaps the newspapers were taking their cues from the new president of the United States, Herbert Hoover, who said: *"We in America are nearer to the final triumph over poverty than ever before in the history of any land."*

We weren't.

In fact, we were further away than lots of "lands." Since the 1890s, almost all European countries had established national unemployment insurance—but the US had none. And so, without wages or social support, soup lines stretched on for blocks and shantytowns cropped up everywhere, named Hoovervilles after the man doing nothing about them.

Perhaps the newspapers were taking their cues from corporate leaders like Henry Ford, who complained: *"There is plenty of work to do if people would do it"* and then turned around and laid off 75,000 workers.

Eventually, other reports crept in . . . reports with more reality to them, but without any more empathy for those who were suffering.

In Detroit, a riot of 500 men broke out when they were *"turned out of the city lodging house for lack of funds."*

In Indiana, 1,500 men *"stormed the plant of the Fruit Growers Express Company, demanding that they be given jobs to keep from starving."*

In Boston, *"twenty-five hungry children raided a buffet lunch set up for the Spanish War veterans. Two automobile-loads of police were called to drive them away."*

History books often blame the crash on wild stock market speculation, making it sound like a momentary loss of sense. Not so, according to economist John Galbraith, who argues that this was no momentary anything. He says the United States economy was *"fundamentally unsound"* due to unregulated corporate and banking structures, shaky foreign trade rules, and poor distribution of income.

Looking back on all the other recessions and depressions in American history, it seems John Galbraith is right. A system where corporate profit is the main (and pretty much only) goal had proved to be volatile. The Great Depression drove 75 percent of Americans below the poverty line.

The above responses from the commercial press, the US government, and big business were consistent with their past behavior. Unfortunately, so was the response of the AFL. With union membership dropping like a rock due to unemployment, the new president of the AFL, William Green, chose to focus on the few people left working.

The Communist Party and the Trade Union Educational League's Unity League (TUEL-UL) did worry about the unemployed. These two organizations began a campaign to help stop the slide into poverty, proposing:

A shorter workday and a shorter work week to keep people employed.

National unemployment insurance, like all those European countries had.

Halting evictions and foreclosures.

Instituting public healthcare.

A plan for the government to increase "public works" (the building of roads, bridges, and schools).

Advocating for social and economic equity for Black, Latine American, and Asian American workers

They did not get any of these things. What did they get? Arrested.

This is a pretty telling exchange between police chief Mr. Scarvada and two men (Mr. Nelson and Mr. Bachman) who sat on a committee for arresting Communist Party and TUEL-UL members:

Mr. Nelson: What charge did you make against them that you might arrest them?

Chief Scarvada: There was not any charge.

Mr. Nelson: You just arrested them?

Chief Scarvada: That is all.

Mr. Bachman (attempting to help the police chief with his job): Why, you arrest them for disorderly conduct, do you not?

Chief Scarvada: Well, possibly that would be a good excuse. There is not any particular law we can act on.

The AFL did not support the unemployed, but they did support the attack on the Communist Party and TUEL-UL by business and government officials for helping to organize Black workers. The AFL's newspaper in Birmingham, the *Labor Advocate*, denounced those who "*openly preach social equality for the Black race. Any man who seeks to disturb the relations between the races is a dangerous character, and should be squelched NOW.*"

But the communists were doing a pretty good job understanding what desperate Americans needed, and the unemployed came out in huge numbers to listen to them, and then to march with them—in Detroit, Chicago, Philadelphia, Cleveland, and San Antonio, as well as smaller places like Shreveport, Louisiana.

They were met with violence everywhere, as reported by the *New York Times*: "*Hundreds of policemen and detectives, swinging nightsticks, blackjacks and bare fists, rushed into the crowd, hitting out at all with who they came in contact, chasing many across the street and into adjacent thoroughfares and rushing hundreds off their feet.*" Instead of headlining this as police violence against the unemployed, the *New York Times* went with: "*Red Riots in Many Cities in America and Europe.*"

Those still employed were now being made to work harder for less money. The chairman of Chase Bank noted: "*It is not true that high wages make prosperity. Instead prosperity makes high wages. American industry may reasonably ask labor to accept a moderate reduction in wages designed to reduce cost.*"

Ask? They didn't. They just cut wages.

And they didn't do it to reduce cost but to pay shareholders.

President Hoover thanked workers in advance of the cuts for being "*responsible.*" In other words, deal with it.

How did workers deal with it? Not well.

Whatever poverty white America was facing, Black America faced worse. Or, as the poet Langston Hughes put it: *"The depression brought everybody down a peg or two. And the Negroes had but few pegs to fall."* In the south, a hate group called the Black Shirts cropped up, attempting to drive Black workers out of the south under the slogan: *"If white men would assert their rights, there would be no unemployment in Atlanta and other cities of the South."*

The Depression was far from fun for working white women either. They were often kept on the job while men were fired because they were cheaper—and once the men were gone, wages were cut even further. On top of this, all women had to endure hostility from male workers and male family members. According to the National Institutes of Health, violence against women rises during economic downturns.

Mexican Americans also suffered severely, but in a very different way. Instead of being paid less *or* let go, they were deported to the tune of almost 2 million people. From Los Angeles to Detroit to Gary, Indiana, and beyond, workers from farms, railroads, steel mills, and auto plants were "repatriated" during a national campaign to rid the country of "undesirable aliens"—although most were US citizens!

Asian Americans were shut out from entering the country altogether. Most Asian countries had already been experiencing major restrictions on immigration for years. But now the Tydings–McDuffie Act of 1934 would join laws like the Chinese Exclusion Act and the Johnson–Reed Act to stop all immigration from the Philippines—a country colonized by the United States.

All this was in order to provide more jobs to white male Americans.

As the Depression deepened—and it kept deepening—the suffering intensified.

President Hoover finally announced a plan to fix things: get the economy back on its feet by handing over $500 million in tax dollars to "*stabilize business*," which would then "*trickle down*" to poor folks.

In the end, Hoover gave over $2.1 billion to American corporations and zero dollars to the unemployed.

What did zero dollars look like?

It can be summed up by a single headline from a Delaware newspaper: "*Starving Mother Kills Self and Four Children*."

DIGGING OUT FROM UNDER
ANOTHER ROCK BOTTOM

It shouldn't take tragedy to bring about change, yet it often does. True to this, the years following the Great Depression saw some of this country's most amazing changes.

Change #1: The Norris–LaGuardia Act.

The act banned federal injunctions in nonviolent labor disputes and gave workers the right to join a union without employers interfering.

Change #2: Franklin Delano Roosevelt.

President Hoover lost the presidential race to FDR in a landslide. The new president took the United States from repression to reform by enacting the New Deal—a group of experimental programs and laws attempting to solve the problems created by the stock market crash and the Great Depression. The New Deal saved capitalism from itself by bringing white working men into the halls of power.

Change #3: Eleanor Roosevelt.

The First Lady helped push through government programs like the men's Civilian Conservation Corps (CCC) and the women's She-She-She, which employed hundreds of thousands of people as part of the New Deal. These government programs brought hope and optimism to working-class people. As one unemployed person said: *"Hoover sent the army, Roosevelt sent his wife."*

Change #4: Frances Perkins.

FDR appointed Frances Perkins as secretary of labor. Perkins was the activist who had witnessed Clara Lemlich being clubbed during the Shirtwaist Strike and all those young women jumping to their deaths in the Triangle Shirtwaist factory fire. She made history as the first woman in a presidential cabinet. Perkins was the author of much of the New Deal—the first time the US government would create programs and laws to help the working class, which in turn helped to rebalance economic and political power in the country.

Change #5: The National Industrial Recovery Act (NIRA).

NIRA was the first law of the New Deal. Its famous section 7(a) gave unions the right to collective bargaining. Remember how English common law had made it illegal for those Philadelphia cordwainers to gather together to ask for higher wages because it was considered *"conspiracy against the good of society"*? It took from the birth of our country until 1933 for workers to finally have this right by law! But—and this is a seriously big but—NIRA hurt marginalized workers by establishing a minimum wage without outlawing discrimination. Since it was now illegal to underpay these workers, corporations fired them. On top of this, southern powers had agricultural workers—virtually all of whom were Black, brown, Asian, and women—excluded from NIRA (7a). The New Deal was mostly a good deal for white men.

Change #6: Social Security.

For the first time, American tax dollars would be used to help support American workers as we aged, became unemployed, or were born/became disabled—allowing all of us the opportunity to give and receive help through our collective hard work, and not through charity.

Change #7: The Wagner Act.

Less than two years after NIRA and 7(a) was enacted, the Supreme Court knocked it down. Democratic Senator Robert Wagner punched back with the most important law in all of labor history: the Wagner Act. It restored the right to collective bargaining and outlawed strikebreaking, private corporate police, and private corporate arsenals, all saving an untold number of lives as violence against workers dropped. On top of this, the Wagner Act formed the National Labor Relations Board (NLRB), which meant that finally, there was a "police force" policing companies. But like NIRA, the Wagner Act did not include a clause to stop discrimination in hiring practices, nor did it employ a single person of color at the NLRB.

Change #8: The La Follette Committee.

Led by Senator Robert M. La Follette Jr., the committee's job was to investigate violations of civil liberties—those rights and freedoms guaranteed by the Constitution in the Bill of Rights. Although the Bill of Rights had been around for almost 150 years, this committee was the first of its kind. It led the fight against all those horrible company towns and private detectives like the Pinkertons who were spying on and disrupting unions. It also helped to protect free speech, free assembly, and the freedom to organize.

Did capitalists change the way they did business based on these new laws and organizations? Absolutely not.

Did the working class take it lying down? Absolutely not.

CHAPTER 40

NUTS, AUTO PARTS, AND PISSED-OFF TRUCKERS

It began with nut shellers in Missouri.

St. Louis was the center of the nut business. Ninety percent of workers cracking pecans for a living were Black women. Ten percent were white women. Black women made three cents a pound. White women made five cents a pound.

In addition to the wage inequality, everyone's wages were spiraling downward. One Black woman who'd shelled nuts for almost twenty years had made $18 a week in 1918 and was making $4 a week in 1933.

The Black nut workers joined the Food Workers Industrial Union (FWIU). Then they wrote to Mr. Funsten of the R. E. Funsten Company—the biggest nut company in town—asking for equal pay, higher wages, and their union to be recognized.

Union recognition means that an employer agrees to bargain with the union. It sounds simple but it's not. Employers don't have to, and often don't, recognize the union. The employer knows if they don't voluntarily recognize the union, then the union (not the employer) must start proceedings to be recognized. These proceedings cost time, money, and effort . . . giving the employer more time to make legal moves to bust the union.

Mr. Funsten said no to it all.

The nut workers walked.

The Norris–LaGuardia Act had made it illegal for Funsten to get an injunction against the strikers. NIRA had given the nut workers the right to unionize and demand a minimum wage. But Funsten didn't care or listen.

The next day, the white women walked out. The day after that, both Black and white women from two other nut companies joined the Funsten nut workers on the picket line—1,500 women in all.

The Communist Party, along with the local Jewish community, fed all 1,500 (and their families) every day while the women walked.

The nut companies cried, *Communism!*

The local rabbi responded: *"The nut pickers' strike was not inspired by the Communists, but it was led by Communists. It was inspired by a wage scale which was un-American, and which did not make possible even the barest subsistence for the workers."*

The nut workers—and the people of St. Louis—did not take the "red" bait. So Funsten made an offer: a slight increase in wages for Black nut workers, but more than that for white nut workers.

They didn't take it. Nothing topples that pyramid of oppression like solidarity.

He tried bringing in strikebreakers—which was now illegal. But without an injunction to stop them from picketing, 1,500 women stood between those strikebreakers and the front doors of the nut companies.

Funsten made a second, better offer: three times their current wage. It included the erasure of wage differences between races and the recognition of their union. The women of Funsten Nuts had won!

Workers poured into unions.

Exactly one year after the nut worker win, auto-parts workers in Toledo, Ohio, would form a union and strike against the Auto-Lite Company for higher wages and union recognition.

But the auto-parts workers had a big problem. On the day of the strike, only half the workers found the courage to walk off the job. Striking is scary business for workers, and now this strike appeared to be lost. Until . . .

Six thousand unemployed workers showed up—not to take jobs as strikebreakers, but to join the picket line. Their solidarity led the rest of the workers to find their courage and walk out.

The Auto-Lite Company fought back. They hired a private police force—also now illegal—and attacked strikers on the street while company management dropped tear gas on strikers from plant windows. The workers and their unemployed allies held on. In came the National Guard with their guns. They killed two people and wounded two hundred. In response, eighty-five local unions announced that they would sympathy strike.

Auto-Lite quickly agreed to raises, the recognition of the union, and rehiring all workers. It turns out, even if laws exist to protect you but don't *actually* protect you, people still feel empowered.

Next came truckers in Minneapolis. The International Brotherhood of Teamsters organized 3,000 truckers and asked the companies of Minneapolis to recognize the union.

They said no. (Gosh, for once you just wish they'd say yes.)

The truckers went on strike, closing down the entire city using what they called "flying squadrons," which were essentially picket lines made up of trucks directed to shut down strikebreakers moving goods. The truckers used old-fashioned phone booths on street corners to call in every ten minutes and get their orders.

"Truck attempting to move load of produce from Berman Fruit, under police convoy. Have only ten pickets, send help."

Off the trucks would fly.

Sympathy strikes were now a thing, and 35,000 building trade workers walked off their jobs in solidarity with the truckers. The Farmers' Holiday Association, a farmers' organization, supplied all the strikers with food.

The Teamsters, the truckers, the building trade workers, and the Farmers' Holiday Association were rocking it, but the opposition wasn't sitting on its hands.

Business in Minneapolis was led by a group called Citizens' Alliance—one of the strongest business associations in the United States. Citizens' Alliance had been shutting out unions in Minneapolis for years, and it planned to continue its success.

The business alliance deputized an army of local upper-class folks as special police. The police and citizens' army occupied the market square in an attempt to break the strike by driving the trucks themselves. Hearing of the plan, hundreds of strikers marched into the square carrying clubs.

The police drew their weapons, and as one worker later noted: *"You can't lick a gun with a club."* The strikers turned to run, but then a single trucker drove straight into the middle of the square, laying on his horn. The market immediately broke down into a massive street brawl that went on for hours.

That night, both sides regrouped, but in the morning, clearer heads did not prevail. Instead, they engaged in a second brawl! This one ended with the strikers driving the citizens' army and the police from the city altogether.

But it was a short-lived victory.

The police and their deputies returned on day three with guns blazing. *"Police took direct aim at the pickets and fired to kill."*

Day four saw the familiar funeral march of the working class—this one 100,000 strong. It also saw the familiar leadership arrests—the governor arrested all strike leaders.

Cut off from their leadership, truck drivers around the city formed small groups called *"curb headquarters"* and led themselves.

The workers dug in. The governor gave up. Things were changing. He released the strike leaders from jail and raided the Citizens' Alliance office. The companies quickly offered an agreement that included wage increases and union recognition.

The truck drivers had won. They rightly celebrated for twelve straight hours.

But the New Deal period wasn't all a party. There were losses. Longshoremen in San Francisco shut down 2,000 miles of the Pacific coastline . . . and lost. Textile workers walked out of mills from New England to South Carolina . . . and lost. The Filipino Labor Union not only lost its lettuce strike, but its workers were run out of town by racist vigilantes.

Between the wins and the losses, workers understood one thing—they had stared down homelessness, starvation, and death during the greatest depression the country had ever seen, and they weren't going back. For the first time in labor history, they were (mostly) winning. Langston Hughes would later write:

> *Who made America,*
> *Whose sweat and blood, whose faith and pain,*
> *Whose hand at the foundry, whose plow in the rain,*
> *Must bring back our mighty dream again.*

CHAPTER 41

A BASEBALL GAME CHANGES EVERYTHING

Driven by that "*mighty dream*," 50,000 rubber workers in Ohio proudly joined a union. Solidarity inside the workplace created solidarity outside it. After making tires all day, rubber workers exchanged their work caps for baseball caps and played ball.

One evening before a game, it was discovered the umpire was a nonunion man. Both teams plopped down on the bench and refused to play until a union ump was found. An hour later, and with a union ump behind the plate, the game was on.

That week on the factory floor, an argument broke out between a supervisor and twelve rubber workers. The workers were just about to give in when the supervisor insulted them, and one of the twelve said: "*Aw, to hell with 'im, let's sit down.*"

They turned off their machines and sat. Their work piled up, log jamming the work of others, and then still others . . . until the entire factory came to a halt.

When workers asked what was happening, other workers called out that it was just like the baseball game—they were sitting down. The company, losing hundreds of dollars every minute, settled the argument in favor of the workers in under an hour.

Sit-downs became a thing.

Rumors of a wage decrease? They sat.

Inspectors roaming the factory in hopes of firing troublemakers? They sat.

A union leader beaten up by company thugs? They *totally* sat.

The sit-down was a literal game changer. But whatever Ohio can do, Michigan must do better.

Welcome to Flint.

In 1936, General Motors was the biggest company in the entire world and Flint, Michigan, was its beating heart.

Working in a GM factory in Michigan was not that much different from working in a textile factory in Massachusetts or a pecan factory in Missouri. The hours were long, the wages were low, and the work was endless. But of all the miseries of factory work, the speedups were the worst.

Assembly-line speed was always being tinkered with—but never in the direction of slowing it down. Workers would go to bed at night shaking from the nervous tension built up from the relentless pace—completing forty cars an hour, then fifty, then sixty.

"We didn't even have time to go to the toilet," complained a Buick worker.

The unskilled workers in Flint needed a union. Would the AFL come to their rescue?

Nope.

Once again, the fight between trade (craft) unions and industrial unions—between skilled workers and unskilled—had reared its ugly head. Out of this old void would rise a new star: the Congress of Industrial Organizations (CIO).

The CIO would follow in the footsteps of the Knights of Labor, the American Railway Union, and the IWW. It would reach out to unskilled workers in the existing industries of mining, agriculture, and railroads, but also in the growing industries of rubber, steel, and auto workers. It would embrace diversity—unionizing half a million Black workers and reaching out to the huge Mexican American community making up the bulk of the workforce across the American southwest. It would give rise to a new power of unions. And it would all begin in Flint.

The United Auto Workers (UAW) was a tiny organization under the umbrella of the new CIO, and General Motors was making sure it stayed that way. It fired anyone even whispering the word *solidarity* and spied on them relentlessly. The company had so completely infiltrated the UAW that in 1936, five of the thirteen UAW board members were GM spies.

GM's efforts paid off. Only 30,000 out of half a million autoworkers were represented by the UAW. Then in walked a young union organizer named Walter Reuther. And he had a plan.

Reuther's research had uncovered that two GM factories were essential to the company's production: one in Cleveland and one in Flint. If the union could tie up these two plants, all of GM—the biggest company on planet Earth at the time—would come to a stop.

Reuther first reached out to GM to discuss the relentless speedups, the terrible wages, and the constant layoffs.

GM refused to talk. And so the plan went into motion.

It was supposed to begin with a sit-down in January of 1937. But a few dozen eager workers at the Cleveland plant jumped the gun—Ohio couldn't stand getting scooped by Michigan—and on December 28, they sat down—forcing all 7,000 workers to stop working.

Michigan clapped back, and on December 30, Flint workers also sat down . . . at the wrong plant!

For Reuther's plan to succeed, they needed Flint's Fisher Body Plant #1 to shut down, but instead, the workers had mistakenly shut down Flint's Fisher Body Plant #2.

General Motors scrambled to capitalize on the error . . . sending out a team to move the machines to another location so production could continue. But before they could get there, workers rushed from Plant #2 over to Plant #1 and quickly shut it down.

The plan was back on track.

The next day was New Year's Eve. GM workers across the country joined their fellow workers in a Sit-Down Celebration at plants in Detroit, St. Louis, Janesville, Toledo, and Norwood.

Reuther's plan was more than working—it was winning. All eyes were now focused on the heart of GM: Flint, Michigan.

Inside the plant, workers ate in the cafeteria and slept on car seats. They formed a governing council, along with committees to deal with food, sanitation, and education. They set up patrols to keep out police and company spies. They even built a theater out of car parts and invited groups in to perform. Instead of building cars all day long at breakneck speeds, they worked with each other in hopes of improving their lives.

Outside the plant, the workers did the same: organizing to feed the sit-down folks inside, setting up picket lines around the plants, and helping the families who now had no money coming in. Inside or outside, the workers were learning just how important they were to the production of cars.

What did GM learn? Nothing. They proceeded to do what corporations in the United States had been doing for almost 200 years: they attacked with police, bullets, and tear gas.

The workers, however, had cleverly covered the windows with sheets of metal in which they'd punched holes. They stuck water hoses through and sprayed their attackers.

After one such six-hour battle, 350 women marched between the plant and the police. Now the guns fell silent, and the corporate lawyers got to work. GM sought an injunction to have the workers arrested for trespassing.

The workers claimed they weren't trespassing but had simply showed up to work and hadn't left. Didn't they have a "property right" to their jobs?

The local judge said they did not and ordered the workers to evacuate the plants.

This could have been the end of the sit-down, but it was quickly discovered that the judge owned GM stock equivalent to $3.6 million today. Because this judge had an obvious personal stake in stopping the sit-down, GM had to take their case to another judge. The workers stayed put.

While they waited for the new judge's ruling, GM tried other ways to get the workers out. They turned off the heat when the temperature dipped to sixteen degrees. They blocked food deliveries. They sprayed tear gas into the windows.

But again, the workers stayed put.

GM demanded the National Guard. The governor sent over 3,000 guardsmen but would not allow them to interfere with the sit-down, only to keep the peace. (The governor also owned stock in GM, but he sold it off.)

President Roosevelt was growing grumpy. He asked, *"Why can't these fellows in General Motors meet with the committee of workers? Talk it out."* Good question.

Frances Perkins met with GM's chairman, Alfred Sloan. He told Perkins he'd meet with the UAW. But a week later, he changed his mind. Perkins was pissed: *"You are a scoundrel and a skunk, Mr. Sloan."*

Things looked bleak . . . until Reuther hatched another plan.

They would take Chevy Plant #4, a plant that built one million Chevy engines a year. As part of the strategy, Reuther had the union leak a fake plan to GM spies that they were going to take Chevy Plant #9. When the police showed up at #9, workers took #4.

Victory was almost theirs . . . until that second judge issued an injunction.

Not only did the injunction say that workers needed to evacuate the plants, it also said—in violation of the First Amendment—they had to stop picketing . . . all by three p.m. that very day.

Now things didn't just look bleak, they *were* bleak. The workers inside the plant wrote to the governor: *"We have decided to stay in the plant. We have no illusions about the sacrifices which this decision will entail. We fully expect that if a violent effort is made to oust us, many of us will be killed."*

Workers on the inside readied for battle. Workers on the outside readied for battle. The National Guard readied for battle. Flint's anti-union city manager, John Barringer, hotly warned, *"We are going to go down there shooting."*

But things had changed in the United States. The laws had changed. The people had changed. The market crash, the devastating depression, the administration in the White House, the New Deal. Instead of *going down there shooting*, the governor sent a message to GM: *Negotiate!*

GM was in a pickle. They'd gone from making 53,000 cars a week to making 1,500 cars a week. They worried how the public would feel about buying cars from their company if they did *go in there shooting*. Finally, GM called Perkins and asked her to ask President Roosevelt to publicly request that GM talk to their workers . . . trying to save face.

Roosevelt publicly requested they talk to their workers.

After forty-four days of sitting inside plants (without a single life lost) and fifty hours of haggling, discussing, and a few screaming matches . . . a deal was made, and the sit-downers stood up and walked out to a union contract.

The *Detroit News* announced: "*Sitting down has replaced baseball as a national pastime.*" Three million workers would join a union in the next few months.

THE BATTLE OF THE OVERPASS

In 1936, there were 48 sit-down strikes.

In 1937, there were 477.

Gravediggers in New Jersey sat down.

Inmates in an Illinois jail sat down.

Even the National Guard who had served during the GM sit-down and had not been paid sat down.

Not only had the GM sit-down inspired other sit-downs, it also inspired companies to come to the bargaining table *without* forcing workers to strike. Corporations were finding it in their hearts to speak to their workers about improving working conditions and pay without beating, jailing, or shooting those workers. This was truly amazing. Even more amazing was the name of the company who came to the table first—US Steel.

US Steel had one of the longest labor rap sheets on record. It had opposed unions since it was Carnegie Steel way back in 1892. Remember the Homestead Strike? Remember Mr. Elbert H. Gary in 1919? The Battle of Blair Mountain? And now here they were, discussing jobs with the folks who worked those jobs.

Walter Reuther would attempt to take advantage of this

moment in history to do the unthinkable: unionize the Ford Motor Company. Henry Ford wasn't much into unions: *"Labor unions are the worst thing that ever struck the earth because they take away a man's independence."*

Ford using the word *independence* was a joke. He ran his company by sticking his nose deeply into the personal lives of the people who worked for him. When Ford Motor Company started, it hired mostly immigrant workers. Ford paid them $5 a day—if they met his standards of cleanliness, did not drink alcohol, and attended English classes twice a week. Upon graduation from his English class, he held a strange ceremony where his employees were asked to hand in clothes they had worn in their native countries (he called them costumes) in exchange for an American flag. If they didn't follow his rules, they only made $2.50 a day—half the pay. Independent men?

Later, when immigrants became what Ford believed to be radical—or in other words, they wanted fair pay and decent working conditions—he hired Black workers. They too were made to meet cleanliness and sobriety rules. On top of this, they also had to be churchgoers. He sent spies into both the factories and the Black community to be sure they were living the way he wanted them to. If they weren't, he fired them. Independent men?

Ford also employed the notorious Service Department—a gang of thousands of ex-cons and ex-cops headed by a man named Harry Bennett. The Service Department was antisemitic, racist, and highly dangerous. They were essentially a terrorist organization hired to scare Ford workers and discourage unions. This was the company Walter Reuther would take on three months after the success of the GM sit-down.

It was May in Detroit. Reuther stood on a public overpass near the Ford Motor Company. He was waiting for the shift change to hand out union leaflets to Ford's 90,000 workers. Before the workers showed up, Harry Bennett did. And he wasn't alone. He brought forty men from the Service Department.

Reuther wasn't alone, either. Like the Ford workers, he knew who Harry Bennett was, and what the Service Department did. In preparation, he brought fellow organizer Richard Frankensteen, news reporters with cameras, staff from the Civil Liberties Committee, and other union members to talk to the Ford workers. He had also obtained a municipal license to distribute the leaflets. But no one was asking for his paperwork.

What happened next? In Reuther's words, *"I didn't fight back. I merely tried to guard my face. They picked my feet up and my shoulders and slammed me down on the concrete and while I was on the ground, they kicked me again in the face, head and other parts of my body. This process went on eight times. After they kicked me down the stairs and slugging me, driving me before them, but never letting me get away. The more we tried to leave the worse it was for us."*

Frankensteen got it bad: *"They at one point put their heel into my stomach and twisted on it, and at another point they held my legs apart and kicked me in the groin."*

Some got it worse. One man suffered a permanently disabling skull fracture, while another man was tossed off the overpass, falling thirty feet to break his spine.

The news reporters, Civil Liberties Committee staff, and other union members tried to run, but the Service Department chased them down, most especially the journalists—ripping notebooks from their hands and smashing cameras on the concrete.

They pursued one reporter five miles before he finally lost them. Another reporter made it to his car, but the Service Department caught him, demanding he hand over the film in his camera. He handed over film . . . just not *the* film.

Following the battle, Reuther and the witnesses put out a statement about what happened. But so did Henry Bennett: *"I know definitely no Ford service men or plant police were involved in any way in the fight. As a matter of fact, the service men had issued instructions the union people could come and distribute their pamphlets at the gates so long as they didn't interfere with employees at work."*

But then the reporter published his photos.

The pictures stunned the American people, who for the first time would see photographic evidence of corporate violence against unions and working people. James Kilpatrick, the photojournalist, would go on to win a Pulitzer for this work.

Henry Ford blew a gasket. He fired 4,000 workers and had his Service Department turn up the terror on workers who remained employed. In the end, he would lose. It took four more years, but Ford Motor Company unionized.

Four days after seeing the pictures of the Battle of the Overpass, Americans would see the first televised massacre in labor history.

Chicago police fired on unarmed strikers of the Republic Steel Company while they picketed outside the company gate. The video, which is still viewable on YouTube, deserves a serious trigger warning for police violence, as it shows them shooting and killing picketing workers as they attempt to flee.

Not put off by this violence, Republic Steel would go on to fight its workers in a second battle in Ohio, where sixteen people died and three hundred were injured. This second one didn't get caught on tape, but it was later discovered that Republic Steel had hired the police and supplied them with 160,000 rounds of ammunition. Republic Steel would keep using physical force to deny its workers the right to unionize for another four years, just like Ford had, but again, the workers would win in the end.

CHAPTER 43

MORE NUTS

Mexican American women shelling pecans in San Antonio were making lousy pay in 1934, just like their pecan-shelling sisters in St. Louis. And just like their pecan-shelling sisters, when their pay was cut, they walked out. San Antonio nut workers lost their first strike. But four years later, wages were cut a second time, and the pecan workers walked out a second time. What would be the difference between 1934 and 1938?

Emma Tenayuca.

Born on San Antonio's West Side—four square miles of seriously bad housing—Tenayuca was arrested on her first picket line when she was sixteen years old. She graduated from high school the next year and began organizing pecan workers. When Julius Seligmann, owner of the Southern Pecan Company and self-proclaimed "Pecan King," cut wages in 1938, Tenayuca called a strike. And like so many organizers before her, she was immediately arrested.

But Emma Tenayuca had spent the last four years working, learning, and growing as an organizer alongside the pecan women who were also working, learning, and growing—and with their young leader now in jail, they simply took over their own strike.

Both Tenayuca and the pecan shellers had some pretty big foes. Foe number one was ye olde corporate and government power duo. The Pecan King undermined the strike by supporting a company union and hiring strikebreakers. Government officials added the fear of deportation using the Texas Rangers and the National Guard. The police layered on the usual violence of beatings, tear-gassing, and arrests.

Foe number two was the Catholic Church. The patriarchal church came out hard against the Mexican American women pecan workers, who were pretty much all Catholic.

The AFL was foe number three. It was also a patriarchy, as well as racist and notoriously not into organizing unskilled workers. Tenayuca and 90 percent of the pecan shellers were women, brown, and considered unskilled. Tenayuca was also a communist, which got everyone even hotter under the collar.

And finally, her own union piled on by replacing her after all the complaints about her being a communist, being a woman, and being brown.

Although Tenayuca was no longer in charge of the strike, she basically stayed in charge of the strike. As soon as she was released from jail, she got to raising money, collecting food donations, and motivating the shellers with her speeches.

After three long months of walking the picket line, the now unionized pecan workers—Local 172 of the United Cannery, Agricultural, Packing, and Allied Workers of America—settled with the Pecan King for higher wages, recognition of their union, and a grievance committee to talk about their working lives with their employer.

If only this were the happily-ever-after end. But it isn't.

Three months later, the Fair Labor Standards Act of 1938 was signed into law, setting the first federal minimum wage at 25 cents an hour. Since the Pecan King had been paying only 16 cents a week, he fired more than two-thirds of the pecan workers and mechanized the plant. With Christmas a month away, the now-starving pecan workers were forced to rely on charity from one of their biggest opponents, the Catholic Church.

But however fleeting the victory against pecan corporations might have been, the women who led the largest strike in San Antonio's history got to keep their confidence, community, identity, and union. Before Emma Tenayuca and the Pecan Strike of 1938, 100 Mexican American pecan workers were union members. After the strike, they were 10,000 strong.

As the 1930s were fast going down in history as the most militant, aggressive, and successful decade for American labor, horror was brewing in Europe.

In 1933, Adolf Hitler became chancellor of Germany. That same year, he dropped out of the League of Nations. In 1935, he broke the Treaty of Versailles and built up Germany's military. In 1938, the German people attacked Jewish synagogues and businesses in what became known as Kristallnacht—the Night of Broken Glass. And in 1939, he started murdering disabled people and invaded Poland, beginning World War II.

With war on the horizon, the clampdown on workers began. The Supreme Court ruled sit-downs illegal. States began passing laws to squash strikes, boycotts, and picketing. Both the AFL and the CIO called for no strikes during wartime. And the United

States House of Representatives formed the House Un-American Activities Committee (HUAC). Its job was to investigate right-wing fascism and Nazism, but it went after communists instead.

Hitler might have been breaking a few international laws and murdering people, but communists were leading the Funsten nut workers, Minneapolis truckers, and San Antonio pecan shellers in successful strikes, and this meant they had to go.

J. Edgar Hoover was back in business.

SECTION SIX

The Second World War,
the Second Red Scare, and
the start of the Cold War
1938–1955

CHAPTER 44

HISTORY REPEATS ITSELF

World War II was different from World War I. Hitler was around this time, with his fascist regime that murdered millions of innocent people and would have murdered even more if allowed. But some things were the same—like the bank accounts of American businesses.

Just as US Steel made a profit of $350 million in a single year of World War I, the second World War saw corporate profits soar from $6 billion in 1940 to $11 billion in 1944. Not only does war make money for many large corporations, it often extends the reach of those businesses around the globe. The US assistant secretary of state, seeing the war coming to a close and the influence of the United States in bringing about peace, said: *"The peace we seem to be making, will be a peace of oil, a peace of gold, a peace of shipping, a peace, in brief, without moral purpose or human interest."*

If you're wondering what the actual secretary of state thought—he was the one dividing up those *peaces*, because he also happened to be the chairman of the board of US Steel and VP of General Motors.

A second bit of history on repeat was the combination of fear and nationalism. These attitudes increased intolerance, sending 120,000 innocent Japanese Americans to jail during the war and helping to institute laws, committees, and institutions to shut down dissenting voices.

Following the 1938 formation of the House Un-American Activities Committee came the reinstatement in 1940 of the Espionage Act of 1917, the Smith Act, and the Nationality Act. Together, they suppressed freedom of speech and freedom of the press and deported folks.

J. Edgar jumped back in with both feet. His reinstated Radical Division had 37 cases of espionage to investigate in 1937. It had 70,000 by 1940.

"Those who cannot remember the past are condemned to repeat it," said Spanish American philosopher George Santayana. But what about the people who do remember the past, and repeat it on purpose?

CHAPTER 45

DISCRIMINATION . . . ON REPEAT

The war brought a war economy, and the war economy brought jobs.

But not for Black folks.

Companies making ships for the war effort were advertising heavily to white women and white youth. Train as welders, they said, with headlines like: *"Keep Our Boys from Dying."* When it was suggested that there were plenty of skilled Black welders around, suddenly the company didn't mind *our boys* dying so much.

The pyramid of oppression is built on purpose. It's a tool to keep workers blaming each other for bad wages, bad hours, and bad working conditions, instead of focusing on the companies in charge of those bad wages, bad hours, and bad working conditions.

A. Philip Randolph—president of the Brotherhood of Sleeping Car Porters—took action. He started the March on Washington Movement (MOWM), which would later introduce the world to Martin Luther King Jr. He called on 10,000 Black people to march on Washington, DC, to end the discrimination in hiring for jobs in the defense industries. He said, *"The Federal*

Government cannot with clear conscience call upon private industry and labor unions to abolish discrimination based upon race and color so long as it practices discrimination itself."

That simple truth hit home, and thousands upon thousands of Black folks signed up.

The white press ignored the whole thing.

President Roosevelt tried that too. But the date kept coming, and the number of people kept growing.

Finally, the president reached out to Randolph. He said the march was a mistake, it would make things worse, and that he'd speak to the companies if Randolph would *please* call it off.

Randolph didn't call it off.

Whenever someone is desperately trying to change the world, the powers that be always seem to throw the same phrases around.

It's a mistake.

It will do more harm than good.

Let's just talk this out.

Randolph held his ground until FDR signed Executive Order 8802—banning discrimination in the employment of workers in defense industries and in the government due to race, creed, color, or national origin, while also establishing the Fair Employment Practices Committee (FEPC) to enforce this order.

Only then did A. Philip Randolph call it off.

CHAPTER 46

DISLOYALTY . . . ON REPEAT

The truckers in Minneapolis who had worked so hard for their union in 1934 watched President Roosevelt arrest their leadership in 1941 for disloyalty.

The leadership were members of the Socialist Workers Party and therefore "radical" and arrestable under the new Smith Act. In their place, FDR promoted a conservative man—and friend of his—named Jimmy Hoffa. Hoffa had links to organized crime and would forever after give American corporations the story they needed to taint all unions with the word *corruption*. The sad irony was that Hoffa was only in charge of the union because a terrible law (the Smith Act) enforced by the president of the United States (FDR) had jailed its perfectly legitimate (and non-corrupt) leadership.

And so it began. Words like *disloyalty* were hyped into hysteria. Hysteria produced bad laws. And those laws rolled back labor's hard-won victories.

J. Edgar Hoover and his FBI jumped right into the "disloyal" muck, keeping records on thousands of American citizens and organizations—not because they were in any way criminal, but because the information was useful to people in power. The FBI—under Hoover's direction—went far beyond investigating alleged disloyalty. It kept files on anybody it wanted to for years, using warrantless wiretapping, illegal opening of mail, and "black bag jobs" (illegal break-ins). This information (and its abuse) would continue for the next forty years and would help to stifle both the civil rights movement and the antiwar movement.

The second Red Scare wasn't repeated by mistake. Being disloyal once again became synonymous with communism, not fascism . . . even though the war the world was fighting was against fascism. Why? Because fascism operates in extremes: extreme nationalism, extreme militarism, extreme leaders—which were the very things people in government and business were using to keep their power.

So disloyalty had to mean communism.

The AFL dutifully threw out all suspected communists from its organizations. Unions are not immune to buying into that pyramid of oppression. The AFL had been proving this for most of its history.

But the CIO fought hard against the expulsion of its communist members, since the communists had been one of the leading forces behind the organization's success. Dr. Mordecai Johnson, president of Howard University, warned the CIO in a speech not to be taken in by the propaganda of the new Red Scare. He asked the big question: What was the United States professing to be defending against? Communist aggression by the Soviet Union—our allies in the war? And what had the United States and Western Europe been doing for the past 150 years if not *"politically dominating, economically exploiting, and socially humiliating over half of the human race"*?

The CIO eventually cracked under the pressure and threw out its communists. This not only weakened the organization but diluted its stance on diversity and equity in unions. The combination of fear and nationalism created a natural "other," and fed the pyramid of oppression.

The CIO, like the Knights of Labor and the IWW before it, had been open to all workers in all industries, skilled and unskilled, without discrimination. Many of the first unions this second Red Scare pressured the CIO to purge were started by people of color, like the United Cannery, Agricultural, Packing, and Allied Workers of America (UCAPAWA) in California, built by Mexican American women workers, and the National Union of Marine Cooks and Stewards (NUMCS), built by Black and Asian workers.

The second Red Scare worked just as well as the first. The war, the government contracts, the jobs, the discrimination, the false patriotism, the laws, the arrests, the deportations . . . all of it depleted the power and influence of the working class and their unions.

How did workers respond? They allowed their unions—the AFL and CIO—to promise a no-strike pledge for the duration of the war. And then they worked for years without a raise at overwhelming speeds. They climbed out of bed and trudged off to work. They created eye-bugging profits for corporations and smashed records on the production lines for the war effort, making:

65,000 naval ships

75,000 tanks
300,000 planes
2 million submachine guns
40 million rounds of ammunition, and
400 million antiaircraft shells.

Workers needed a break. Instead, history would continue to repeat itself.

CHAPTER 47

A NEVER-ENDING RED SCARE

Victory in Europe!

World War II was over and everyone couldn't be happier. Everyone, that is, but the president of General Motors.

Capitalism, it seemed, didn't cope well with peace. War, however, was a profit machine. World War II had seen $117 billion in US tax dollars go to corporations in defense contracts. GM now suggested a "*permanent war economy.*"

But could America just stay at war?

Since hundreds of thousands of Americans had just finished dying in one, it didn't seem like a good time to suggest another. But maybe Americans would be up for a pretend war, with the pretend enemy being the nemesis of capitalists: Russia.

In real wars, the United States had only fought alongside Russia—never against it. But both Red Scares and both world wars had done wonders for American business. Could we live in a permanent Red Scare?

The new president of the United States, Harry S. Truman, said yes, we could. And he slowly guided the United States into what today we call the Cold War. Instead of being rivals for economic power with Russia following World War II, the American public was led to believe the Russians might attack at any moment.

Most Americans didn't believe the Cold War hype at first. Soviet Russia had been a great ally in the war. The American public saw the Red Army as heroes. The country had led an astonishing fight against Hitler in which more than 6 million Russians had died. General Douglas MacArthur—the American general in charge of the Allied powers—described what the Russians had accomplished in World War II as: "*The greatest military achievement in all history.*"

Not true, the people benefiting from fear and nationalism began shouting. They installed air raid bells in schools and made children practice hiding under their desks from potential atomic weapons being dropped by Soviet Russia.

The US had recently dropped these bombs on Japan and watched the devastation they caused. Government officials well understood the reactions people would have if they raised the possibility of the same thing happening to American children. It was all about the fear.

Fact check: In the first ten years of the Cold War, the United States built 1,500 atomic bombs (enough to destroy every major city in the world) to Russia's approximate seventy-five ballistic missiles (which had the capacity to blow up a one-mile radius) . . . in other words, there was no competition.

The Cold War gave the United States the excuse for a constant war economy—just like GM wanted. In the next ten years, America's military budget would grow to 50 percent of the total US budget. American corporate profits would rise to $113 billion in half that time. What would happen to the wages of workers?

They would fall by 5 percent.

CHAPTER 48

EVERYBODY EATING PIE IS SOCIALISM

The working class had just endured four long years of war, hard work, and frozen wages. Walter Reuther—now head of the United Auto Workers GM department, the largest division of the UAW—had a good idea: unfreeze them.

His plan called for a 30 percent raise.

GM said they could only raise wages if they raised the price of cars.

Businesses love to say this—that paying labor more has to include higher prices. Another name for higher prices is inflation. Inflation can happen for many reasons besides wage increases, like when supply is low and demand is high for products, or taxes are increased, or when the price of raw materials rise. No one likes inflation. Businesses know this. They also know that when prices rise for a wage increase, Americans will blame "greedy" unions, and not "greedy" corporations. They know this because they were sure to say it in their commercial newspapers . . . a lot.

Reuther pointed out the important fact that GM profits had risen 50 percent since 1941 and were still rising. The carmaker could very much afford to raise the wages of its workers without raising the price of its cars.

GM scoffed at Reuther. Who was he to tell them how to price their cars? And as to the raise? GM said: *"We shall resist the monopolistic power of your union to force this 30 percent increase in basic wages."*

Monopolistic power was a pretty funny term coming from a company that at this time in history owned close to 50 percent of the entire car market in the United States. Even Ford—GM's next biggest competitor—commanded only about 30 percent of the market, with the rest of the automakers down around 3 percent.

GM refused to unfreeze war wages, and workers walked— 75,000 of them from eighty factories, across nineteen states.

Newspapers, business leaders, and congressmen cried that unions were greedy, and that workers were looking to get more than their fair share of the pie.

Reuther fought back, saying: *"Labor is not fighting for a larger slice of the national pie. Labor is fighting for a larger pie."* He went on to say that we needed a *"more realistic distribution of America's wealth."*

GM's chief negotiator shot back, saying Reuther was *"exposing his socialist desires."*

Reuther was okay with this: *"If fighting for a more equal and equitable distribution of the wealth of this country is socialist, I stand guilty of being a Socialist."*

President Truman stepped in. He appointed a team to figure it out. The team decided that an 18 percent raise in wages and no raise in car prices was fair.

Reuther agreed to the president's plan.

GM didn't.

But before GM could feel the squeeze . . .

1946 HAPPENS

On January 19, 1946, 800,000 steelworkers walked out on strike.

350,000 coal workers walked next.

250,000 rail workers followed.

Meatpackers walked off the job. Miners walked off the job. Electrical workers walked off the job. Even municipal workers walked off the job. Rochester, New York, saw the largest mass arrest in its history when police who were supposed to be rounding up strikers just arrested everybody they saw, including a teacher on her way to work and a dog, who was definitely not on its way to work, but nevertheless ended up in jail.

In total, 1946 saw 5,000 strikes of 5 million workers.

The continuing wartime wage freeze combined with rising prices were making workers miserable. But in this great strike wave—the largest in American history—business and government saw its opportunity to sell America its new pretend war.

The House Un-American Activities Committee, along with that old villain, J. Edgar Hoover, had already been working hard on the plan. Now they upped their game. Nothing was too over the top. Newspapers and radios blasted fear:

Red Army submarines were spotted off the coast of California.

Every plane crash was the Reds.

Every murder was the Reds.

It was even reported that the Red Army was planning an invasion of Detroit.

Instead of stepping in to speak for and with labor during the strike wave, President Truman shut labor down. First, he seized the railroads to end a mounting nationwide strike and then he "injunction-ed" the United Mine Workers. The injunction was illegal under the Norris–LaGuardia Act, but somehow that didn't matter. The UMW was fined $700,000 and the miners were forced to return to work.

Truman followed this repression of the working class with the Truman Doctrine—a series of government policies pledging support to nations around the world fighting authoritarian threats. This could have meant fascist threats but really meant communist threats. And fighting them around the world also meant fighting them at home.

Following the introduction of his doctrine, whenever Truman wanted to do something—like invade a country—he called it fighting communism. Whenever Truman didn't like something, he called it communism. At the same time, he upped the loyalty thing by appointing a Commission on Loyalty, along with loyalty tests to assess the patriotism of American citizens.

The country was really in the soup now.

Joe McCarthy—a Wisconsin senator, and, like A. Mitchell Palmer, someone who knew how to gain fame and position by using fear and nationalism—became the king of ferreting out disloyal Americans. Using Truman's loyalty commission, McCarthy charged anyone he wanted with disloyalty, because Truman had never defined exactly what disloyal meant.

Many of the formal charges against Americans, like this one, were ridiculous: *"You have during most of your life been under the influence of your father, who was an active member of the Communist Party."*

People accused of disloyalty were asked completely nutty questions, such as this actual example: *"There is a suspicion in the record that you are in sympathy with the underprivileged. Is this true?"*

Gosh, you hope it was true. Although if it was, it would have made this unfortunate person disloyal.

Disloyalty—once again—became criminal. And many thousands of innocent people lost their jobs, were jailed, or were deported.

Ironically, this behavior on the part of the US government might have been called authoritarian . . . a mindset Truman had supposedly vowed to rid the world of.

Not so surprisingly, this ideological war eventually led Americans into real wars, which included real death. We call this kind of war a proxy war—a war fought between smaller countries that really represents the interests of major powers, with those major powers also directing, fighting, and funding them. Some but not all these conflicts took place in:

Korea (1950–53)
Vietnam (1954–75)
Cuba (1961–62)
Cambodia (1967–75)
Chile (1973)

Middle East (1973–89)

Afghanistan (1978–92)

Angola (1976–88)

El Salvador (1980–92)

Nicaragua (1979–90)

Very much on purpose . . . communism became the big bad again. Also very much on purpose . . . workers' dreams of bettering their lives became "*socialist desires.*" And since socialism was— on purpose—another word for communism, thirty states passed anti-union laws allowing for more open shops, more injunctions against unions for lesser offenses, and more laws against boycotts.

By 1947, Congress had jumped in the game, passing the Taft– Hartley Act, which, to his credit, President Truman vetoed, calling it a "*shocking piece of legislation.*" This set of laws—still on the books today—basically wiped out the Wagner Act and the Norris– LaGuardia Act. It was written by business leaders and pushed through by auto and steel lobbyists. *Business Week* announced the Act as "*A New Deal for American's Employers*" because . . .

It included an eighty-day injunction against striking for any business that affects the national welfare. Many businesses successfully claimed they affected the national welfare.

It outlawed mass picketing.

It denied unions the right to contribute to political campaigns.

It allowed corporations to demand workers hold an election to certify their union, where previously a simple signing of a card of the majority—called a card check—had created a union. These elections took forever and gave corporations time to kill the union . . . which was the whole point.

It was also the beginning of the push for state "right-to-work" laws, allowing workers not to pay union dues, and so in other words, not to pay for union staff salaries, office rent, lawyers, organizing, trainings, benefit plans, or the ever-essential strike fund (money that went directly to workers in the event of a strike). Yet at the same time, by law, the union was made to represent those workers not paying dues.

Taft–Hartley did its job:

Strikes fell by 40 percent. Speedups returned. Injunctions returned. Labor spies returned. Forcing union leadership into oaths against communism returned.

And just like that, the massive gains of the 1930s were gone.

CHAPTER 50

THE TREATY OF DETROIT

Back to Walter Reuther.

With 1946 (and '47) driving working folks into the ditch, Reuther quickly settled with GM for a 17 percent raise without a peep about the pricing of cars.

GM accepted the contract, and then turned around and raised the price of cars.

Inflation shot up 18 percent. (Cars have an oversized impact on inflation because they have an oversized impact on American lives.) It was as if the workers hadn't gotten a raise at all, because essentially they hadn't. Due to the inflated price of food, homes, and cars, they now made less than they had before.

But in 1950, Charlie Wilson, the president of GM, saw the writing on the wall for his company—and it was all dollar signs. General Dwight D. Eisenhower had been promoting an interstate highway program since World War I. With Eisenhower a contender for the White House, his idea of a massive highway system was not far off. Charlie planned to invest billions in producing cars for all those new roads.

But the plan only worked if GM workers worked. Because

workers are essential, and Charlie Wilson knew it.

He called Walter Reuther and presented his plan for workers:

A two-year contract. Until now, all labor contracts had been one year.

A raise of 11 cents an hour. Workers had just finished striking for 113 days for a 15-cent-an-hour raise, and here was Wilson offering up 11 cents more.

A cost-of-living adjustment. Today, we call it a COLA for short. For the first time in American history, workers would receive a raise based on inflation. If the price of stuff went up, their wages would go up.

A 2 percent annual improvement factor. This was an added raise if GM was productive—and GM would be productive. For the first time, workers would share in the profit of a corporation along with owners and shareholders.

The only catch for workers: they couldn't strike during the contract.

GM workers agreed to the plan in a heartbeat.

For the next two years, GM workers—who, BTW, were almost entirely white men—went to work building cars with a lot less worry in their lives. And they built hundreds of thousands of cars. GM management went to work with a lot less worry in their lives—and they made money. Billions and billions of dollars.

When the end of the contract neared, Wilson and Reuther met again. By now, Reuther was the president of the entire UAW. This time, Wilson offered another first: a five-year contract.

It would come to be known as the Treaty of Detroit and would go on to become an inspiration and model for other businesses.

The *Washington Post* called it *"a great event in industrial history."* And it was.

But more interesting is how a professor from Harvard saw it: *"GM may have paid a billion for peace but it got a bargain."* Why? Because GM would now be able to schedule production for five years, something they had not been able to do with workers striking constantly over low pay.

In other words, corporations had been bringing on their own pain for centuries. Now for the first time, corporations could count on workers not to strike, and workers could count on making money. Good money.

For the first time, some in the working class could also be called the middle class.

Bread *and* roses.

But while Walter Reuther's autoworkers were taking their first baby steps as the middle class, things weren't going all that well for workers who weren't white men.

CHAPTER 51

"SOMETHING NEW IS COOKING ON THE FREEDOM TRAIN"

Despite the Treaty of Detroit, the country belonged to corporations once again.

The second Red Scare and Cold War were a whopping success at making profit and stomping unions. The new president of the United States, Dwight D. Eisenhower, believed the New Deal to be *"creeping socialism"* and dismembered it. He then handed more than $50 billion worth of public land to Standard Oil, General Electric, and the DuPonts. J. Edgar Hoover, still working it, presented Congress with a plan to throw close to 500,000 Americans into concentration camps as the United States headed toward war in Korea. And after both the CIO and AFL purged all the "communists" from their ranks, the business community announced: *"A union doesn't need to be communist-dominated or to be led by communists to constitute a potential danger to industrial society."*

So goes the confessional quotation from German pastor Martin Niemöller during World War II's Holocaust . . .

> *First they came for the socialists, and I did not speak out—*
> *Because I was not a socialist.*

Then they came for the trade unionists, and I did not speak out—
Because I was not a trade unionist.

Then they came for the Jews, and I did not speak out—
Because I was not a Jew.

Then they came for me—and there was no one left to speak for me.

But it's never too late for solidarity.

Out west, a group of independent unions, CIO unions, and AFL unions came together to help win an hourly raise for oil workers across all three. In Pennsylvania, electrical workers, mine workers, and smelters from the CIO and the AFL unions joined one another to successfully unfreeze their wages. Togetherness won out big-time in 1955, when the CIO and AFL agreed to combine into a single organization—the AFL–CIO—bringing together 145 unions and 15 million members.

Who needed this solidarity most of all?

Black workers in the south.

In the 1950s, corporations were moving south to prey on unorganized and easily exploited Black workers. Jim Crow laws and white terrorist groups made it almost impossible for southern Black workers to organize. During one campaign in Florida, an organizer named Joseph Shoemaker was seized by Tampa police without reason or warrant. They released him a couple of hours later to the waiting Ku Klux Klan, who flogged him, castrated him, tarred and feathered him, and then dipped his legs into boiling tar. He died within a few hours.

There was no trial. No one went to jail for his murder. This created a ripe environment for vigilantism. Black workers went without the protection of their government or a union, at the mercy of corporations and vigilantes.

Despite these dangers, Black workers did unionize in the south. And despite rampant racism, some white union members stood with Black workers, like this white worker in Georgia: "*We left the colored people out when we first organized, and we lost two Labor Board elections. Then we asked them to join the union. We won the election with their votes. They have made good union members, and we are mighty glad they are with us.*"

Taking Black people and their votes for granted seems to be a national pastime in the United States, and mostly discrimination was the rule inside unions and on the job. In the past, the CIO had taken many more risks for racial equality than the AFL ever did. However, when the second Red Scare threw communists out of unions, the push for racial equality left with them.

Black workers stood in lines to apply for jobs, only to be told there were no openings. Experienced Black workers went unemployed while inexperienced white workers were hired. And if Black workers were hired, they were almost universally denied advancement, seniority rights, and apprenticeship training programs, all while dealing with racially segregated collective-bargaining agreements denying them higher-skilled jobs.

As always, this system worked for corporations. Divide and

conquer. Keep that pyramid of oppression firmly in place.

Workers were once again at a crossroads. How would they respond?

In the words of William R. Hood, leader of the UAW's Local 600 in Detroit, and the keynote speaker to the first conference of the National Negro Labor Council: *"We come to announce to all America and to the world that Uncle Tom is dead. Something new is cooking on the Freedom Train. We come here today because we are conscious at this hour of a confronting world crisis. We are here because many of our liberties are disappearing in the face of a powerful war economy and grave economic problems face working men and women everywhere. No meeting held anywhere in America at this mid-century point in world history can be more important nor hold more promise for the bright future toward which humanity strives than this convention of our National Negro Labor Council. For here we have gathered the basic forces of human progress, the proud [B]lack sons and daughters of labor and our democratic white brothers and sisters whose increasing concern for democracy, equality, and peace is America's bright hope for tomorrow."*

Solidarity: it has and will always be America's bright hope for working people.

SECTION SEVEN

The Golden Age of Capitalism and Labor Peace
1955–1975

CHAPTER 52

NEITHER GOLDEN NOR PEACEFUL

The twenty years between 1955 and 1975 are called the Golden Age of Capitalism and Labor Peace, but they were neither golden nor peaceful.

1955

* Fourteen-year-old Emmett Till is brutally murdered by white supremacists.
* Rosa Parks sits down, igniting the Montgomery bus boycott.
* US deports 3.8 million Mexican immigrants/Mexican American citizens in the racist Operation Wetback.

1956

* COINTELPRO is formed. This FBI program illegally surveilled, infiltrated, discredited, and disrupted Black civil rights organizers.

1957

* Dr. Martin Luther King Jr. forms the Southern Christian Leadership Conference (SCLC).
* The Civil Rights Act of 1957 passes, making it a crime to stop people from voting—but it goes unenforced.
* Nine Black students—the Little Rock Nine—need the National Guard to escort them into school past an angry white mob during desegregation.

1958

* In response to Little Rock, 10,000 students march in DC for desegregation.

1960

* Four Black college freshmen use the sit-down for civil rights when they sit in at a segregated lunch counter in Greensboro, North Carolina.
* In response to the Greensboro sit-in, Black students form the Student Nonviolent Coordinating Committee (SNCC) to promote civil rights.
* The Civil Rights Act of 1960 passes, establishing federal inspections of local voter registration polls and instituting penalties for obstruction. Again, it goes unenforced.

1961

* The Vietnam War begins. It will go on for eleven years.
* Freedom Riders protest segregated bus terminals by riding buses across the south. Participants are beaten with fists, clubs, and iron bars, and their buses are set on fire; the police do not stop the violence but instead arrest Freedom Riders by the thousands.
* Women Strike for Peace (WSP) forms, protesting the war in Vietnam.
* Indigenous students form the National Indian Youth Council (NIYC), advocating for the civil rights of Indigenous people.

1962

* A mostly white student-led labor group—Students for a Democratic Society (SDS)—grows to include antiwar and civil rights.

1963

* The March on Washington for Jobs and Freedom takes place; Dr. King gives his "I Have a Dream" speech.
* Four Black children are murdered when a bomb planted by white supremacists explodes inside a church in Alabama.
* *The Feminine Mystique* is published by Betty Friedan, suggesting women have their own dreams and setting off a second women's movement.

* The Community Mental Health Act is passed, beginning necessary change in mental health services.
* John F. Kennedy is assassinated.

1964

* The Civil Rights Act of 1964 outlaws discrimination on the basis of gender, creed, race, or ethnicity—but leaves out disability. Again, the law goes unenforced.
* Patsy Takemoto Mink becomes the first Asian American woman elected to Congress.
* Protesting the removal of their tribal fishing rights, the Puyallup Nation engages in the first fish-in, receiving a violent reaction from police.

1965

* The SNCC and the SDS lead the first antiwar march in Washington, DC.
* Thurgood Marshall becomes the first Black Supreme Court justice.
* The Immigration Act of 1965 passes, ending racist quotas on immigration that disproportionately discriminated against Asian, Black, and brown countries.
* The Voting Rights Act outlaws racial discrimination in voting. Enforced, it creates major change—10 percent of Black people in the south voted pre-law, 60 percent vote post-law.
* Black folks rise up against the long history of police

violence and the criminalization of Black people during the Watts Rebellion.

* Malcolm X is assassinated.

1966

* The Black Panther Party for Self-Defense forms in response to police brutality and civil rights violations perpetrated by imperialist countries around the globe.
* Muhammad Ali declares himself a conscientious objector and refuses to fight in Vietnam. He is jailed for three years.
* National Organization for Women (NOW) is formed and brings over a thousand sex discrimination lawsuits against US corporations.

1967

* Black folks rise up against the long history of police brutality and the criminalization of Black people during the Detroit Rebellion. The anger and frustration continues through the summer (the Long Hot Summer), sparking more police violence.
* Ironically, that same year, the Summer of Love takes place in San Francisco, when close to 100,000 mostly white youth come together with the hope of forming a more liberal American culture.
* The League of Revolutionary Black Workers forms out of the Detroit Rebellion with the goal of joining forces with white workers on the issue of class exploitation.

* Dr. Martin Luther King Jr. is assassinated.
* The Civil Rights Act of 1968 is passed, strengthening laws against violence on Black folks. The law does not include the police.
* The Architectural Barriers Act is passed, mandating all buildings be made physically accessible to disabled folks when designed, constructed, altered, or leased with federal funds.
* Senator Robert F. Kennedy is assassinated.
* Shirley Chisholm becomes the first Black woman elected to Congress.
* Ten thousand Chicano high school students walk out of school in Los Angeles, protesting underfunding in what comes to be known as the Chicano Blowouts. This leads to blowouts across Texas.
* The Indian Civil Rights Act is passed. It gives Indigenous people access to the Bill of Rights, but also gives the federal courts the right to intervene in intra-tribal disputes.
* The American Indian Movement (AIM) is founded in Minneapolis, with the goal of protecting the rights of urban Indigenous people.

1969

* Queer folks rebel against the long history of police violence and the criminalization of LGBTQIA+ people during the Stonewall Rebellion in New York.

* Indians of All Tribes (IOAT) occupies Alcatraz Island in protest for freedom, justice, and equality.
* Chicago police, under the direction of the FBI and armed with submachine guns, raid the apartment of twenty-one-year-old Black Panther leader Fred Hampton. They fire over eighty-two rounds, murdering Hampton and Mark Clark (defense captain for the Peoria chapter) while they sleep.

1970

* Four students at Kent State University in Ohio are shot and killed by the National Guard during a protest against the Vietnam War.
* "Poor Black Women" is published by Patricia Robinson, tying male supremacy to capitalism.

1971

* The Pentagon Papers are leaked to the press. This top secret study by the US military stated that the Vietnam War was going terribly, revealing the government had been lying to the American people about the conflict.
* Inmates at Attica Prison protest inequality within the prison system.

1972

* Four men are arrested for breaking into the Democratic National Committee headquarters in the Watergate office

building in Washington, DC.

* Title IX of the Education Amendments of 1972 (often called just Title IX) is enacted, prohibiting discrimination based on sex in education programs and activities (schools) that receive money from the federal government. This includes over 20,000 public schools and colleges/universities across the US.

1973

* The Supreme Court rules in *Roe v. Wade* that a woman cannot be prevented by a state from having an abortion.
* Oil-producing Arab nations refuse to sell oil to the US after the start of the Arab–Israeli war because the US supports Israel. This begins the 1973 energy crisis.

1974

* President Richard M. Nixon resigns, admitting he played a part in the break-in of the Democrats' headquarters at Watergate (his opponents in the upcoming election).
* Congress passes the Equal Educational Opportunities Act, creating more equality in public schools by offering bilingual education.

1975

* Vietnam War ends with over 3 million people dead.

In 1940, the richest 10 percent made 50 percent of all income. In 1970, the richest 10 percent made 30 percent of all income. Where did that 20 percent go?

The rise of union contracts—like the Treaty of Detroit—was pipelining that money to a rising white middle class. In these twenty years, income inequality between white men at the top and white men at the bottom was at its lowest in all of American history. It has never gotten this close again. But growing inequality within the working class itself was helping to fuel a lot of "-isms" (racism, sexism, ableism, etc.).

White men who were doing better economically due to a combination of new laws and good union representation were being sold the story that they were doing better because they were working harder. They *deserved* (they were told) not just higher wages but also better jobs, better education for themselves and their kids, better seats on buses, better everything.

But the truth is, white working men hadn't just begun to work hard in 1955. Another truth: Black folks, brown folks, Asian folks, disabled folks, queer folks, Indigenous folks, and white women were also working hard. So it would make sense that they *also* deserved better everything.

And since they weren't getting better *anything*, these folks rebelled . . . and in doing so, brought together the labor movement and the civil rights movement.

The fight against the dividing nature of the pyramid of oppression was never fought so hard as in these twenty years.

THE BODY YOU'RE BORN IN

For most working-class folks in 1955, the "choice" between a decently paid job and a poorly paid job had nothing to do with hard work or training, and everything to do with the body they'd been born with. A worker's color, gender, religion, and disability were what stood at the employment office door and often stood between that worker and a decently paid job.

Black workers standing at that door in 1955 earned 56 percent of what white workers earned. By 1975, this number hadn't budged. A government report on hiring practices stated, "*the employment of [Black workers] in white-collar, administrative, and technical jobs is practically unheard of.*" A study of discrimination in defense hiring gave this typical example of bias: in two aircraft plants, only a single Black worker was found among a workforce of 5,000.

People were (and are) poor because they were (and are) kept poor. They need laws to help get them out of poverty. Rich people were (and are) rich because they were (and are) kept rich. They enact laws that help them stay rich.

What was the AFL–CIO doing to change this?

Well, Black bricklayers were denied jobs building the new AFL–CIO headquarters in Washington, DC, even though the AFL had had a "no discrimination" clause in their bylaws since 1886.

So. Not much.

The National Association for the Advancement of Colored People (NAACP) called the AFL–CIO out for doing nothing about discrimination. The response from the AFL–CIO sounded a lot like when A. Philip Randolph threatened his March on Washington if the government didn't take action on defense jobs. Union leaders said:

"Criticism doesn't help."

"These are difficult times."

"Now is a time for unity."

In essence, they said, *Stop complaining; at some point in the future, things will change.*

A. Philip Randolph proposed the AFL–CIO deny affiliation to any union that practiced racial or other discrimination. The now-president of the combined AFL–CIO, George Meany, was pretty blunt when he told the press: *"Randolph's request is not likely to be granted."*

Randolph responded: *"The fight has just begun."*

The AFL–CIO leadership obviously had a poor relationship with Black workers. When Rosa Parks sat down, prompting 40,000 Black workers to walk miles back and forth to their jobs instead of ride segregated buses (the Montgomery bus boycott), the AFL–CIO leadership remained silent. But individual unions inside the AFL–CIO did not. The socially conscious United Packinghouse Workers, the female-heavy service workers of

District 65, and the Jewish drugstore clerks of Local 1199 sent funds from their unions, and their rank and file raised money to support their fellow workers.

Unfortunately, these unions were attacked by white supremacist organizations like the Ku Klux Klan and the White Citizens' Council (today called the Council of Conservative Citizens) and ended up on the government's communist lists—remember, the second Red Scare had now turned into the never-ending Cold War.

Not all AFL–CIO leadership kept silent. One top-ranking white organizer spoke out in support of the millions of Black workers, especially workers in the south. *"Since [the] merger did we grow in the South? No. Who did? The Klansmen and the White Citizens' Council."*

He was accused of *"looking only at the negative side of the picture."*

People trying to invoke real change are often charged with being negative. A. Philip Randolph was constantly accused of being a downer, especially at a time when white working people were doing so well. It was often a slippery slope from there to suggesting that marginalized folks *would* be doing well if something wasn't wrong with them.

John Galbraith, the economist who said unregulated corporate and banking structures were what made the US economy unsound, now wrote in his bestselling book *The Affluent Society* that poverty was limited to rural or depressed areas and to people who showed *"mental deficiency, bad health, inability to adapt to the discipline of modern economic life, excessive procreation, alcohol, insufficient education."*

Galbraith's answer to a recession or depression was that a market needed rules to steady it. Yet his answer to poverty was that if you were still poor at this point in US history, it was on you, and not that our government, institutions, and corporations needed rules to stop discrimination.

A. Philip Randolph's take on Black poverty? "*[B]lack labor never had a chance.*"

The United States Labor Department, the United States Commission on Civil Rights, and the New York City Youth Board all agreed with Randolph. True to his brand, Randolph proposed another March on Washington in August of 1963 to demand jobs for Black workers, an end to discrimination in industry, and unions for all marginalized folks.

The AFL–CIO Executive Council refused to endorse it. But Randolph didn't go unsupported. Behind him stood a towering number of acronyms from the Black community (NALC, CORE, SCLC, SNCC, NCNW, and the NAACP), from the religious community (AJC, NCC), and from the working-class community (BSCP, WDL, UAW, ILGWU, TWU).

This all led to—surprise, surprise—President John F. Kennedy asking for the march to be stopped, saying they could talk this out.

Randolph had been here before. He said no.

JFK next called Randolph to DC to tell him that the march was a bad idea, that it would turn out violent, that it was not a good look for Black workers. Again, Randolph refused to cancel, and the Negro American Labor Council announced the March on Washington for Jobs and Freedom.

About this time, a second book on poverty was published:

The Other America: Poverty in the United States. It said the opposite of *The Affluent Society*, pointing out that poverty existed on a massive level in the United States, and that Black people suffered overwhelming discrimination in both industry and in unions.

This book said nothing that Black Americans didn't already know. On August 28, 1963, the March on Washington for Jobs and Freedom took place.

Two hundred and fifty thousand Black and white people from all over the United States showed up. Forty thousand were union members, the largest group of unionists gathered in one place in American history.

A. Philip Randolph was seventy-four years old when he heard the words, *"I have a dream."* Randolph had been dreaming that dream for a very long time. His march physically brought together the labor movement and the civil rights movement. This strong Black-labor alliance helped to push through the 1964 Civil Rights Act, finally removing "whites only" clauses from union constitutions.

CHAPTER 54

HUELGA!

Two years later and across the country, California grapes were ripening on the vine. Time to harvest. But in a story that is now centuries old, grape corporations decided to increase hours and decrease wages. Grape pickers would be expected to begin at four a.m. (instead of six) to pick grapes for $1.20 a day (instead of $1.40). Everyone has a breaking point, and these workers had just reached theirs.

Led by Larry Itliong, they walked out of the fields.

Itliong had arrived in the United States from the Philippines when he was fifteen years old. He spent his life picking lettuce, asparagus, and grapes. He also canned the fruits and vegetables he picked, losing three fingers to a canning accident. It wasn't an easy life. To change things, Itliong founded the Filipino Farm Labor Union, became president of the Filipino Voters League, and headed the AFL–CIO Agricultural Workers Organizing Committee (AWOC).

When Itliong and 1,000 of his fellow workers walked away from the harvest, he knew they were taking a huge risk. In the past, when Filipino American grape pickers asked for more money and better conditions, the corporations fired them and hired Mexican Americans in their place. Everyone needed to work to live, and corporations used this fact to reinforce the pyramid of oppression.

That very afternoon, California grape corporations hired Mexican Americans to cross the picket line, and Itliong's grape strike was doomed.

Desperate, he called Cesar Chavez and Delores Huerta for help.

Like Itliong, Cesar Chavez had grown up in the fields. He was just fourteen years old when he left school to pick avocados and peas. Also like Itliong, he was actively seeking change, and when Chavez met Delores Huerta, they decided to change things together. They formed the National Farm Workers Association (NFWA) in an effort to help Mexican American farm workers.

But when Larry Itliong begged Chavez and Huerta to stop the Mexican workers from crossing the picket line, they said no. The NFWA was not yet three years old and barely had any money. A strike could kill the new organization. When workers strike, their union dues help to feed and house them. The NFWA couldn't afford to do this.

The Filipino American workers continued to picket, and the Mexican American workers continued to cross the picket line. Both were suffering.

Do you know who wasn't suffering? The grape corporations. The pyramid of oppression is not just Black and white but includes all people who can easily be divided. Poor people are often in this situation. And agricultural workers were poor.

They lived in crowded single-room shacks next to the fields. They shared broken-down latrines. The shacks and latrines were company-owned. After picking the field clean of lettuce, grapes, avocados, oranges, or whatever was growing there, workers shuffled off, walking for miles to the next field and the next shack and the next dirty communal latrine, year after year after year.

For many, it was a crushingly lonely life. Under the Johnson–Reed Act of 1924 and the Tydings–McDuffie Act of 1934, Filipino immigration was so severely limited that the men who immigrated to the United States were now unable to bring over their mothers, sisters, wives, and daughters. Other segregationist laws forbade Filipino men from marrying white women. Generations of Filipino men lived their lives far from and without family.

This was who the Mexican Americans had to walk by each day as they crossed the picket line. Chavez and Huerta might have been worried about keeping their young organization alive, but the workers couldn't stand it. They called for a meeting.

Twelve hundred Mexican American workers crammed inside Iglesia Nuestra Señora de Guadalupe to vote on what to do. Should they join the struggle? Outside the church, the Filipino Americans waited.

The vote was taken. The Filipino Americans heard the cry.

"Huelga!"

But they didn't know what that meant.

The cry became a chant.

"Huelga! Huelga! Huelga!"

Strike!

It would last five years.

It would grow into a 300-mile march.

It would become one of the most successful boycotts in American history.

It would force some of the wealthiest people in the United States to recognize the humanity of some of the poorest people in the United States.

CHAPTER 55

I AM A MAN

While Itliong, Chavez, and Huerta were busy marching across California to change their backbreaking lives, Black sanitation workers in Memphis, Tennessee, were dealing with their own garbage.

You'd think that, in a country born out of a statement like *"all men are created equal,"* dignity would be easy to come by. It wasn't . . . and still isn't. It took five years for the California farm-workers to win a single grape strike. We're still fighting to protect many civil rights today.

These sanitation workers were called "tub-toters," because they carried giant tubs on their backs to collect garbage from cans behind people's homes. Tub-toting was the most difficult and dirty job in the sanitation department, and due to this, almost all tub-toters were Black.

After a day of tub-toting, many workers would walk for miles to get home instead of taking the bus because they smelled so bad. Showers in the sanitation department in Memphis were for whites only.

Also for whites only: regular hours, benefits, and safe working conditions.

On a rainy day in February, Echol Cole and Robert Walker jumped into the back of the sanitation truck to stay dry. The hydraulic plate activated due to an electrical error. Stuck inside, Cole and Walker were crushed to death.

This wasn't the first time a truck had malfunctioned. This wasn't the first time workers were crushed to death because of it. Tub-toters received no worker's compensation or death benefits. And Walker's wife was pregnant. Like the Filipino American grape pickers, Black tub-toters had had enough.

A thousand tub-toters crowded into the Union Labor Temple on Second Street. T. O. Jones—once a tub-toter himself, and now an organizer with the American Federation of State, County and Municipal Employees (AFSCME)—was waiting for them. Together, they wrote up a list of their concerns to take to the city's public works commission.

The commissioner said no to everything.

The next morning, eleven days after Cole and Walker died, the tub-toters walked off the job. In the words of tub-toter Taylor Rogers: "*You keep your back bent over, somebody's gonna ride it.*"

But striking in Tennessee for Black workers was no easy feat. In the words of AFSCME organizer Peter J. Ciampa, who was sent down to help these workers win: "*My God, what the hell am I going to do with a strike in the South?*"

The mayor visited the picket line, informing the men that striking against the city of Memphis was illegal. This is true in almost all states in the US—it is against the law for public employees to strike. It is also against the law for federal employees to strike.

Ciampa responded: *"What crime have they committed, Mr. Mayor? They are saying they don't want to pick up stinking garbage for starvation wages. Is that a crime?"*

Newspapers charged the workers with the regular:

Being greedy.

Attempting blackmail.

Being communist.

But garbage piled up in the streets of Memphis. So the city council sat down with the strikers. After listening to them speak, the men agreed to a resolution to raise wages and recognize the union. (All the city council members were men . . . and white.)

The workers celebrated, but the mayor hit back hard. The resolution was voted down.

Furious, the sanitation workers marched. The police came out in force, driving their vehicles within centimeters of the marchers. When one of the cars drove over someone's foot, workers surrounded the police car and started rocking it. The police leapt from their vehicles, clubbing and spraying and arresting marchers. Onlookers were shocked. It was as if the police had been waiting for an excuse to use force.

One of the marchers, a Black minister, said, *"This was done to me for one reason, and that's because I was [B]lack, no other reason."*

The ministers got together. They formed a group called Community on the Move for Equality (COME), inspired by the Bible verse: *"Come let us reason together."*

Once again, labor and civil rights were bonding, not because work is our lives but because work so often determines the quality of our lives. COME called on Black folks in Memphis to boycott white businesses to pressure the mayor into signing the resolution. They also printed up giant placards that read: *I Am a Man*, because "*we hold these truths to be self-evident, that all men are created equal.*"

Paid poorly to carry maggot-filled buckets all day long. Not allowed a shower. Possibly being crushed to death. And having no say in any of it, ever. This was not equality.

On went the strike. The mayor stopped all food stamps to the strikers' families. AFSCME's money began to run out.

The city was busy hiring new tub-toters—just like the Mexican Americans who took the jobs of the Filipino Americans, people need to work to live. It's a hard choice. And just like the Filipino Americans, the Black sanitation workers were desperate.

They called on Dr. Martin Luther King Jr.

King had been tirelessly working to change the racial inequality coursing through the laws and culture of the United States, but he was now refocusing his efforts on economic inequality. His next big organizational idea was the Poor People's Campaign. The problem, he said, wasn't just about Black people (race), but also about poor people in general (class): "*If America doesn't use its vast resources and wealth to bridge the gap between the rich and poor in this nation, it, too, is going to hell.*"

He headed for Memphis, where he was met by a huge and enthusiastic crowd. "*You are demanding that this city will respect the dignity of labor. You are here to demand that Memphis will see the poor. You are reminding the nation that it is a crime for people to live in this rich nation and receive starvation wages. It isn't enough to integrate lunch counters. What does it profit a man to be able to eat at an integrated lunch counter if he doesn't earn enough money to buy a hamburger and a cup of coffee?"*

A second march was suggested, this time led by Dr. King.

This march also turned ugly, as police beat, maced, and arrested hundreds of marchers, causing concussions, broken bones, and damaged lungs from the mace. In the end, a seventy-five-year-old man was beaten so badly that he clung to life and a sixteen-year-old boy was shot dead.

The Memphis newspapers shouted that King had led a riot and the police were beacons of restraint. The governor sent in the National Guard, and army tanks and soldiers with bayonets patrolled Memphis streets. The FBI, still led by J. Edgar Hoover, sent out memos to newspapers and news organizations across the country saying: *"King's famous espousal of non-violence was vandalism, looting, and riot."*

The national newspapers reported that the Poor People's Campaign would also turn violent. King had always been hounded by the press and the government—back then he wasn't at all celebrated or respected as he is today—and now they let him have it. Perhaps Dr. King hit an American nerve with his fight for poor folks' rights.

Black American rights involve Black Americans. Filipino American rights involve Filipino Americans. Mexican American rights involve Mexican Americans. Poor people's rights involve . . . so many Americans. Winning those rights requires us to tear down the pyramid of oppression.

King spoke a second time to the sanitation workers.

"Like anybody, I would like to live a long life. Longevity has its place. But I'm not concerned about that now. I just want to do God's

will. And He's allowed me to go up to the mountain. And I've looked over. And I've seen the Promised Land. I may not get there with you. But I want you to know tonight, that we, as a people, will get to the promised land! And so I'm happy tonight. I'm not worried about anything. I'm not fearing any man! Mine eyes have seen the glory of the coming of the Lord!"

He would be shot to death that night while standing on a hotel balcony. His idea to unite poor Americans against economic inequality would die with him.

CHAPTER 56

A FINAL GIFT

In Dr. King's last speech, he said, *"Either we go up together, or we go down together."*

Solidarity was his final gift.

The morning after King was murdered, President Lyndon B. Johnson sent the undersecretary of labor to Memphis to speak to the mayor.

The mayor still said, *"We are not going to recognize this union."*

Three days later, Coretta Scott King marched through the streets of Memphis. King's young children marched. Rosa Parks and Walther Reuther marched. The sanitation workers marched. They marched in silence, 40,000 strong.

The mayor agreed to a deal. The tub-toters won raises, labor recognition, a say in their jobs, protections against discrimination, safety regulations . . . and showers.

T. O. Jones called for the vote to accept the council's contract, asking those to stand up to vote yes.

Everyone stood.

Jones had gone from a tub-toter to a union organizer to a

civil rights leader—he couldn't stop himself from crying when he spoke. *"We have lost many things. But we have got the victory."*

So many things had been lost, especially by Black folks, between the day Christopher Columbus arrived from Spain to a night on a Memphis hotel balcony.

But so many things had also been won.

The 1960s would end, and the 1970s begin. And with it, more of these victories.

The Occupational Safety and Health Act (OSHA) became law—creating an enforcement agency that had the power to inspect and examine workplaces. Finally, quarrymen inhaling deadly chemicals, printers ingesting arsenic, coal miners contracting lung cancer, cannery workers losing fingers, and sanitation workers being crushed to death by their own trucks had an agency that just might save their lives.

The Environmental Protection Agency (EPA) became law. After one hundred years of factories, mines, railroads, highways, and massive corporate farms, the environment had taken a hit. Pollution was so bad that in 1971, the Cuyahoga River in Cleveland burst into flames multiple times. (Don't worry about the fish; the pollution in the river had killed them off years earlier.)

Finally, in 1975, forty-two years after the National Industrial Recovery Act had given industrial workers the same right, the California Agricultural Labor Relations Act granted grape pickers the right to form unions and collectively bargain.

Hard-won victories. *"Either we go up together, or we go down together."*

But 1979 was coming . . . and workers would be pulled apart and stacked back on top of each other once again. A single word would define the next two generations (and counting) of workers and their lives.

Oil.

SECTION EIGHT

Neoliberalism and the Labor Movement Decline
1975–2008

CHAPTER 57

OIL

The Seneca Nation harvested the black crude for use as mosquito repellent.

Colonial missionaries marveled when encountering oil seeping from the ground for the first time: *"As one approaches nearer to the country of the Cats, one finds heavy and thick water, which ignites like brandy, and boils up in bubbles of flame when fire is applied to it."*

By the early 1800s, the United States was using oil in medicines. At the end of that century, they were extracting kerosene from oil and using it to fuel lamps, giving poor whales a break.

Later came J. D. Rockefeller with his mega-monopoly, the Standard Oil Company. Oil was fast replacing coal and whale oil, while also keeping electricity out of American houses because at this time, oil was cheaper than electricity.

It wouldn't stay that way. The more we used it, the more we seemed to need it. First, oil companies tried to make deals with Indigenous nations for oil from their lands, and then oil companies tried to make deals with foreign nations for oil from their lands. Standard Oil (which later became Mobil, and then ExxonMobil) bought rights from the government of Saudi Arabia to search for oil in their country. They found it.

Not long after this, plastic was invented—using oil. Oil was showing up in our cars, our homes, and our food packaging. We needed even more when World War II began. It would be the first time the United States rationed oil. After World War II, oil would begin starting its own wars.

The Central Intelligence Agency (CIA), the agency in charge of US national security overseas, backed a plan to over-throw Iran's democratically elected government in 1953, helping to return the shah (king) to power. Why? Because the new Iranian government was about to nationalize oil, meaning the government would control the oil industry and not individual companies. The US oil industry wanted nothing to do with a national oil company—they wanted oil to stay in private hands for private profit.

Why would our government help out oil companies? The same reason the US government sent in the National Guard to put down strikes. There is an undeniable connection between the wealthy in the United States and the people who govern it. In the words of historian Howard Zinn: "*Corporate influence on the White House is a permanent fact of the American system.*" Or in the words of a presidential campaign adviser to a meatpacking executive, while a $25,000 contribution was appreciated, "*for $50,000 you get to talk to the President.*"

In 1970, oil production would reach its peak in the US— meaning we were sucking as much oil out of the ground as we could as fast as we could—but Americans were using it even faster. This brings us to 1971 and the first energy crisis. Demand for oil was greater than the supply of oil, and this made the price rise (inflation).

And things were about to get worse.

A group of countries in the Middle East stopped selling oil to the United States because we were supporting Israel, and these countries were at war with Israel.

Without oil from the Middle East and with our own oil "peaked," supply dropped even further and demand grew even higher. American oil corporations didn't help the situation. They raised the price of oil per barrel by 350 percent between 1973 and 1974. According to the *New York Times*, oil companies "*had the highest volume of profits of any industrial sector.*" How high? Eight billion dollars to the auto industry's $3.3 billion.

When oil is in private hands, private hands can do what they like.

What does oil have to do with the working class? A lot. The working class was searching for it, drilling it, refining it, trucking it, and pumping it to the tune of millions of jobs. Oil was everywhere and in everything, and without it, the country fell into a recession.

The United States was dependent on this slick mosquito repellent. Without enough of it, our economy hit the skids in the worst economic downturn since the Great Depression. Unemployment rose as oil industry workers, construction workers, and manufacturing workers lost their jobs—over 3.5 million in a single year.

Instead of looking for ways to cut back or use other resources, we looked for more oil.

In 1975, President Gerald Ford pushed Congress to pass laws removing regulations controlling oil and gas. In 1977, Jimmy

Carter took office as president of the United States and followed Ford's plan. With fewer rules in place, these presidents were hoping to open the market to competition and allow the "free market" to solve the energy crisis.

The free market means an unregulated market—or a market with no rules.

Next, the Iranian Revolution broke out—the country tried again to remove the shah from power after the US government helped him regain it in 1953. In response, the oil-producing countries of the Middle East raised oil prices.

Even less oil. Even higher prices. President Jimmy Carter said: *"Those citizens who insist on driving large, unnecessarily powerful cars must expect to pay more for that luxury."*

Rich people pay more? He was voted the heck out of office and Ronald Reagan was voted in. Reagan said: *"First we must decide that 'less' is not enough. Next we must remove government obstacles to energy production."*

Following in the footsteps of both Ford and Carter, Reagan issued an executive order removing all remaining federal regulations on the domestic production and distribution of oil and gasoline. Following this, he sent 300,000 US troops into the Middle East to "protect the world's oil supply" . . . or rather, the United States' access to it. In response to his policies, twenty-three oil executives thanked the president by donating $270,000 to redecorate the White House living quarters.

Oil.

It would dominate our economy for decades. It would wreak havoc on our environment. It would lead us into horrendous wars. It would make some people a lot of money. Of course, all our country's problems can't be blamed on this "*heavy and thick water, which ignites like brandy, and boils up in bubbles of flame when fire is applied to it*" . . . just a lot of them.

One of these problems was the dredging up of an old economic theory from the nineteenth century called liberalism: the idea that "the market" should be allowed to make major social and political decisions. To distinguish the nineteenth-century version from the twentieth-century version, it became new liberalism, or "neoliberalism."

This is not the same as social liberalism, as in liberals and conservatives. This is economic liberalism . . . as in liberating (or freeing) the market from rules and regulations and allowing it to make all the decisions. It is the idea that the market (private individuals) should be in charge of the economy and not governments or communities.

Neoliberalism has never been good for workers because the market doesn't care if your child is sick and you can't come to work, and more often than not, the private individuals in charge turn out to be people who wear dead cats to parties, sell guns that shoot your thumb off, or are strangely proud of themselves for lighting tents on fire with families asleep inside of them.

THE FREE MARKET

The United States celebrated its two hundredth birthday in 1976, but the American working class was not in a partying mood. Inflation was up, meaning everything cost more money. Unemployment was up, meaning jobs were hard to come by. Poverty was up, due to inflation and lack of jobs. The war in Vietnam was lost, costing the country so many precious lives, and after the US government had repeatedly reported it was winning it. And on top of this, the country had just witnessed many populations of marginalized Americans and Indigenous folks being hosed, clubbed, and murdered in their beds while attempting to win civil rights. Anybody might be blue after all this. The United States needed change.

Marginalized people needed to be protected by laws. Union contracts needed to include marginalized folks. The progress between corporations and unions that had brought both reasonable profit for shareholders and reasonable wages for workers needed to be celebrated and continued. OSHA and the EPA needed to be strengthened to protect workers and the environment. And the energy crisis needed to be solved.

Anybody waiting for the above to happen is still waiting because the free market was now in charge . . . and it wasn't doing any of this.

What did it do? The free market created international business associations. The old-fashioned triangle of worker repression—corporations, government, and the press—upped its game to the international level. One example was the US-based Trilateral Commission. Along with associations like it, they oversaw what became known as multinational companies—although 98 percent of their executives were American. By the mid-1970s, these multinational companies made so much money that they were the third-largest economy in the world (second to the US and Russia).

The free market decided that the Federal Communications Commission Fairness Doctrine wasn't necessary. The law—requiring news programs to devote airtime to both sides of controversial matters of public interest—was removed.

The free market gave tax reductions to businesses because it said these breaks stimulated the economy, even though the government agency whose job it was to track these things—the United States Department of Commerce—stated this was (and is) not true. Their research shows that low corporate taxes produce a sluggish economy.

The free market slashed benefits for poor people, like free school lunches. *"President Reagan trimmed $1.46 billion from $5.66 billion earmarked for child nutrition programs."* This *trim*, critics reported, was about equal to the $1.44 billion spent that same year on the Pentagon's executive dining rooms for military officers.

The free market minimized worker safety. Regulations

disappeared, leading to increased tragedies. Instead of workers locked in a burning textile factory in New York, workers were locked in a burning chicken processing plant in North Carolina. Imperial Food Products had three previous fires at its Hamlet plant in eleven years of operation and had never received a safety inspection. In the fourth fire, one-third of the workers died. They might have lived if the building had a fire alarm, the sprinkler system wasn't broken, and the exit doors weren't locked.

The free market ditched the environment. As with school lunch programs, the EPA's budget was cut. In the next two years, over 250,000 violations of the Safe Water Drinking Act by businesses and 80,000 complaints about clean drinking water by individuals piled up on the EPA's desk, but most went uninvestigated. On top of this, the agency whose job it was to protect the environment allowed manufacturers to increase the release of hazardous pollutants into the air by 245 tons a year.

What would the free market think about the unusual equality that had been growing between labor and industry since Walter Reuther's Treaty of Detroit, an equality that had taken so many lifetimes—and so many lives—to win?

THE UNFRIENDLY SKIES

The first union to find out was the Professional Air Traffic Controllers Organization (PATCO). It was 1981, and each air traffic controller was guiding a plane into, or out of, the sky about every twenty seconds. Thousands of lives depended on these folks. It was and is a super high stress job.

A study done by the Federal Aviation Administration (FAA) reported that controllers were not only stressed because they went to work each day holding the lives of thousands in their hands, but also because they worked long shifts with no breaks, were regularly working in understaffed situations, and continued to have their pay decreased year after year.

They were also stressed because of the free market. Fewer rules meant a harder job for controllers. The money the airlines saved by cutting safety and environmental checks, they spent on more planes. More planes meant more people for controllers to get up and down. Fewer safety checks meant a higher rate of safety issues. But the free market felt hearing about these issues was a real bummer, and so the program for controllers to report them without retaliation from the airlines was removed.

– 294 –

Like the tub-toters in Memphis, the controllers sent a list of concerns to their employer, the government of the United States. Just like the tub-toters, the controllers were government (public) employees, and so were not allowed to strike. Unlike the tub-toters, the controllers were pretty hopeful that they wouldn't need to strike. But if they did, they had two big reasons to believe they'd win the strike.

The first reason was that the newly elected president of the United States, Ronald Reagan, would surely have their union's back since PATCO had supported his presidency. Ronald Reagan had written to them, saying: *"You can rest assured that if I am elected president, I will take whatever steps are necessary to provide our air traffic controllers with the most modern equipment available and to adjust staff levels and workdays so that they are commensurate with achieving a maximum degree of public safety."*

The second reason they were hopeful was that unlike the poor, Black Memphis sanitation workers, air traffic controllers were mostly professional white men—a group that had seen some of the most stunning union successes during the Golden Age of Capitalism and Labor Peace.

But they *would* need to strike, and they would lose that strike—badly—for two pretty big reasons.

First, the controllers didn't read the room. Neoliberalism had begun—the free market was in charge. There would be no Treaty of Detroit because treaties are created by people. The free market was not a person.

Second, PATCO didn't have the support of other unions. The AFL–CIO told PATCO, *"You can't win this strike,"* and the UAW said the strike would cause *"massive damage to the labor movement."* The country was in a recession. The president of the United States had just survived an assassination attempt, making him popular and therefore able to take chances. And it was summertime, the time of year when airline pilots make most of their salaries and so need to be flying planes.

The air traffic controllers still walked off the job. That same day, President Reagan walked into the Rose Garden of the White House. In front of a horde of cameras, he basically said the air traffic controllers were greedy as hell, and that any raises would *"impose a tax burden on their fellow citizens."*

Calling the wages of government workers a burden to citizens is seriously distorting the facts. Plenty of things cost the average American much more in taxes: things like the Vietnam War, aid to companies during recessions, and tax breaks to corporations. Nevertheless, the president pointed out that the controllers were breaking the law and gave them forty-eight hours to report to work or be fired.

The controllers were stunned. They were even more stunned when forty-eight hours later they *were* fired, and their union leaders were arrested.

The strike devastated the controllers. Many were charged with felonies, some did prison time, others went bankrupt. PATCO was made to pay the airlines millions in damages, after which the government decertified the union and it dissolved.

All labor suffered along with the controllers. Historian Willis J. Nordlund said the United States government had sent a strong message: *"Organized labor—unionism—was essentially incompatible with the emerging free-market philosophy of the administration."*

So the free market's thoughts on unions?

What's a union?

THOSE DAMN MINING COMPANIES

Corporations watched that Rose Garden speech and jumped for joy. The president of Phelps Dodge—yes, that Phelps Dodge, the second-largest mining company in the US and the very one that deported the miners in Bisbee, Arizona—said, *"Suddenly people realized, hell, you can beat a union."* Which was a weird thing to say since unions were quite often being beaten.

It was now 1983, and the copper industry was taking a hit in the ongoing recession. When negotiating union contracts, most copper companies froze wages for three years but kept a cost-of-living adjustment. Workers were living through the same long recession as the copper companies, and so they accepted these freezes and went on with their lives.

But not Phelps Dodge.

Phelps Dodge negotiated a three-year wage freeze but didn't stop there. They said no to the cost-of-living adjustment, made workers pay a share of their healthcare, and created a lower wage scale for new hires called a two-tiered wage scale.

This two-tiered scale meant that while everyone was doing the same job, some people made more and some people made less—forever—no matter how many years those new workers worked for Phelps Dodge. The United Steelworkers union, who represented the copper miners, believed that this two-tier wage system would destroy uniform wages (and they were right). They went back to the table attempting to negotiate the same deal as the other copper companies.

Phelps Dodge said no.

The workers walked out.

The strike went on for two years. Phelps Dodge hired strikebreakers—most likely encouraged by President Reagan's replacement of federal air traffic controllers. The company also evicted workers from company homes—the first time a company had done this since the Golden Age of Capitalism and Labor Peace had begun.

With the mines back up and running with new workers living in their houses, the strikers were literally out in the cold. And there was more bad news. After a union-busting campaign led by Phelps Dodge, the new workers voted to decertify the union—resulting in the largest mass decertification in the history of the United States. Phelps Dodge workers were now un-unionized in Arizona, New Mexico, and Texas.

Many companies followed in the footsteps of Phelps Dodge: freezing wages, removing cost-of-living adjustments, instituting two-tier systems to pay workers less, making workers pay a share in health costs—and if workers walked out, they simply hired new ones. Once these new workers were in place at lower wages, the company would hire newly cropping-up union-busting companies. These companies would bury workers in anti-union propaganda, force them to attend anti-union meetings, and generally intimidate the workforce into de-unionizing. *Fortune* magazine wrote: *"Managers are discovering that strikes can be broken, that the cost of breaking them is often lower than the cost of taking them, and that strike-breaking (assuming it to be legal and nonviolent) doesn't have to be a dirty word."*

"Assuming it to be legal and nonviolent." According to the Economic Policy Institute, 42 percent of what union-busting companies do is illegal. But fines are not only rare, they're cheap. And companies like Phelps Dodge can very much afford them. Copper's economic downturn took an upturn not long after, and Phelps Dodge went from $30 million in profits to $420 million in just a few years.

"Strike-breaking doesn't have to be a dirty word" according to who?

The workers who lost their jobs, their healthcare, and their homes? Or the new workers who would be stuck forever in a second tier?

But the union was gone, and with it the voices of the workers.

CHAPTER 61

THEY'VE GONE TOO FAR

Greyhound bus company signed up for the Phelps Dodge plan. It froze wages, removed the cost-of-living adjustment, yada yada. After trying to negotiate and getting nowhere, bus drivers walked off on strike. Greyhound's CEO, John W. Teets, was thrilled. He hired replacement drivers at a lower cost and went on with his life, saying: *"There's a place for unions, but they've gone too far."*

That phrase was picked up by every CEO in the country and repeated over and over in the commercial press: unions, they've gone too far. Behind the scenes, a lawyer who represented employers told it like it was: *"Companies just want to get rid of unions."*

The strike had been labor's biggest weapon, and now corporations couldn't wait for employees to walk off the job so they could replace them with lower-paid workers. The recession caused by the oil crisis had made jobs harder to find, and workers were once again opting for feeding their families over solidarity. It was a brutal choice.

The recession deepened across the United States, with the Midwest hit the hardest and factory workers hit even harder. Steel mills, auto plants, and more started shutting down. The sad name "Rust Belt" was introduced to describe all the empty factories rotting in the Midwest. Manufacturing hit the skids, and with it went the beating heart of unions.

Worker givebacks were everywhere. They gave back wages. They gave back vacation time. They gave back health coverage. They gave back cost-of-living adjustments. They gave back everything they could, and then were asked to give more.

Unemployment, international competition, and the moving abroad of manufacturing industries were stripping workers bare. The talk was all about how workers in other locations worked for less. Companies would hop off to take advantage of those workers. As the CEO of General Electric said: *"There's a bunch of guys in Thailand, Korea, and Brazil who get up every morning and try to figure out how to eat your lunch and take your market share."* Where was that good ol' patriotic nonsense when you needed it?

Piling on the fear was talk that technology would replace all workers before long. Although technology never seems to actually wipe out human work, it did have the effect it always has on workers: turning skilled jobs into unskilled jobs and higher-paying jobs into lower-paying jobs. Where once workers spent years learning the anatomy of a cow in order to butcher it, they now spent weeks learning to run machines that butchered cows.

The proud moment in US history when wages and profits rose together was over. By the end of the 1980s, wage inequality would be at the highest level it had been since the 1930s, and it would continue to rise until the present day. In 2023, three Americans held more wealth than the entire financial bottom half of the country. The lower class was growing. The middle class was shrinking. The poor in America were becoming poorer.

The United States entered the 1990s with the Business Roundtable—a club of all the big CEOs of America's leading companies—stating their mission: *"Corporations are chartered to serve both their shareholders and society as a whole."* By 1997, the Roundtable had changed its tune: *"The paramount duty of management and boards of directors is to the corporation's stockholders."*

What happened in between? The North American Free Trade Agreement, or NAFTA.

Conceived of by President Reagan and signed into law by President Clinton, this agreement allowed corporations to cross the borders of the United States, Canada, and Mexico and sell their products to all three countries tax-free. Workers, on the other hand, were not allowed to freely cross the borders of the United States, Canada, or Mexico to sell their labor.

NAFTA would immediately throw 10,000 US workers—and eventually 700,000 US workers—out of a job as US companies moved to Mexico. Once south of the border, all those American companies caused major trauma to Mexico's small businesses, uprooting millions of Mexican workers and sending many of them north into the US for jobs. Since they were people and not capital, their moves were illegal.

Now there were lots more people looking for work in the United States and lots fewer jobs, giving corporations that stayed in the United States the power to pay all workers less. If those poorly paid workers complained or organized, companies said, *Push us and we will move to Mexico.* Some companies actually loaded machinery onto trucks to increase the threat.

Over the years, free movement for capital (and none for

workers) would spread in the form of the World Trade Organization, the World Bank, and deals between the United States and China—giving capital free access to the world, while national borders tightened around workers.

The prevailing story of the day shifted to one where unions were over, and the stock market was the answer to all problems.

Blockbuster movies glorifying the men who were wheeling and dealing down on Wall Street were raking in crowds. Workers were given a pat on the head and told that eventually all the success of these men would trickle down to them. That word, *trickle*, was used a lot when it came to talking about working-class folks.

To speed along the demise of unions, the trifecta of corporations, government, and the press did their thing, financially supporting government officials, instituting laws, and yapping through the media:

"Unions are divisive."

"They're just a big business."

"Unions are just political."

"They cause taxes to go up."

Union busting became the hot new thing, and thousands of companies whose sole business was to union bust were making millions of dollars doing it. According to research from Cornell University, under the tutelage of union-busting companies:

89 percent of corporations force workers to attend anti-union meetings.

63 percent of corporations interrogate workers one on one.

57 percent of corporations threaten to close the company location.

47 percent of corporations threaten to cut wages.

34 percent of corporations fire union supporters.

22 percent of corporations bribe workers.

Union membership dropped like a rock.

But folks who work for a living were also living, and so no matter what story was being touted by the powers that be, workers knew the truth. They knew their wages were dropping. They knew jobs that paid the rent and the bills were rare. They knew they'd lost their healthcare, their vacations, their pensions. They knew the trickle never reached them.

As bad as things looked for the working class, it looked equally bad for spotted owls.

CHAPTER 62

"SAVE A LOGGER, EAT AN OWL"

Neoliberalism's free market wasn't just kicking workers' butts but Mother Earth's as well. In 1988, hundreds of scientists around the world joined the Intergovernmental Panel on Climate Change (IPCC), publishing the first worldwide paper on what was happening to our environment. They also announced the root of the problem: man-made greenhouse gases.

The IPCC urged world governments to take action. One of its lead scientists described the response: "*Unfortunately, strong vested interests have spent millions of dollars on spreading misinformation about climate change.*"

Those "vested interests" were corporations, invested in profit from producing the stuff making the world so sick.

Environmentalists joined with scientists to push against corporations. One of those pushes happened in Northern California, where environmentalists attempted to slow the lumber industry's deforestation of the redwoods. Corporations quickly added those environmentalists to the pyramid of oppression, pitting loggers against environmentalists in what became known as the Timber Wars.

Northern California, Oregon, and Washington were (and are) logging country. Nearly every forest that hasn't already been protected for conservation has been harvested at least once in the past century. Environmentalists wanted more than a few acres of forest protected, and they wanted to stop certain practices like clear-cutting: a harvesting practice where all the trees are cut down, or "cleared," en masse over a huge area. Clear cuts hurt wildlife, rivers, and people.

The lumber industry wasn't having it. The president of Louisiana-Pacific, one of the world's largest building materials manufacturers, said, *"It always annoys me to leave anything on the ground when we log our own land. We log to infinity. It's out there, it's ours, and we want it all. Now."*

The environmentalists took a militant stance toward saving the forest. They climbed up into the trees and stayed there—a tactic taken from the sit-downs of the automotive workers in Ohio and Michigan decades before. They blockaded the roads so the loggers couldn't get to the trees, sometimes with rocks and debris and sometimes with their bodies. They also engaged in civil disobedience by dismantling equipment so it couldn't be used to cut down trees. And they lobbied their government officials to pass laws to protect the environment.

The lumber corporations fought back. They also lobbied their government officials—and they often had a lot more money than the environmentalists. They sued individual environmentalists in an attempt at intimidation. They tried to ban *The Lorax* by Dr. Seuss from schools because they felt it portrayed logging in a bad light. They felled trees onto demonstrators. But their most successful tactic of all was to pit loggers against environmentalists.

It worked. The pyramid of oppression often does. Loggers just wanted to do their jobs well and then return home to friends and family, like everyone else in the world.

Unlike everyone else in the world, they had a job that was one of the most dangerous out there, and environmentalists weren't making it any easier. Logging involves working with heavy equipment and falling trees, sometimes as tall as 200 feet. It also includes chain sawing and moving those large trees. In 1990, OSHA and the CDC reported logging as one of the top ten most hazardous occupations. And now they had a bunch of environmentalists taking apart their equipment, climbing trees, and messing around. The company found it easy to point the finger at environmentalists, telling the workers they would end up costing the loggers their jobs.

Blaming environmentalists got even easier when environmentalists tried to save the spotted owl by having it listed as an endangered species. Logging companies were clear-cutting too much of the owl's habitat and it was slowly disappearing. When the US Fish and Wildlife Service hearing date arrived, Louisiana-Pacific closed for the day and bused in 5,000 loggers wearing T-shirts that read: "*Save a Logger, Eat an Owl.*" It was the environmentalists versus the workers according to Louisiana-Pacific. But it was really the company versus regulation.

Louisiana-Pacific fueled the fight until it was done logging the area. With 96 percent of the original old-growth redwoods now gone, the company took off, leaving workers behind. It even closed down the Potter Valley Mill—one of the company's longest running mills—throwing 136 loggers out of work in a town of just 500 people.

Again, the president of Louisiana-Pacific had something to say: "*I feel sorry for Potter Valley and all the people that are there. But when you look at the total picture, our future is so bright, even though some product lines are at their end.*"

Who won the Timber Wars?

Not the environmentalists.

Not the workers.

Not the owls or the "*product line*"—those redwood trees.

The free market—the capitalists—won.

CHAPTER 63

WHAT HAPPENED IN VEGAS, SHOULD NOT STAY IN VEGAS

The free market was proving to be a real winner, with businesses, governments, and commercial presses around the world having its back. But could it succeed in Vegas, where the house always wins?

Not if that house included the waitstaff, dishwashers, cooks, room attendants, and bartenders.

The Culinary Workers Union Local 226—repping all these workers—limped through the 1980s. Then, in 1989, it got what Vegas calls a hot break.

Nevada was considering a plan to collect taxes from foreign gamblers. Foreign folks having to pay taxes meant fewer of them flying over to gamble. Casinos were bummed.

At the same time this new tax was being proposed, Las Vegas's first mega-resort was about to open—the Mirage Hotel and Casino. The new hotel had built a giant volcano that would erupt outside its front door every single night of the week.

Over the top? Yes. Very cool? Also yes.

And it inspired some over-the-top thinking from Local 226. The union proposed teaming up with Mirage to block Nevada's proposed foreigner tax.

The buy-in? Mirage had to agree to "card check" neutrality if the plan won. Card check neutrality just meant Mirage wouldn't fight unionization if its workers voted for a union. People who build daily-exploding volcanoes are usually up for going about things differently, and Mirage agreed.

Together, they blocked the tax. Then . . .

Mirage didn't fight the vote.

Workers voted for a union.

Mirage recognized the union.

The real juice was that a host of other large casinos followed Mirage and unionized.

Two years later, another mega-resort was set to open, the MGM Grand. This hotel would be the largest in the entire world. And as a Vegas first, it would brush off the adults-only persona of the city to welcome children. Unfortunately, MGM was determined not to unionize, and they hired almost all their workers from Los Angeles.

Local 226 was pissed. They met opening day of the 5,000-room hotel with 5,000 protesters.

MGM was unmoved.

So Local 226 held a rally outside the new casino, where 500 people ended up getting arrested. Not a good look for the new family-friendly MGM. Yet the big hotel continued to hold out.

Now Local 226 was really pissed, and they decided to hit MGM directly in their corporate truck nuts: Wall Street.

After some research—even labor organizers do homework—they prepared a report for MGM investors that revealed the chunk of change that MGM had borrowed to build and run the hotel. They made sure to let investors know what a strike of MGM employees might look like for their bank accounts. They called the report: *"Would You Bet a Billion Dollars on a Single Roll of the Dice?"*

Turns out, the investors wouldn't. They fired their anti-union chairman and hired a new one, who immediately signed with Local 226. Following MGM, even more hotels and casinos unionized.

The new chairman of MGM loved the unionized workers. They were happy. They worked hard. They were paid well. He said: *"When you're in the service business, the first contact our guests have is with our guest-room attendants or the food and beverage servers, and if that person's unhappy, that comes across to the guests very quickly."*

Local 226 continued its winning streak. Tripling in size since 1989, it is one of the most diverse unions in the United States, representing people from 173 countries from around the world. It is also the largest Latine organization in the state of Nevada. Waitstaff, dishwashers, cooks, and room attendants—working class one and all—have solid jobs that support themselves and their families.

How? That winning combination of Local 226's innovation and its 1989 roll of the dice.

So many workers across the country needed an innovative union and some luck. But neoliberalism's free market had unions on the ropes. Who would step into the ring as the next face for working people?

CHAPTER 64

THE TOMATO WARS

A small but plucky social justice group in the Sunshine State, that's who.

Florida grows 90 percent of the US's "winter tomatoes"—the tomatoes we eat from December to May. Most of those are grown in the town of Immokalee, Florida (pronounced like *broccoli*). Though fun to say, picking tomatoes in Immokalee in the 1990s was not fun.

Workers lined up at five a.m. to climb onto run-down buses owned by tomato corporations and be driven to the fields by six a.m., where they would:

Pick a bucket in the hot sun.

Drag the bucket to be weighed.

Get paid 40 cents for a 32-pound bucket.

Pick another bucket.

The workers were often cheated out of money by crew leaders under-weighing the buckets. If a worker complained, they were fired. Most of the tomato pickers were on work visas from Mexico and Central America just to pick these tomatoes, and being fired meant they would be sent home. So no one complained.

Getting cheated sucks. But there were far worse abuses. Picking tomatoes under a hot sun with no breaks and no bathrooms. Drinking water from putrid wells. Sleeping in a locked semi-truck and then being charged $20 daily rent. Being sexually assaulted. Being raped.

And this Floridian hell was nothing new.

Way back in 1960, a famous documentarian filmed the migrant workers in *Harvest of Shame*, where he said: "*These are the forgotten people, the underprotected, the undereducated, the underfed.*" Over thirty years later, these workers were still underprotected, undereducated, and underfed.

In 1993, a ragtag group of community organizers were about to change this. They met in Immokalee's Our Lady of Guadalupe Roman Catholic Church and founded the Coalition of Immokalee Workers (CIW). CIW was not a union and could not directly bargain with employers on behalf of workers. It was a community-based social justice group whose single goal was to stop the abuse of workers in the tomato industry.

They began by educating and entertaining workers: putting on skits, holding classes, and operating a small radio station. But when Pacific Tomato Growers—one of the largest tomato corporations in Florida—cut wages in 1995, CIW helped workers strike.

The strike worked, and Pacific pulled back on the wage cut. But the reinstated wage of 40 cents a bucket had been the same for fifteen years.

In 1997, CIW helped workers strike again, this time against Gargiulo, the largest tomato grower in the United States. Gargiulo raised wages by 10 cents a bucket. Still, that's 50 cents per 32-pound bucket. A worker needed to fill six buckets just to buy a gallon of milk.

Two years later, the CIW organized a third strike. None of the corporations raised wages. So CIW tried marching.

Workers marched 200 miles from Fort Myers to Orlando with a list of their concerns. The march ended with a protest at the Florida Fruit and Vegetable Association—yes, another business association. But tomato corporations refused to speak with CIW about wages, about water, about bathrooms, about sexual abuse, about anything.

CIW was stuck. Corporations didn't have to worry about workers unionizing because, as agricultural workers, they didn't have the same federal right to collective bargaining given to industrial workers. Remember, the governor of California had given agricultural workers the right to collective bargain in 1975, but Florida did not. On top of that, the tomato corporations sold to companies, not to people, so CIW struggled to get consumers to care.

But then an article appeared in the tomato industry magazine *The Packer*. (The lesson here is always be reading.) It broke the news that Taco Bell was going to start buying discounted tomatoes from Six L—a major tomato corporation in Immokalee.

CIW jumped on it. Perhaps Taco Bell didn't know under what conditions those discounted tomatoes would be harvested. Maybe they didn't know who would actually be paying for that discount. It was also possible that Taco Bell didn't know that tomato pickers were almost 100 percent Latine, the culture the company used to sell their restaurant.

CIW called Taco Bell. Taco Bell didn't care.

CIW announced a boycott of Taco Bell, asking the fast-food company for two things to end the boycott:

Require the corporations it bought its tomatoes from to sign a code of conduct to stop abuses like sexual assault and no drinking water.

Pay a penny more per pound of tomatoes—with that penny passed on to the pickers, not the corporations.

Taco Bell said no.

Now CIW got serious. Maybe Taco Bell didn't care about tomato pickers, but they knew who Taco Bell did care about: college students.

College kids were Taco Bell's market. CIW reached out to college students across the United States. Did they care how the tomatoes in their burritos were being picked?

They cared a lot!

Students quickly formed their own group, called the Student/Farmworker Alliance, and jumped in on the campaign with the slogan *"Boot the Bell."*

Not only did college students boycott Taco Bell, but they petitioned their colleges and universities to remove Taco Bell from their campuses. Eventually, students not only helped to involve their churches and communities but convinced the federal government to investigate the poor practices of tomato corporations.

Taco Bell cracked like the Liberty Bell. In 2005, they signed the code of conduct and paid the penny more. With the help of the AFL–CIO and another year of protests (nothing seems to come easy for workers) McDonald's also agreed to sign the code of conduct.

Next they went after Burger King. But their CEO said: *"It's not our job to tell the growers how much to pay their workers.*" BK VP Steven Grover got involved, calling the protest "*a colossal waste of time.*" Horrible comments began to show up on all the online news stories about CIW's fight with Burger King. "*The CIW has given the workers nothing. . . . The CIW is lining the leaders' pockets. . . . The CIW is a self-serving attack organization. . . . The CIW spreads overly simplistic misinformation to unquestioning students.*"

Not only were the comments absolutely false, but they also insulted students. In the end, intrepid journalists tracked down the commenter . . . and discovered it was Steven Grover, using his seventh grader's Myspace account, an old-school social media platform.

Burger King fired him, signed the conduct agreement, and agreed to pay the penny-a-pound. They were followed by Whole Foods and Subway. It was now 2008, and it still wasn't time for celebration.

The Florida Tomato Exchange—the business association of tomato growers—wasn't happy with the success of the workers. Under its mandate to set industry standards, it shut down the penny-a-pound program and fined any tomato corporation that paid it $100,000.

But things came full circle when Pacific Tomato Growers paid the penny in defiance of the association. Not only did they pay the penny, they also agreed to a health and safety program and a training program to teach workers about the code of conduct to be kept by the corporations.

Jon Esformes, an operating partner and family member in the family-owned Pacific Tomato Growers, signed the deal right before Yom Kippur, the Jewish Day of Atonement. He said, "*It's the time of year when you are supposed to put your sins behind you. The transgressions that took place are totally unacceptable today and they were totally unacceptable yesterday."*

With those words, the Tomato War ended with Pacific. But the work of that revolutionary group who met in Immokalee's Our Lady of Guadalupe Roman Catholic Church was not done. And neither was the Student/Farmworker Alliance. Both groups are still working for the human rights of farmworkers today.

After all, as of this writing, Wendy's still hasn't signed that agreement.

Boycott!

CHAPTER 65

AGAIN

The working class entered the twenty-first century just as it had entered the twentieth century: Down and out. Again.

President Clinton had presided over another period of "historic economic growth"—just not historic economic growth for the working class. Again.

Vegas and Immokalee workers might have seen successes after literally decades of struggle, but the free market had taken its toll on the working class, and on their unions. Again.

How would unions enter the new century? Helping out the pyramid of oppression by infighting. Again.

The AFL–CIO decided that upping its political game and taking on labor law was the way to bring back union strength. But others inside the mega-federation believed organizing was the key. These organizers called themselves Change to Win (CTW), and they split away from the AFL–CIO, creating their own federation and taking seven big unions with them.

What happened? Not much.

The AFL–CIO didn't make great progress with their legal moves and CTW didn't make great progress on its organizing. A few years later, four of the seven unions rejoined the AFL–CIO federation, while the others created the Strategic Organizing Center (SOC).

What were corporations doing while unions divided up and then reunited? Prowling the globe for cheap workers and loose environmental rules. What was the United States government doing? Supporting the interests of US corporations around the world over the interests of humans around the world, as was made clear by the Human Rights Watch when it criticized powerful nations, *"particularly the United States,"* for failing to improve human rights internationally for fear of losing access to rich markets. Meanwhile, ignoring human rights was causing humans living in these abused markets to stockpile bad feelings toward our country.

What was happening inside the United States?

Inequality and poverty were rising. In 1990, CEO pay was 85 times the average worker's pay. By 1999, CEO pay was 475 times the average worker's pay. Forty million people had no healthcare. Our jails were filling. And every February, politicians got busy quoting Dr. King's speech about having a dream, but never quoting him about *"the evils of capitalism"* or mentioning that he thought *"a radical redistribution of economic and political power"* was necessary in the United States.

In short . . . things were going south. Again.

And again, working-class folks and a heap of others started howling.

Students on campuses across the country held weeks-long sit-ins to force their colleges and universities to pay the people who worked at their schools a living wage.

The Poor People's Economic Human Rights Campaign toured the United States by bus, putting together stories of the working class who could not feed their families.

Religious leaders joined in on the call for change as reported by the *New York Times*: "*More than any other time in decades, religious leaders are making common cause with trade unions, lending their moral authority to denounce sweatshops, back a high minimum wage and help organize janitors and poultry workers.*"

All this howling came to a head in Seattle in 1999.

The World Trade Organization—a body of the richest and most powerful organizations on the face of the earth—was to hold their yearly meeting in the city to set the global rules of trade between nations. The idea that they could set rules for the free market made it clear that it was not free at all, but a market set up, driven, and run by and for those rich and powerful organizations.

Over 40,000 people took to the streets in protest. Thousands more signed petitions condemning the power of the WTO—unions, churches, environmentalists, Indigenous nations, farmers.

While the commercial news focused on a few window-breakers, the smaller presses like the *Progressive* picked up on why people came out to protest, and on the beauty of their solidarity and diversity:

"*Farmers from around the world came together. The AFL–CIO rally cheered speakers from close to a dozen countries. And after events organized to highlight the devastating impact that globalization was having on women in the Third World, throngs of women from Africa, Latin America, India, Europe, and the United States marched together in human chains through the streets of downtown Seattle.*"

Regular folks were so over the free market. They were ditching the pyramid of oppression and standing up for living wages; medicines moving across borders; an end to poverty, corporate greed, and environmental abuses; and improvements to the conditions of workers around the world.

But then the election of 2000 hit: Al Gore vs. George W. Bush.

Gore vs. Bush wasn't the most exciting matchup. There wasn't much difference between these two. Both were rich white men. Both supported the death penalty. Both were "tough on crime." Both supported an ever larger military. And neither had a plan for universal healthcare, for housing, or for the environment—back then, Gore wasn't Mr. Climate Change yet.

In the words of a gas station cashier who wasn't sure she'd even vote: "*I don't think they think about people like us.*" And in the end, the presidential election wasn't won by votes at all. It was decided by the Supreme Court.

What happened? Gore won the popular vote by hundreds of thousands of ballots. But that doesn't decide our election. The electoral college system does. Everybody in a state votes. The candidate that wins in the state gets all the electoral votes in that state. Electoral votes are based on the state's population (California has about 40 million people and 54 electoral votes, while Delaware has about 1 million people and gets 3 electoral votes). We count up the electoral votes to choose a president, not the actual number of votes—so a candidate can get way more actual votes (meaning more people wanted that person) but still lose the election.

The origin of the electoral college can be traced back to slavery and the south's desire to maintain political power. Slave states were allowed to count enslaved people in their population numbers to gain more electoral votes, though these enslaved people were not allowed to vote. Strange things happen when you're busy making moral concessions. This was certainly true back then, as well as in the 2000 election.

When all the votes except Florida's were counted, it turned out that whoever won in Florida would be president of the United States. So who won in Florida?

The votes were super-di-duper close. So count them again, right? Wrong.

Bush's team and his supporters held rowdy rallies outside the recount rooms where folks screamed that recounting the ballots was stealing the vote from Bush. Bush needed to stop the recount because he understood Gore would win the election if they actually counted the votes. In other words, if a democratic election was completed.

These frenzied "Stop the Steal" rallies succeeded in stopping the recount. (This strategy of losing an election and calling it stolen would be tried again twenty years later when President Donald Trump lost his reelection.)

Bush and his team used the pandemonium they created to push the election to the Supreme Court. For the first time in the history of the United States, the judicial branch of the US government chose our president. And just as Bush knew they would, they chose him.

Later, one of the justices, Sandra Day O'Connor, would regret her decision to allow the court to decide the presidency. *"Maybe the Court should have said, 'We're not going to take it, goodbye.'"*

But they didn't say goodbye, and the American people were

given President Bush.

What did that presidency look like? Tax cuts for the wealthy. Opposition to environmental regulation. Privatization—aka, giving away government responsibilities (tax dollars) to private corporations. The presidency looked like all the things that the people in Seattle had protested against. Would Gore have done these things? To be fair, probably. If we look back at history, statistics show that both parties supported these policies at the time. So what's the difference?

The difference came on September 11, 2001.

Hijackers on four different planes crashed them: two into the World Trade Center, one into the Pentagon, and one in rural Pennsylvania. Everyone onboard was killed, as well as thousands of people in the buildings and on the ground. It was a horrific assault. It was also a moment where the world might have come together, against war, destruction, death. It was a moment that Gore might have handled differently, but a moment that Bush met with the "War on Terror." He started a war in Iraq—a country that had no connection to the hijackers. But it did have oil.

Oil.

Again.

Seattle in 1999 happened. Again. But this time, the entire world showed up. Millions of people in over 600 cities protested the invasion of Iraq. It was one of the biggest protests in history.

The American government brought out the usual. The commercial press denounced protesting as unpatriotic and instituted laws like the USA PATRIOT Act. A younger sibling to the Espionage Act and the Sedition Act, the USA PATRIOT Act worked to suppress dissenting voices during the war.

Next came privatization. Again. Tax dollars were handed to private corporations. The United Stated paid more private companies in Iraq than in any other war. In fact, there were times when American contractors outnumbered the military in Iraq. These corporations would make $72 billion from the War on Terror.

And then—in 2008—the stock market crashed.

Again.

SECTION NINE

Progressive Neoliberalism
2008–the present

COMMON SENSE

The cause of the 2008 crash and the recession that followed sounds very much like the cause of the over fifty other recessions and depressions that have occurred since the United States was established. According to John Galbraith, unregulated corporate and banking structures.

In the early 2000s, so many people had become homeowners that bankers needed new targets to sell mortgages to. They marketed home ownership to poor folks, charging them extra high interest rates because they were poor—essentially charging the largest amount of money for a mortgage from the people who made the smallest amount of money. This made it much more likely that borrowers would default—not be able to pay—and bankers knew it. Yet instead of mentioning this risk to investors, the financial industry turned around and sold the loans as super solid. Investors invested. Bankers got rich. Then—just like the bankers knew they would—folks started to default, and the bottom fell out for homeowners and investors.

We know why bankers did it. Money. But how were they allowed to do it? Because of free market deregulations like the repeal of the Glass–Steagall Act, a group of laws that would have prevented thousands of people from losing their homes and jobs.

What happened to the finance industry that caused the crash and the other industries hit by it?

Just as the US government gave land to the railroads in the nineteenth century and land to Standard Oil, General Electric, and the DuPonts in the 1950s, under President Barack Obama, the United States government gave $498 billion to American corporations during what became known as the Great Recession of 2007 to 2009. "Recovery" money *for* them, instead of laws *reforming* them.

Because corporations give people jobs.

Because the money will trickle down.

Because private business runs things better.

Because the rich are somehow more deserving.

Common sense.

Two years after the crash, working-class Americans were still on the ropes, but corporate America was flush. They'd been handed the tax dollars of those working-class Americans in the form of recovery funds. It was at this moment that the Supreme Court ruled in *Citizens United v. Federal Election Commission* that restricting corporate spending in politics was a violation of a corporation's First Amendment rights. This meant regulations were removed for campaign spending by corporations. They were now free to lawfully spend as many billions of dollars as they'd like to elect candidates. Unions, meanwhile, are still restricted in how much they can spend politically by the 1947 Taft–Hartley Act.

"Corporate influence on the White House is a permanent fact of the American system."

The world those 40,000 protesters in Seattle had stood against continued on:

> *to see the regrowth of the finance industry, fresh from tanking the economy,*
>
> *to see the rise of the service industry out of the Rust Belt of lost manufacturing jobs,*
>
> *to see an increase in carbon emissions bringing on climate change,*
>
> *to see racism popping its head up so often and against so many marginalized groups, it was like a scary jack-in-the-box.*

Through it all, the working class kept working under the mounting pressure that longer hours and less social support had on their families and communities.

Because corporations give people jobs?

Because the money will trickle down?

Because private business runs things better?

Because the rich are somehow more deserving?

Common sense?

THE TERRIBLE, HORRIBLE, NO GOOD, VERY BAD LAW

Scott Walker—the newly elected governor of Wisconsin in 2011—certainly believed he knew better when he proposed Act 10.

It was a modest bill, he said. It would help support the state budget, he said. It's time to put our differences aside and find ways to work together to move forward, he said.

The law Walker was proposing would:

> end the right of public unions in Wisconsin to collectively
> bargain over benefits and working conditions while
> capping raises,
>
> force unions to hold an election every year just to win the
> right to negotiate for the capped raises,
>
> make that yearly election be won by a majority of all eligible
> members, not just those who cast votes . . . so any worker
> who doesn't vote is counted as a no,
>
> make union dues optional.

In other words, if this bill passed, it would suck for teachers, clerical workers, prison guards, childcare workers, nurses, home healthcare workers, sanitation workers, and others. In an attempt to put "*differences aside and find ways to work together*" these workers agreed to a cut in their benefits if they'd be allowed to keep bargaining rights. Walker said no.

Within days, thousands of Wisconsin workers flooded the capital to protest.

But this was 2011. Workers and unions had now been painted as greedy and unnecessary for thirty years. Echoing Ronald Reagan in the Rose Garden, Walker said: "*We can no longer live in a society where the public employees are the haves and taxpayers who foot the bills are the have-nots.*" (BTW, public employees are also taxpayers.)

Now over 100,000 workers showed up at the state house to protest. Chanting. Singing. Beating drums. Sleeping on the floor so they could wake up and do it again the next day.

The bill still passed into law. And the workers went home to a depleted union, less money, less healthcare, smaller retirement pensions, and harder lives.

It was a terrible, horrible, no good, very bad law.

And Walker wasn't done. He proposed another—the "right-to-work" law—allowing private workers to opt out of paying union dues.

Before this law, workers in a company with a union chose whether to join the union, but—whether they joined or not—they had to pay union dues, because the union was legally responsible for making sure all workers received the benefits of the union (contract negotiation, safety concerns, hiring practices, etc.).

Governor Walker argued his "right-to-work" law would protect workers from being *forced* to join a union—but federal law already said no one can be forced to join a union, and Walker knew this. What Walker was really doing was removing dues from the pockets of unions—and thereby weakening their power.

Act 10 attacked public unions. Right-to-work attacked private unions.

Twenty-seven states joined Walker in enacting right-to-work laws, giving workers the "right" to not pay union dues. What is it like to be a worker in one of these twenty-eight states? Twenty-two sit at the bottom of the country when it comes to worker income.

So did the "have-nots" become the "haves" in Wisconsin?

Not necessarily. Since the passing of Act 10, Wisconsin has fallen behind the rest of the country in economic growth—making all citizens of Wisconsin the "have-nots."

Wisconsin workers marched in the original May Day parade. They sat in solidarity during the great GM sit-downs. They were first to give the right of collective bargaining to public workers. And they rushed by the thousands to their capitol to stop a law that would greatly diminish their jobs and workplaces.

Because they knew something Scott Walker didn't . . . we are all deserving.

CHAPTER 68

HEY, KIDS, HAND OVER THE MONEY

The very next year and one state to the south, 26,000 Chicago public educators walked out of 580 schools. This time, it wasn't only unions under fire, but all public education.

Way back in 1834 when the first national union was organized, working people proposed a list of demands. Topping that list was public education for all. Even back then, the working class understood that education was a route to changing their economic circumstances.

Today, public schools remain one of the single most important ways in which opportunities might be divided more equally, making them not just a foundation of American life, but a foundation of democracy.

But the free market, in charge since 1975, had its eye on public education. Public schools weren't making anyone any money—which is the free market standard of what matters. Just like when the World Trade Organization met to set up the global rules of trade between nations so those within the WTO would be sure to profit, American corporations met to set up the rules of privatizing public education, so those running the corporations would be sure to profit.

But how to get their hands on the tax dollars funding American schools? Before long, a new "common sense" idea began to circulate—the government stinks at running things.

Is this true?

Only if you believe our military is poorly run. Our libraries are poorly run. Our fire departments are poorly run. Or any number of well-run government organizations are not really well-run.

Meanwhile, to believe corporations would be better at running things, folks would have to forget the entire history of working-class America—forget the fired, the cheated, the poisoned, the clubbed, the beaten, the bayoneted, the hosed, the crushed, the burned, the homeless, the jailed, and the murdered.

But people can forget when they're buried under an avalanche of media easily triggered because that media is 90 percent owned by just eight multinational companies, and because regulations like the Federal Communications Commission Fairness Doctrine, which once legally forced news organizations to tell other sides of a story, had been killed off in 1987.

TV and computer screens across the country blasted story after story about this fast-becoming-common-sense decree: privatization is better for everyone! And nowhere was the cry to hand over public-school money to businesses louder than in Illinois. The only thing standing in the way was a bunch of teachers, paraprofessionals, school social workers, and school librarians—a group of people who no one should ever underestimate.

Business underestimated them.

Familiar battle lines were drawn: government, business, and

the press vs. the Chicago Teachers Union, parents, students, and communities.

Helping Team Business was President George W. Bush's No Child Left Behind, which normalized constant standardized testing. Kids in grades K–12 were now taking an average of 112 standardized tests—tests written and sold by corporations to the tune of millions of dollars, whose results could be manipulated to fit any narrative. Years later, statistics would show that this testing did not help students, and worse, it often hurt them—yet public schools still test, and corporations still make millions.

Also helping out Team Business was President Barack Obama's Race to the Top, which introduced more charter schools. Charter schools are funded by tax dollars but run by private organizations . . . exactly what corporations were looking for. Race to the Top also introduced more testing without more success, but with lots more data pointing the finger for failing schools at teachers and school staff.

To "fix" schools in Chicago, Team Business went with the familiar plan of cutting wages and increasing working hours while refusing to reduce class size, repair buildings, or increase staff.

Did Chicago or the country want the free market running its schools with its profit-over-people philosophy? Or did they want people in control of public schools, teaching children that a meaningful life is not derived from profit?

Led by chemistry teacher Karen Lewis, Chicago teachers and staff chose the latter by a vote of 98 percent. They donned their red union T-shirts (red being the color of revolution) and took to the streets. Partnering with thousands upon thousands of students, parents, and community members, they marched for their right—and the right of 400,000 children—to be taught (and live their lives) through the lens of a more meaningful way of life.

Note: It might sound like this crowd of people literally showed up overnight. But it didn't. It took the power of years of organizing—much like when Clara Lemlich jumped on the stage during the rise of the garment workers, and all those women knew exactly who she was and what she'd say. In Chicago, folks had been watching the clouds of the free market gathering overhead for years. They'd been talking, connecting, building within the community to hold back the coming storm. So when lightning struck, they were prepared for the weather.

Out they came, marching, chanting, singing, eating, chatting, communing, and growing as citizens and people. They were out there with each other and for each other, and because of this, there was a great sense of joy in the strike.

What did Team Business do?

They did *all the things* . . . but that list gets seriously old, so let's skip to the part where the teachers, school staff, students, parents, and community win.

They won!

After days of striking under the weight of *all the things*, they were handed a contract. The rank-and-file workers sat down on the sidewalks outside their schools and read through it together. And then they voted for it with the highest approval rating ever recorded for a teachers' contract, ending the strike and preserving the "good" in the public good called public education.

We run things better together.

CHAPTER 69

UNIONS ARE COMMUNITIES AND
COMMUNITIES ARE UNIONS

Workers were beginning to shake off the "common sense" of the free market. Like the Chicago Teachers Union teaming up with the community to save public education in the third-largest school district in the country, depleted unions were finding new strength by teaming up with the many social justice groups rising out of gutted American communities. One such team was the Service Employees International Union (SEIU) and New York Communities for Change (NYCC).

The SEIU and NYCC—together with forty Brooklyn fast-food workers from McDonald's, Burger King, and KFC—would join forces to raise the minimum wage of fast-food workers to $15 an hour, calling it the Fight for $15 (FF15).

America's first fast-food chain was White Castle. It opened in Wichita, Kansas, in 1921. Its claim to fame was cheap square hamburgers. White Castle made them square so the entire grill surface area could be covered with meat. Factories and mechanization were all the rage back then, and working people were fascinated with being able to eat at a restaurant where a hamburger tasted the same today as it did yesterday . . . the same as it would taste tomorrow.

In 1921, this was different and cool. Walking into a McDonald's or Taco Bell today doesn't have the same feel, but there is something to be said for familiar and cheap.

Over the years, keeping it familiar meant keeping it mechanized—and keeping it cheap meant low-quality food and underpaid workers. By 2012, not much had changed. The forty Brooklyn workers in that first meeting made minimum wage ($7.25) whether they'd worked at Burger King for five days or five years.

Much like sugar workers in Louisiana, copper miners in Idaho, or grape pickers in California, many of those forty workers didn't have a real place to call home. After working at McDonald's by day, at night they slept in homeless shelters, on the couches of friends and family, or in large groups inside single-bedroom apartments.

Fast-food workers weren't just underpaid, they were "underworked." Most of the fast-food chains limited worker hours so they wouldn't have to pay the healthcare, sick days, or vacation time required when workers were full-time. Often these workers would do a shift at McDonald's in the morning and then head over to Burger King to do a second shift in the afternoon, attempting to cobble together a living.

Now they were demanding $15 an hour. Why $15? The workers agreed that at $15 an hour, they might pay rent *and* live a little . . . bread *and* roses.

How would they get that little bit of living?

Unionizing was out of the question because their industry was franchised. Instead of working directly for massive corporate headquarters, companies like McDonald's sold the rights to their restaurants to around 13,000 franchise owners, who *then* employed the staff. Even if those workers were covered from head to toe in clothing bearing the name of the company, showing up to work at buildings with the corporate name splashed across it, and selling food covered in the company logo, the company could say they weren't employees.

Without a union and its bank of union dues, fast-food workers couldn't strike because they couldn't support themselves through that strike. Still, deciding they didn't have much to lose, the workers agreed to walk off the job for a single day. When asked if she was scared of the coming protest, one worker said she was *"more scared of coming home and not being able to feed my child."*

They walked out on November 29, 2012, and they weren't alone. They were joined by workers from the SEIU and by NYCC community members.

No one got raises. But even so, it was a good moment. Standing up matters. It may not always change your salary, but it always changes you. Standing up felt so good that they kept standing up.

On April 24, 2013, in Chicago. On May 8, 10, 15, and 30 in St. Louis, Detroit, Milwaukee, and Seattle. Six more cities walked in July. Fifty more cities walked in August. And by the end of the year, over a hundred cities saw fast-food workers walk off the job in a single day of protest.

People started to pay attention. Academics at the University of California and the University of Illinois conducted a study detailing how the bad pay of fast-food workers was affecting more than just fast-food workers. It was affecting all of us.

The study found that because fast-food workers received poor wages and no benefits, over 50 percent of them were on public assistance, to the tune of $7 billion in taxes. In other words, because McDonald's wasn't paying its workers enough to feed their families, the government needed to help feed their families. Because Burger King wasn't allowing folks to work full-time and receive healthcare, Medicaid had to support these workers.

The study concluded that Americans, not corporations, were paying the wages of corporate employees. We were all making profit for fast-food corporations.

Did fast-food corporations know this was happening? Well, when McDonald's employees called its helpline to ask for more hours to make ends meet, helpline spokespeople suggested workers use food pantries, apply for food stamps, and sign their children up for Medicaid. They knew.

Were they convinced by the protests and the studies to raise their workers' wages? They were not.

By 2015, with fast-food corporations still refusing to raise minimum wage, the Fight for $15 followed in the footsteps of Vegas's Local 226 and Florida's CIW: they looked for a back door. In this case, it was an airport door.

Seattle's airport was filled with low-wage, nonunionized immigrants (baggage handlers, cleaners, etc.). The airlines had kept these folks from unionizing, and because of this, their pay was downright sad.

In came the FF15. But instead of trying to convince the airlines to increase wages, they turned around and convinced the town of SeaTac (where Seattle's airport is located) to vote for a town-wide $15 minimum wage. The people of SeaTac voted, and for the first time in the United States, a town voted in a minimum wage. Everyone in the town now needed to be paid $15 an hour, including fast-food workers.

Not long after SeaTac voted in the minimum, the cities of Seattle, San Francisco, and Los Angeles followed. Finally, in 2016, four years after the fight started, New York City voted in $15. And then . . . the entire states of California, Massachusetts, New Jersey, and Illinois. Corporations hopped on board—big ones like Facebook, Aetna, and Disney, along with smaller ones like local hospitals.

Fast-forward to 2022, when the state of California enacted the Fast Food Accountability and Standards Recovery Act (AB 257)—a law fast-food corporations are working overtime to overturn. The first of its kind, AB 257 created a Fast Food Council that includes fast-food workers to set standards on wages, hours, and working conditions. It gives a voice to those who work in the industry, and if allowed to continue, could be a first step toward the powerful old-fashioned industrial unionism of the Knights of Labor, the ARU, the IWW, and the CIO, where workers across an industry could bargain collectively.

Those forty fast-food workers from Brooklyn who had nothing to lose, had won.

Forget the trickle; workers needed it to rain.

DUMB BUNNIES

Things were changing. But whenever people try to change the world, the powers that be tend to dig in their heels. In December of 2017, Congress voted in more than $1 trillion in corporate tax cuts. Merry Christmas, corporate America.

In January 2018, Jim Justice—the governor of West Virginia, a billionaire coal heir, and the richest man in the entire state—announced a 1 percent raise for all public employees. Happy New Year, working class?

Public employees didn't celebrate, teachers especially. West Virginia ranked 48 in the country for teacher salaries. This 1 percent raise, alongside an increase in their healthcare costs, had many teachers actually seeing smaller paychecks. Like those autoworkers back in Walter Reuther's day had known, a small raise plus increased costs of living really equals no raise—and sometimes even a pay cut.

The state's corporations had received $425 million in tax cuts in the last ten years, with more planned for the new year. Tax cuts mean less money coming in, which means less money to pay public employees. Meanwhile, teachers hadn't had a raise in four years, and were now slated for 1 percent.

The same week as the raise announcement, the state introduced a new healthcare app that was really an exercise app. Workers were forced to join and forced to use it. If they didn't, their healthcare costs went up. Many of these workers were already working a second or third job to support their families, and now they'd have to pay more if they didn't take a certain amount of steps every day?

In a spontaneous burst of anger, 1,000 teachers took some serious steps—right to the state capitol door, where they staged a one-day strike.

Governor Jim Justice called a town meeting where he told the teachers their message had been heard. But then he added: *"Now if you choose to respond to somebody that's a politician, that's running through the streets that didn't stand with you any more than I can fly through the sky, then you're being dumb bunnies. If you stand with somebody who absolutely has shown how much he loves you, I won't let you down."*

Confusing quote, but basically, he was calling them stupid. And absolutely no one needed his creepy love talk; they needed this elected state official to do his job by instituting a fair wage and reining in healthcare costs.

Jim Justice said no.

So . . . 10,000 teachers descended on Charleston, West Virginia.

Like the tub-toters and the air traffic controllers, public workers in West Virginia were not allowed to strike. The attorney general threatened the teachers with fines for not showing up at work. But superintendents had their teachers' backs, and they closed the schools.

The community and parents also had their teachers' backs.

They came out in droves . . . feeding strikers, marching with them, and wearing red for revolution. Nine days later, Jim Justice signed a 5 percent raise into law and promised to fix their healthcare.

West Virginia teachers were like, yay!

Their colleagues in Oklahoma were like, hmm.

West Virginia may have been forty-eighth in pay for teachers, but Oklahoma was forty-ninth. And Oklahoma teachers hadn't received a raise in over ten years. Meanwhile, oil and gas companies had been given a tax cut from 7 percent to 2 percent—reducing the state's money by $300 million a year. At the same time, funding to schools had dropped by 28 percent.

Oklahoma teachers were seeing red.

They quickly joined what was becoming known as the Red for Ed fight, demanding raises, more school staff, better healthcare, and a bunch of money to fund schools.

The governor, seeing the writing on the wall, increased wages and improved healthcare, but she wouldn't budge on school funding.

The teachers walked.

The governor of Oklahoma was pissed. Like Jim Justice, she too attempted to insult the school staff, saying: *"Teachers want more. But it's kind of like having a teenage kid that wants a better car."* All she succeeded in doing was insulting both teachers *and* teens.

A senator joined in, saying: *"I'm not voting for another stinking measure when they're acting the way they're acting."* He was talking about professionals who were publicly protesting for better schools.

Nevertheless, Oklahoma's government wasn't about to budge, and school staff didn't get the extra money for their schools. Not giving up, several of the teachers ran for office, and in doing so, ran out twelve members of Congress who hadn't supported schools.

Up next?

The state of Arizona.

Arizona's school funding had dropped by almost 30 percent while classroom size had risen—Arizona classrooms were the second most crowded in the country. School counselors worked caseloads of over 900 students each, while thousands of teaching and counseling positions went unfilled because of those class sizes and caseloads. Who could teach or counsel under these conditions?

To top it off, just like in West Virginia, their governor had only offered them a 1 percent raise.

The protest was on, and school staff descended on the capitol building. One teacher carried a sign that read *"Don't make me go all West Virginia on you."*

You've probably guessed that Arizona made school staff go all West Virginia. On April 26, close to 75,000 staff, parents, students, and community members flooded into downtown Phoenix—the city was a sea of red shirts. Increased funding and raises for all school staff were written into law.

Red for Ed would continue to blow through Georgia, Colorado, Kentucky, and Tennessee, finally reaching the California coast when 32,000 Los Angeles teachers walked out on strike. The city's educators were weighed down under large class sizes, no librarians, no nurses, and low staff pay. At the same time, the state had $23 billion in surplus funds.

Although the LA teachers quickly won their raise, they remained out on strike for nurses, librarians, class size, after-school programs, adult education, and community-based buildings—the very things that make public education a safe and inviting place to learn and grow.

They won it all.

Corporations and governments may "give" people jobs, but it is workers who get those jobs done. Red for Ed 2018 would go into the books as one long battle by working-class folks in defense of public education. Solidarity prevailed . . . mostly.

One outlier that year was a guy named Mark Janus, an employee of the Illinois Department of Healthcare and Family Services. Janus didn't have to join the union at his job, but he did have to pay union dues for the services the union provided because Illinois was not a right-to-work state. He sued to get out of paying union dues. His case went all the way to the Supreme Court as *Janus v. AFSCME* (American Federation of State, County, and Municipal Employees Union).

Why would a case about one guy suing to get out of paying $50 a month in union dues go all the way to the Supreme Court?

Because it wasn't one guy.

Janus was represented by lawyers from the National Right to Work Legal Defense Foundation and the Liberty Justice Center— two extremely rich and powerful groups that name themselves (and speak) like they're helping working people but are not.

Backed by the rich and powerful, Mark Janus won his case.

The Supreme Court ruled that public employees didn't have to pay unions, even though unions legally had to support all the Mark Januses in the country. Allowing people to opt out of dues hurts unions in their wallet, which is exactly what Janus's allies had intended all along.

CHAPTER 71

COOL NICKNAME, STILL DYING

After centuries of being called names like reptiles, scum, and dumb bunnies, the working class would now be anointed with a more flattering name: essential.

In March of 2020, COVID-19 hit—a deadly virus that sent most people around the world into their homes to stay safe. But lots of other folks couldn't stay home. They had jobs that needed them to show up in person. So despite the risks, these "essential" workers went out into a deadly pandemic.

The commercial press took to calling these working folks "heroes," just like they often called soldiers "heroes." After all, like soldiers, these workers went out to die for their country while making very little money doing it.

Were they heroes? Maybe. But one thing these workers definitely were, and more important, always had been, was essential. Working people are essential.

For almost two straight years, John Deere workers were on this list of essential workers, making bright yellow-and-green tractors for farming, which in turn helped to grow food for the country.

That essential work paid off—for the company.

In 2021, John Deere made a record-breaking net income of $6 billion (compared to $3.5 billion prepandemic). The company thanked its CEO with a raise, from $6 million a year to $16 million a year. How did it thank its workers? The company offered its once-essential workers—who had risked their lives and the lives of their families to help produce those record-breaking profits—a two-tiered contract where longtime employees would continue to make a solid salary with solid benefits, but newer employees would make much less with bad benefits and absolutely no retirement plan.

Ten thousand John Deere workers walked off on strike under the banner: *Deemed essential in 2020, prove it in 2021. You can't build it at home.*

Tractors can't be built at home. But perhaps they can be built in a factory run by office workers? John Deere forced its office employees onto the shop floor to make tractors. In the words of one labor journalist following the move on Twitter, it did not go well: *Day 1: A non-union salaried worker just crashed a tractor inside the plant. Whoops!* It seems you can't build it in the factory either . . . without the people who know how to do it.

John Deere workers didn't walk off the job alone in 2021—140,000 workers across the US joined them. Group home workers, baristas, delivery drivers, nurses, miners (always the miners), steelworkers, bus drivers, distillery workers . . . even theatrical stage workers walked out. The commercial press called this wave of postpandemic strikes Striketober because the crest of the wave hit in the month of October. The pandemic, with its extra stress of sickness and death, seemed to be driving workers over the edge.

Kellogg's and Nabisco workers were part of the walkout.

Cereal and snack workers had been putting in twelve- to sixteen-hour shifts throughout the pandemic. Nabisco even ditched the weekend. When asked why shifts were stretching into forever, a corporate spokesperson cited "*business needs.*"

Those *business needs* turned out to be a high demand for their products combined with the fact that it cost a lot less to over-work existing workers than it did to pay for recruitment, hiring, and benefits for new workers. In other words, it was cheaper to mandate overtime. Like John Deere, Kellogg's and Nabisco both reported record-breaking profits during the pandemic along with huge CEO raises. Yet here were workers once again reduced to fighting for basics like an eight-hour workday and a weekend.

While John Deere, Kellogg's, and Nabisco workers had unions helping them navigate their fight, so many other workers didn't. In the postpandemic United States, unions were still effectively squashed by the now forty-year-old "common sense" story calling them useless. Union strength and membership were at their lowest levels since the 1850s! Without a union to fight for fair wages and normal working hours, many workers quit.

How many?

According to the Department of Labor, 4.3 million of them in January of 2022 alone. The commercial press named it the "Great Resignation," and many were quick to ditch the essential title, returning to the tried and true drunk and lazy insults. In the words of one journalist referring to the unemployment insurance and COVID-19 stimulus checks keeping workers housed and fed: "*When the government trains people to stay at home, and they said that's our patriotic duty to stay home and to close their businesses, and that the government will take care of you, you train people to be drunk on entitlements, you train people to be lazy."*

That is one way to look at it. Another might be that working your life away for poor wages under the duress of sickness and death just didn't sound like a good idea anymore.

However, the ending for many of these essential workers is still in play. In the fall of 2021, John Deere workers did win a new six-year contract with substantial raises, and were able to fend off the two-tiered wage system. But remember NAFTA? In the summer of 2022, John Deere announced it was moving two of its largest plants to Mexico.

CHAPTER 72

GIGS AND CLICKS

Hailed as heroes or belittled as lazy, workers gotta work. This hasn't changed. Even when the laws do.

Eight months after the pandemic began, California voted in Proposition 22, a new law allowing app-based companies to classify their 300,000 workers as independent contractors—basically, as self-employed.

Self-employed and delivering food for a single company.

Self-employed and delivering packages for a single company.

Self-employed and delivering people—to work, to dinner, to anywhere—for a single company.

Welcome to the world, little gig worker.

Hailed as freedom for workers by tech corporations, the reality of gig work is much less romantic: working a bunch of jobs without being paid minimum wage, healthcare, overtime, vacation time, or sick time. Corporations like Uber, Lyft, DoorDash, Postmates, and Instacart poured $218 million into the "Yes on Prop 22" campaign to pass the law, because not paying people benefits saves them heaps of money.

Following their big win, the DoorDash CEO said: *"Now,*

we're looking ahead and across the country, ready to champion new benefit structures that are portable, proportional, and flexible."

No championing of any benefits came. Instead, other states followed in the footsteps of California. App-based corporations began shelling out millions to keep the status of their workers as self-employed. Not only did this save corporations money in benefits, it made it nearly impossible for these workers to unionize.

Under antitrust laws created in the 1800s and meant to limit the power of corporate monopolies, self-employed workers are not legally allowed to form a union. A group of self-employed workers uniting would ironically be considered a monopoly. A monopoly is one company or one group of workers in total control of an industry and able to set prices and wages.

These laws are in place to stop both corporate monopolies and worker monopolies. But like those Philadelphia cordwainers centuries earlier being considered a *"conspiracy against the good of society,"* antitrust laws more often come down hard on workers and soft on business.

So gig work is awesome for corporations. They don't have to pay benefits because "no one works for them," and they don't have to give workers a say in their jobs because "no one works for them."

But gig work is not at all awesome for workers. They have no say in their rates, can be fired at any moment (called by the ominous name *deactivated*), and go unpaid while waiting for these companies to deploy them.

In financial filings to the government, Lyft reported it employed 4,500 people. Meanwhile, it also reported it *didn't* employ 1.1 million drivers. Under a heading called Key Benefits to Drivers, Lyft listed the "benefits" these 1.1 million workers who don't work for them enjoy: *We work hard to serve the community of drivers on our platform, empowering them to be their own bosses and providing them the opportunity to focus their time on what matters most.*

Best not to define what matters most, because if it is a worker's health or spending time with family, Lyft isn't providing it. No healthcare coverage or paid time off are mentioned in the filings.

While gig workers were eking out a living racing around the country on bikes, scooters, and cars, another new group of workers were eking out a living inside four walls.

Welcome to the world, little microworker.

The wonder of technology is made possible by these millions of working-class folks. They mine, collect, and process data—inputting minute pieces of information that build artificial intelligence systems to diagnose cancer, run online security systems, build self-driving cars, or locate a single face in a crowd. Together they create the digital world as we know it today. In the words of one Google worker: *"Artificial intelligence is not that artificial; it's human beings that are doing the work."*

Microworkers log into sites like Amazon Mechanical Turk and Clickwork to take on five-hour jobs, five-minute jobs, or five-second jobs. This piecemeal work is called Human Intelligence Tasks, or HITs: mind-numbing data collection jobs that corporations say are "freeing" for workers—so freeing, they refer to their workers as "players."

The number of "players" exploded following the 2008 recession, and then again following the COVID-19 pandemic, meaning that people without good jobs were taking the HITs. The number of workers collecting data for Clickwork and other data corporations is now close to 20 million.

Twenty million people without benefits.

Twenty million people without job security.

Twenty million people without a voice in their workplace.

Twenty million people making a few cents a click.

Many of these people aren't working out of homes in Minneapolis or Kansas City, but out of refugee camps in Kenya, slums in Palestine, and prisons around the world. Like app-based corporations who sell poorly paid jobs to the public as offering "flexibility" to "*focus their time on what matters most*," tech corporations sell microwork with mottos like: "*Give work, not aid*," or boast that they're providing "*the most underprivileged people in the world access to new forms of micro employment.*"

These jobs are no different from the tenement sweatshops of the nineteenth century, where women and children lived and worked—or rather, worked and barely lived—being paid for each piece they sewed. Even the "sweatshop" environment is mirrored in the description of a microworkplace in Dadaab, Kenya—one of the world's largest refugee camps: "*Cramped and airless workspaces, festooned with a jumble of cables and loose wires . . .*"

When Prop 22 passed, the Yes on Prop 22 website celebrated: "*Prop 22 represents the future of work in an increasingly technologically-driven economy.*"

The Utopian Socialists would have given this future a thumbs-down.

CHAPTER 73

WE ARE HERE-ISH

A lot will have changed by the time you're reading this last chapter. A lot has changed since the beginning of the book.

The US economy has moved from agriculture (farming) to manufacturing (factories) to service and distribution (brewing coffee and delivering packages). Corporate spyware has replaced factory speedups—with anxiety due to constant surveillance replacing nervous tension from ramped-up assembly lines. Hard-won laws against child labor are being lifted—making it easier to hire kids in low-paid, dangerous jobs. Debt, inflation, and overwork are causing social stress—not to mention climate change, gun violence, mass incarceration, and police violence. Stress can lead to illness and injury, yet access to healthcare for the working class is declining. And economic inequality is higher than it has ever been.

But one important thing hasn't changed—the only group with the will and the means to turn this all around is the working class.

In 2022, 15,000 nurses in Minnesota went on strike against an understaffed and exhausted healthcare system. The strike was the largest private-sector nurse strike in US history. In 2022, 50,000 University of California graduate student workers went on strike against increasing teaching responsibilities in response to dropping numbers of professors. The strike was the largest higher education strike in US history. In 2022, workers at two of America's most iconic corporations—Starbucks and Amazon—voted to unionize. Nurses, students, baristas, and packagers weren't alone . . . in 2022, striking and unionizing rose 50 percent.

Unfortunately, something else hasn't changed—corporations.

Today, US employers are charged with violating federal labor law in 41.5 percent of all union election campaigns. This is after corporations have legally delayed the vote for as long as possible. And if workers succeed in voting for a union, corporations often follow up by legally denying the vote's validity. When all this does not stop a union, corporations can stall negotiations for months or years while shifting work to nonunion places of business.

As of this writing, neither Starbucks nor Amazon workers have a contract. Starbucks says it is negotiating in good faith. The union says, *"Starbucks has never accepted a single proposal and never offered a single counterproposal."* Amazon contested the union vote of its workers. The National Labor Relations Board upheld the vote. Amazon is appealing the decision.

In the beginning of 2023, corporations began laying off massive numbers of workers despite making record-high profits in 2022. Why? According to one CEO, *"We need to see unemployment rise. We need to see pain in the economy."*

But fear isn't working this time.

In 2023, 340,000 UPS workers said they'd strike unless their new contract paid part-time workers better and removed tiered wages. They got both.

In 2023, pilots at American and Southwest airlines voted to strike, along with flight attendants at American, United, Alaskan, and Southwest. Pilots and attendants say endless work schedules are killing their quality of life.

In 2023, 11,000 writers from the Writers Guild of America (WGA) walked out on strike against the Alliance of Motion Picture and Television Producers (AMPTP). A few weeks later, the writers were joined by 160,000 actors from the Screen Actors Guild and the American Federation of Television and Radio Artists (SAG-AFTRA) . . . a combo strike that hasn't happened since 1960.

How does it feel to negotiate with corporations as the working class? In the words of SAG-AFTRA president Fran Drescher, *"They stayed locked behind closed doors; they continued to cancel our meetings with them. We thought, 'Well, maybe they're really getting into it,' but then what we ultimately received from them was what my mom would call 'a leck and a schmeck.'"*

Workers have been experiencing a leck and a schmeck for centuries—from the Founding Father who said, *"Those who own the country ought to govern it,"* straight on to the abovementioned CEO who, besides wishing pain on the economy and workers, said, *"We need to remind people that they work for the employer, not the other way around."*

Who owns this nation . . . millions of Americans or one Gary?

In 1920, when steelworkers struck against US Steel's CEO Elbert Gary, the answer was, sadly, one Gary. In the fall of 2023, Gary better sit his ass down.

Sixty-four thousand nurses are gearing up to strike across

California, Oregon, and Washington. One hundred and forty-eight thousand autoworkers have begun to strike across the Midwest. One hundred and seventy thousand writers and actors are striking on both coasts. Amazon packagers, Starbucks baristas, Alaskan school-bus drivers, Trader Joe's grocery workers, Temple and Rutgers University graduate students, Los Angeles and Oakland teachers, Gannett journalists . . . 2023 has seen them all walk out. Maybe it's barely surviving a deadly pandemic. Maybe it's thirty years of dropping pay. Maybe it's that an average worker needs to work sixteen years to make what a CEO makes in a single week!

"As the past has clearly shown, nobody wins in a strike," said the GM president on the heels of the 2023 United Auto Workers strike. He is wrong. As the past has clearly shown, striking has led to five-day workweeks, eight-hour workdays, sick time, vacations, pensions, and the invention of the weekend.

When workers struck a few hundred years ago, capitalists shouted that the working class couldn't handle the money. When workers strike today, the commercial media shouts that the working class is "causing" economic strife. NBC worried businesses may close: *"Stellantis could close 18 facilities under UAW deal."* While Yahoo! Finance pointed out that workers were only hurting themselves: *"Ford, GM to layoff workers due to ripple effects."*

But it doesn't take much to reimagine this actual headline from CBS: *"Looming auto workers strike could cost $5 billion in just ten days,"* into this headline: "Looming auto workers strike could lead to billions more in the hands of the working class." Now keep on imagining . . . because this is how change begins.

Imagine we give workers a say in their working lives.

Imagine people—not profit—is what we choose to center.

Imagine a society that recognizes class conflict, racial injustice, sexual and gender inequality, disability discrimination, and false patriotism.

Imagine a country that rejects the pyramid of oppression and chooses instead to embrace diversity, community, solidarity . . .

and one another.

ACKNOWLEDGMENTS

I am solely responsible for the content in this book, along with all its opinions and any of its errors. The inspiration for it sprang from the following workers, coworkers, labor organizers, scholars, journalists, and friends.

Thank you . . .

to the two people who first heard the words "young adult nonfiction on US labor history" and said "Yes!"

Michael Bourret

Stephanie Guerdan

to this brave group who took a look at their times and said "No."

The carters who wouldn't get off the road for the governor of Massachusetts

Sam

John Brown

the worker who derailed the train in Martinsburg

Henry and George Cox

Eugene V. Debs

Jack

Clara Lemlich

Joseph and Gasper

William Snyder

Frank Little

the kids who raided the veterans' buffet

Ben Fletcher

Emma Tenayuca
A. Philip Randolph
Frances Perkins
Walter Reuther
William R. Hood
Larry Itliong
T. O. Jones
Coalition of Immokalee Workers
everyone who participated in the 1999 Seattle WTO protests
American teachers
to the folks whose strong shoulders this book stands on.
Cinzia Arruzza
Lana Barnes
Tithi Bhattacharya
Thomas Blanchet
Jane Little Botkin
Angela Y. Davis
Daniel Denvir
Marc Doussard
Melvyn Dubofsky
Philip S. Foner
Nancy Fraser
Jonah Furman
Beverly Gage
Jillian Goeler
Lawrence Goodwyn
Steven Greenhouse
Doug Henwood
Ken Jacobs

Robin D. G. Kelley
Kim Kelly
E. Tammy Kim
Alison Klapthor
Caitlin Lonning
Deborah J. Lucas
Kekla Magoon
Karl Marx
Tia McCarthy
Jane F. McAlevey
Daisy Pitkin
Paul Robeson
Marta Russell
Noam Scheiber
Dean Strang
Rich Thomas
Daniel M. Thompson
David Treuer
Ahmed White
Jessica White
Howard Zinn
to the four who always have my back.
Cate Berry
Miriam Chernick
Adrienne Kisner
Mary Quattlebaum
With special thanks to Robin Galbraith, Jackson Mann, and Grace Mann for reading and commenting on this book over and over and over again.

SOURCE NOTES

Chapter 2: Somebody's Gotta Work

"great profit" . . . "more hands.": Philip S. Foner, *History of the Labor Movement in the United States*, Vol. 1, 13.

"Servants served masters": Foner, *History of the Labor Movement in the United States*, Vol. 1, 15–16.

"drain from the Mother-Country the disaffected and the vicious": Foner, *History of the Labor Movement in the United States*, Vol. 1, 16.

"any work in which the employer shall employ them": Foner, *History of the Labor Movement in the United States*, Vol. 1, 16–17.

"seduced children using gingerbread": James Kelly, "'This iniquitous traffic': The Kidnapping of Children for the American Colonies in Eighteenth-Century Ireland," 233.

"The golf links lie so near the mill . . . men at play.": Sarah N. Cleghorn, *Portraits and Protests*, New York: Henry Holt and Company, 1917, 75.

Chapter 3: Running, Rioting, and Revolting

"to deter him & others . . . he shall live.": "Punishment for a Negro Rebel," *William and Mary College Quarterly Historical Magazine* 10 (1902): 177–178.

"the scum of the people": Foner, *History of the Labor Movement in the United States*, Vol. 1, 30.

Chapter 4: Capitalism Goes Viral

"be content to abate their wages according to the fall of the commodities": Foner, *History of the Labor Movement in the United States*, Vol. 1, 25.

"to save the American Workingman from himself": Ibid.

"high wages more frequently . . . ruining their health": Ibid.

"we think it reasonable . . . our Mistrisses Husbands.": Foner, *History of the Labor Movement in the United States*, Vol. 1, 27.

"for not obeying the Command . . . in their Place.": Ibid.

"I am as good flesh and blood as you, you may go out of the way.": Foner, *History of the Labor Movement in the United States*, Vol. 1, 29.

"A poor honest man is preferable to a rich knave.": Foner, *History of the Labor Movement in the United States*, Vol. 1, 30.

"misled" . . . "men of the Low class.": Ibid.

Chapter 5: A Riotous Mob Founds a Nation

"A handful of English capitalists . . . millions of Americans.": Foner, *History of the Labor Movement in the United States*, Vol. 1, 3.

"The mob begin to think and to reason . . . the parent state.": Foner, *History of the Labor Movement in the United States*, Vol. 1, 34.

"reptiles": Charles S. Olton, "Philadelphia's Mechanics in the First Decade of Revolution 1765–1775," 311.

"Have we not an equal Right . . . Body of the Inhabitants.": Foner, *History of the Labor Movement in the United States*, Vol. 1, 37.

"was carried on by a mob . . . the utmost freedom.": Foner, *History of the Labor Movement in the United States*, Vol. 1, 39.

Chapter 6: An Orgy of Fraud

"an orgy of fraud": Foner, *History of the Labor Movement in the United States*, Vol. 1, 61.

Chapter 7: Fatal Flaw

"conspiracy against the good of society": Foner, *History of the Labor Movement in the United States*, Vol. 1, 78.

"government of the worst": Foner, *History of the Labor Movement in the United States*, Vol. 1, 84.

"Those who own the country ought to govern it.": Ibid.

"fatal to religion and morality": Alexander Hamilton, "A Full Vindication of the Measures of the Congress, &c." founders .archives.gov/documents/Hamilton/01-01-02-0054.

"This abomination must have an end . . . hasten it.": E. Paul Yarbro, *Forged in the Fires: How Providence, Purpose, and Perseverance Shaped America*, 269.

"people's movement" . . . "the Bible will be cast . . . legal prostitution.": Foner, *History of the Labor Movement in the United States*, Vol. 1, 87.

Chapter 8: You Made It!

"exert a very unhappy influence" . . . "seducing them from . . . ensure them.": Foner, *History of the Labor Movement in the United States*, Vol. 1, 102.

"un-American" . . . "foreigners" . . . "a spirit of discontent . . . been strangers.": Ibid.

"The laws are made by the rich and of course for the rich.": Foner, *History of the Labor Movement in the United States*, Vol. 1, 121.

"lost to society . . . robbery and murder.": Foner, *History of the Labor Movement in the United States*, Vol. 1, 133.

Chapter 9: Heaven and Hell

"Employ no men . . . thoroughly broken up.": Foner, *History of the Labor Movement in the United States*, Vol. 1, 167.

"We could not travel . . . with necessaries.": Foner, *History of the Labor Movement in the United States*, Vol. 1, 187.

"Our salvation must, through the blessing of God, come from ourselves.": Foner, *History of the Labor Movement in the United States*, Vol. 1, 192.

"increase crime, suffering, wickedness, and pauperism" . . . "hours spent in dissipation": Philip S. Foner, *Women and the American Labor Movement*, 36.

"Deprive us, after working . . . every wind.": Foner, *History of the Labor Movement in the United States*, Vol. 1, 198.

"a premature grave": Foner, *History of the Labor Movement in the United States*, Vol. 1, 210.

"The mills could not be improved by any suggestion of ours.": Ibid.

Chapter 10: Foreigners and Frightful Atrocities

"who feed upon the coarsest . . . any society.": Foner, *History of the Labor Movement in the United States*, Vol. 1, 225.

"The feeling of animosity . . . to you.": Foner, *History of the Labor Movement in the United States*, Vol. 1, 226.

"The frightful atrocities of slave holding must be seen to be described.": Foner, *History of the Labor Movement in the United States*, Vol. 1, 251.

"You know we are not a quarter . . . thank the Lord.": Foner, *History of the Labor Movement in the United States*, Vol. 1, 275.

"come 1,200 miles from . . . to Pennsylvania.": Foner, *History of the Labor Movement in the United States*, Vol. 1, 253

"In the South we hear . . . slavery and bondage?": Foner, *History of the Labor Movement in the United States*, Vol. 1, 277.

"Slavery is the natural and normal . . . a delusion.": Foner, *History of the Labor Movement in the United States*, Vol. 1, 280.

"The truth is that Republicanism . . . than Radicalism.": Foner, *History of the Labor Movement in the United States*, Vol. 1, 284.

"dared the whole world . . . a man do?": Eugene Debs, "Eugene Debs's Stirring, Never-Before-Published Eulogy to John Brown at Harpers Ferry," *Jacobin*.

"Capital is the fruit of labor. . . superior to capital.": Foner, *History of* the *Labor Movement in the United States*, Vol. 1, 292.

"had tenderness for the Ethiopian race" . . . "shut their eyes to the squalor around them, and shed crocodile tears over the imaginary ills of slavery" . . . "disastrous event" . . . "blow to every working man": Foner, *History of the Labor Movement in the United States*, Vol. 1, 294.

Chapter 11: Busted Dreams

"There is one truth which . . . ought to be slaves.": Foner, *History of the Labor Movement in the United States*, Vol. 1, 312.

"Col. Montgomery and his gallant . . . a glorious consummation.": Foner, *History of the Labor Movement in the United States*, Vol. 1, 319.

Chapter 12: Welcome to the New Hot Mess

"sap the foundation of that independence of character, and that reliance on one's own resources": Foner, *History of the Labor Movement in the United States*, Vol. 1, 443.

"thoroughly communistic": Ibid.

"were hunted like mad dogs": Foner, *History of the Labor Movement in the United States*, Vol. 1, 440.

"already the cry of the dying children begins to be heard": Howard Zinn, *A People's History of the United States*, 245.

Chapter 13: All Hell Breaks Loose

"Many of us have reason to know what long hours and low pay mean.": Foner, *History of the Labor Movement in the United States*, Vol. 1, 469.

"All the men killed were shot through the head or heart": Foner, *History of the Labor Movement in the United States*, Vol. 1, 466.

"settle this business with Philadelphia troops": Foner, *History of the Labor Movement in the United States*, Vol. 1, 468.

"is a wild beast who needs to be shot down": Foner, *History of the Labor Movement in the United States*, Vol. 1, 469.

"The ignorant rabble with hungry mouths needs to be fed a diet of lead.": Ibid.

"The only way to deal with a mob is to exterminate it.": Robert J. Goldstein, *Political Repression in Modern America from 1870 to 1976*, 29.

"Labor Revolution": Foner, *History of the Labor Movement in the United States*, Vol. 1, 471.

"We are asking the public . . . railway men.": Ibid.

"white and colored men . . . rights of workingmen.": Foner, *History of the Labor Movement in the United States*, Vol. 1, 473.

Chapter 14: Eat the Rich

"the greatest march of economic growth in human history": Zinn, *A People's History of the United States*, 254.

"Wilkerson & Company received car of oil Monday 13th . . . Please turn another screw.": Zinn, *A People's History of the United States*, 257.

"Federal aid in such cases . . . national character.": Zinn, *A People's History of the United States*, 259.

Chapter 15: Hope Between the Pages

"The philosophy of a new social order . . . as unnecessary.": Emma Goldman, "The Reckoning," 212.

"The Negro population of the South deserves our kindest and most careful attention.": Foner, *History of the Labor Movement in the United States*, Vol. 1, 503.

"an injury to one is the concern of all": Foner, *History of the Labor Movement in the United States*, Vol. 1, 510.

Chapter 16: 1886

"I can hire one-half of the working class to kill the other half.": Foner, *History of the Labor Movement in the United States*, Vol. 2, 50.

"We mean to make things over. . . for what we will!": Foner, *History of the Labor Movement in the United States*, Vol. 2, 103.

"Hold them personally responsible . . . make an example of them": Zinn, *A People's History of the United States*, 270.

"Hang them first and try them afterwards!": Jeremy Brecher, *Strike!*, 46.

"No disturbance of the peace . . . cooly executed murder.": Ibid.

"If I had a little strained the law, I was to be commended for so doing.": Foner, *History of the Labor Movement in the United States*, Vol. 2, 108.

Chapter 17: Sugar, Spies, and Suppression

"We break strikes . . . no friction.": Foner, *History of the Labor Movement in the United States*, Vol. 3, 44.

"penniless, ragged, and carrying their bed clothing and babies": Zinn, *A People's History of the United States*, 274.

"God Almighty has himself drawn the color line": Philip S. Foner, *Organized Labor and the Black Worker*, 60.

"At such times and upon such occasions . . . lawful rights.": Zinn, *A People's History of the United States*, 274.

Chapter 18: Oh, Frick

"savage beasts who deserve no pity": Foner, *History of the Labor Movement in the United States*, Vol. 2, 210.

"full of men with Anarchist principles": Foner, *History of the Labor Movement in the United States*, Vol. 2, 214.

"Our victory is now complete and most gratifying.": Brecher, *Strike!*, 62.

Chapter 19: Death by Devil Fish

"If the year 1892 taught . . . of degradation.": Zinn, *A People's History of the United States*, 278.

"leaden" diet: Goldstein, *Political Repression in Modern America from 1870 to 1976*, 27.

"It is a waste of taxpayers . . . receive it.": Foner, *History of the Labor Movement in the United States*, Vol. 2, 239.

"In a society where such . . . human family.": Foner, *History of the Labor Movement in the United States*, Vol. 2, 240.

"acts of God": Zinn, *A People's History of the United States*, 278.

"to eliminate the aristocracy of labor": Zinn, *A People's History of the United States*, 279.

"We do not expect the company . . . work any longer.": Brecher, *Strike!*, 80.

"add to our treasuries thousands upon thousands of dollars": Foner, *History of the Labor Movement in the United States*, Vol. 2, 259.

"the greatest battle between labor and capital that has ever been inaugurated in the United States": Brecher, *Strike!*, 82.

"the complete annihilation of the American Railway Union": Foner, *History of the Labor Movement in the United States*, Vol. 2, 263.

"It is the government's duty . . . lawless men": Brecher, *Strike!*, 84.

"From a Strike to a Revolution" . . . "Mob Bent on Ruin" . . . "Anarchists and Socialists said to be Planning the Destruction and Looting of the Treasury": Foner, *History of the Labor Movement in the United States*, Vol. 2, 269.

"They might as well try to stop . . . in this country.": Brecher, *Strike!*, 96.

Chapter 20: Blowing That Shit Up

"The issue is Socialism versus . . . for civilization.": Zinn, *A People's History of the United States*, 281.

"secure to our people freedom . . . powerful corporations": Zinn, *A People's History of the United States*, 286.

"Wall Street owns the country. . . . thus far beware.": Zinn, *A People's History of the United States*, 288.

"The sentiments now animating . . . shooting them dead.": Foner, *History of the Labor Movement in the United States*, Vol. 2, 339.

"We are aware of the fact . . . just like we are.": Zinn, *A People's History of the United States*, 290.

"This year is going to be a year of patriotism . . . of the flag.": Zinn, *A People's History of the United States*, 295.

Chapter 21: God and Science Prefer the Rich

"That you have property . . . laziness and vices.": Foner, *History of the Labor Movement in the United States*, Vol. 2, 28.

Chapter 23: What Justice Is

"There is no color line in the furnace hells of the steel trust and there will be none in the One Big Union.": Foner, *Organized Labor and the Black Worker*, 111.

"The working class and the employing class have nothing in common.": Foner, *History of the Labor Movement in the United States*, Vol. 4, 39.

"Tie 'em up! Tie 'em up! . . . and the One Big Strike.": Richard O. Boyer and Herbert M. Morais, *Labor's Untold Story*, 173.

"Hanging is none too good for them. They would be much better dead.": Ibid.

"There is one thing I can tell you . . . We can always get some more.": Foner, *History of the Labor Movement in the United States*, Vol. 4, 174.

"They took turns lecturing about . . . knee-high in the cells.": Zinn, *A People's History of the United States*, 332.

"The prosecuting attorney . . . I know what justice is.'": Zinn, *A People's History of the United States*, 333.

Chapter 24: Broken Noses and Busted Ribs

"I have listened to all the speakers, and I have no further patience for talk.": Steven Greenhouse, *Beaten Down, Worked Up*, 53.

"The brutality of the police . . . noses broken open.": Greenhouse, *Beaten Down, Worked Up*, 56.

Chapter 25: Better Working Conditions, or Not Having to Jump to Your Death

"I learned a new sound . . . Sixty-two thud, deads.": Greenhouse, *Beaten Down, Worked Up*, 64.

Chapter 26: Stop the Change

"Engaged in a game of bathing . . . reward for his find.": Foner, *History of the Labor Movement in the United States*, Vol. 3, 147.

"The United States as government . . . of machine-rule.": Foner, *History of the Labor Movement in the United States*, Vol. 5, 35.

"Mr. Gompers betrays his . . . the corporations.": Foner, *History of the Labor Movement in the United States*, Vol. 3, 303.

"The greatest and most dangerous rock in the course of any republic is the rock of class hatred.": Foner, *History of the Labor Movement in the United States*, Vol. 3, 311.

Chapter 27: A Magical Combination

"Our lives shall not be sweated . . . give us roses.": James Oppenheim, "Bread and Roses," *The American Magazine*, December 1911.

"Better to starve fighting than to starve working": Foner, *History of the Labor Movement in the United States*, Vol. 4, 316.

"Never before has a strike . . . human beings.": Foner, *History of the Labor Movement in the United States*, Vol. 4, 320.

"poor, ignorant" . . . "a reign of terror" . . . "the destruction of the present social order": Foner, *History of the Labor Movement in the United States*, Vol. 4, 332, 333.

"Take the Children" . . . "Send us Your Children": Foner, *History of the Labor Movement in the United States*, Vol. 4, 325.

"would become in time veritable breeders of anarchy": Foner, *History* of the Labor Movement in the United States, Vol. 4, 326.

"for the purpose of tiring out or starving strikers": Foner, *History of the Labor Movement in the United States*, Vol. 4, 341.

"labor buzzards" . . . "social vultures": Foner, *History of the Labor Movement in the United States*, Vol. 4, 345.

Chapter 28: One Step Forward Is Not Enough Steps

"That old man with the burning eyes . . . believe it myself.": Zinn, *A People's History of the United States*, 339.

"I know that my father has followed . . . and satisfaction.": Boyer and Morais, *Labor's Untold Story*, 190.

"For God's sake, save my children": Ibid.

Chapter 29: Submarines, a Luxury Liner, and Some Really Big Loans

"Britain has the earth, and Germany wants it.": David Frum, "The Real Story of How America Became an Economic Superpower," *The Atlantic*, December 24, 2014.

"Perhaps our going to war . . . panic averted.": Boyer and Morais, *Labor's Untold Story*, 915.

Chapter 30: Parades and Propaganda

"new and startling disclosures": Foner, *History of the Labor Movement in the United States*, Vol. 7, 82.

"filled our unsuspecting communities . . . intrigues everywhere": Goldstein, *Political Repression in Modern America from 1870 to 1976*, 107.

"the masters of Germany" . . . "liberals" . . . "socialists" . . . "the leaders of labor" . . . "carry out their designs": Ibid.

"Wars throughout history have . . . fought the battles." . . . "I wish Wilson was in hell, and if I had the power, I'd put him there.": Zechariah Chafee Jr., *Free Speech in the United States*, 139–141, 184.

Chapter 31: Collinsville, Tulsa, Bisbee, and Butte

"had been a good thing": Foner, *History of the Labor Movement in the United States*, Vol. 7, 279.

"the authorities" . . . "without gloves" . . . "sedition" . . . "treasonable tirades": Foner, *History of the Labor Movement in the United States*, Vol. 7, 287, 288.

"A Little hanging goes a long way toward labor peace": Dean Strang, *Keep the Wretches in Order*, 7.

Chapter 32: The "Right" Kind

"I can shoot quickly . . . begin in Washington.": Strang, *Keep the Wretches in Order*, 42.

"In a great industrial nation . . . kind of leadership.": Foner, *History of the Labor Movement in the United States*, Vol. 7, 303.

"The world must be made safe for democracy.": Woodrow Wilson, 1917, "Joint Address to Congress Leading to a Declaration of War Against Germany," National Archives, www.archives.gov /milestone-documents/address-to-congress-declaration-of-war -against-germany.

Chapter 33: The "Wrong" Kind

"look lawful": Strang, *Keep the Wretches in Order*, 54.

"someday, some of them would commit substantive crimes": Ibid.

"dispirit, disorient, and disable": Strang, *Keep the Wretches in Order*, 60.

"main man": Strang, *Keep the Wretches in Order*, 81.

"No one understands the distinction better or states it more forcibly.": Strang, *Keep the Wretches in Order*, 114.

"Patriotism may be the inspiration . . . believe in war.": Strang, *Keep the Wretches in Order*, 15.

"Take this same organization . . . one hundred years ago.": Strang, *Keep the Wretches in Order*, 155.

"War in the modern world . . . a political war.": Foner, *History of the*

Labor Movement in the United States, Vol. 7, 2.

Chapter 34: Don't Rock the Boat

"The right of the employer . . . or questioned.": Foner, *History of the Labor Movement in the United States*, Vol. 8, 9.

"It is not good now to rock the industrial boat.": Foner, *History of the Labor Movement in the United States*, Vol. 7, 348.

"ringleaders of anarchy": Zinn, *A People's History of the United States*, 379.

"The general strike . . . dangerous because quiet.": Ibid.

Chapter 35: A Villain Origin Story

"My one desire is to acquaint people . . . the Red Movement.": Robert K. Murray, *Red Scare*, 194.

"The surest way to preserve the public against those disciples of destruction is to send them back forthwith to lands from which they came.": Adam Hochschild, "When America Tried to Deport Its Radicals."

"Today, we hear the hiss . . . hold most dear.": Ibid.

"We should place them all . . . be hell.": Foner, *History of the Labor Movement in the United States*, Vol. 8, 24.

"be deported permanently to the Island of Guam": Hochschild, "When America Tried to Deport Its Radicals."

"foreign agitators acting on behalf of the Bolsheviks in Russia": Foner, *History of the Labor Movement in the United States*, Vol. 8, 24.

"use the other so well that five radicals required treatment by ambulance surgeons.": Murray, *Red Scare*, 77.

"The capitalist papers may shout . . . explosion occurred.": Murray, *Red Scare*, 80.

"actively stirring up trouble because they know on which side their bread is buttered": Hochschild, "When America Tried to Deport Its Radicals."

"We believe that the reason the perpetrators . . . to discover them.": Murray, *Red Scare*, 81.

"Ninety per cent of communist and anarchist agitation is traceable to aliens.": Hochschild, "When America Tried to Deport Its Radicals."

"If I had my way, I'd . . . bridles first.": Murray, *Red Scare*, 83.

Chapter 36: Bodies and Blood

"foreign element" . . . "no good American reason" . . . "not between workers and employers, but between revolutionists and America.": Foner, *History of the Labor Movement in the United States*, Vol. 8, 161.

"Stand by America, Go Back to Work": Murray, *Red Scare*, 143.

"We have conclusive evidence that the strike is in the hands of the Reds and we can prove it.": Foner, *History of the Labor Movement in the United States*, Vol. 8, 163.

"Who owns this nation, one hundred and ten million people or one Gary?": Foner, *History of the Labor Movement in the United States*, Vol. 8, 158.

"Out of the sly and crafty eyes . . . criminal type.": Murray, *Red Scare*, 219.

"dirty Bolshevik terrorists": Murray, *Red Scare*, 216.

"a lion-hearted man" . . . "order out of chaos" . . . "Little Red Riding Hood with a cry of 'Wolf'": Murray, *Red Scare*, 198, 253.

"We believe in and uphold civil liberties . . . rich and poor alike.": "An Open Letter to President Harding," 21–22.

Chapter 37: Rags to Rags

"All the chief avenues to mass opinion were now controlled by large-scale publishing industries.": Zinn, *A People's History of the United States*, 383.

"their little stomachs busted open": Foner, *History of the Labor Movement in the United States*, Vol. 11, 122.

"The individual is hopeless.": Foner, *History of the Labor Movement in the United States*, Vol. 9, 222.

"airplane bombings of miners' villages could happen in America": Foner, *History of the Labor Movement in the United States*, Vol. 9, 225.

"Don't you know where you are? . . . in West Virginia." Ibid.

Chapter 38: Profit over People

"Samuel Gompers Dead Since 1917": Foner, *History of the Labor Movement in the United States*, Vol. 9, 363.

"Brokers Believe Worst Is Over," "Stocks up in Strong Rally," "Very Prosperous Year Is Forecast": "The Crash of 1929 Headlines," PBS.org, www.pbs.org/wgbh/americanexperience/features/crash-headlines/.

"We in America are nearer to . . . any land." Foner, *History of the Labor Movement in the United States*, Vol. 11, 18.

"There is plenty of work to do if people would do it": Zinn, *A People's History of the United States*, 387.

"turned out of the city lodging house for lack of funds": Zinn, *A People's History of the United States*, 364.

"stormed the plant of the Fruit Growers . . . from starving": Ibid.

"twenty-five hungry children raided . . . them away.": Ibid.

"fundamentally unsound": Zinn, *A People's History of the United States*, 361.

Transcript of conversation between Mr. Scarvada and two men: Goldstein, *Political Repression in Modern America from 1870 to 1976*, 204.

"openly preach social equality for . . . squelched NOW.": Foner, *History of the Labor Movement in the United States*, Vol. 11, 28.

"Hundreds of policemen and detectives . . . off their feet.": Foner, *History of the Labor Movement in the United States*, Vol. 11, 33.

"Red Riots in Many Cities in America and Europe": Foner, *History of the Labor Movement in the United States*, Vol. 11, 34.

"It is not true that high wages . . . reduce cost." Foner, *History of the Labor Movement in the United States*, Vol. 11, 42.

President Hoover thanked workers in advance of the cuts for being *"responsible."*: Foner, *History of the Labor Movement in the United States*, Vol. 11, 41.

"The depression brought everybody down a peg or two. And the Negroes had but few pegs to fall.": Foner, *Organized Labor and the Black Worker*, 188.

"If white men would assert their rights . . . the South.": Foner, *History of the Labor Movement in the United States*, Vol. 11, 47.

"stabilize business" . . . "trickle down": Foner, *History of the Labor Movement in the United States*, Vol. 11, 61.

"Starving Mother Kills Self and Four Children": Foner, *History of the Labor Movement in the United States*, Vol. 11, 56.

Chapter 39: Digging Out from under Another Rock Bottom

"Hoover sent the army, Roosevelt sent his wife.": Goldstein, *Political Repression in Modern America from 1870 to 1976*, 210.

"conspiracy against the good of society": Foner, *History of the Labor Movement in the United States*, Vol. 1, 78.

Chapter 40: Nuts, Auto Parts, and Pissed-Off Truckers

"The nut pickers' strike was not inspired . . . the workers.": Foner, *History of the Labor Movement in the United States*, Vol. 11, 134.

"Truck attempting to move load . . . send help.": Brecher, *Strike!*, 162.

"You can't lick a gun with a club.": Brecher, *Strike!*, 163.

"Police took direct aim at the pickets and fired to kill.": Brecher, *Strike!*, 165.

"curb headquarters": Brecher, *Strike!*, 166.

"Who made America . . . mighty dream again.": Langston Hughes, "Let America Be America Again," *Esquire*, July 1, 1936.

Chapter 41: A Baseball Game Changes Everything

"Aw, to hell with 'im, let's sit down.": Brecher, *Strike!*, 181.

"We didn't even have time to go to the toilet.": Greenhouse, *Beaten Down, Worked Up*, 81.

"Why can't these fellows . . . Talk it out.": Greenhouse, *Beaten Down, Worked Up*, 89.

"You are a scoundrel and a skunk, Mr. Sloan.": Ibid.

"We have decided to stay in the plant. . . . will be killed.": Greenhouse, *Beaten Down, Worked Up*, 90.

"We are going to go down there shooting.": Greenhouse, *Beaten Down, Worked Up*, 91.

"Sitting down has replaced baseball as a national pastime.": Greenhouse, *Beaten Down, Worked Up*, 92.

Chapter 42: The Battle of the Overpass

"Labor unions are the worst thing . . . man's independence.": Timothy J. Minchin, "Gigantic Struggles."

"I didn't fight back. . . . was for us.": Nelson Lichtenstein, *Walter Reuther: The Most Dangerous Man in Detroit*, 84.

"They at one point put their heel . . . the groin.": Ibid.

"I know definitely no Ford service men . . . employees at work.": "Ford Men Beat and Rout Lewis Union Organizers; 80,000 Out in Steel Strike," *New York Times*, May 27, 1937.

Chapter 44: History Repeats Itself

"The peace we seem to be making . . . human interest.": Zinn, *A People's History of the United States*, 414.

"Those who cannot remember the past are condemned to repeat it.": George Santayana, *The Life of Reason: Introduction and Reason in Common Sense*, 172.

Chapter 45: Discrimination . . . on Repeat

"Keep Our Boys from Dying": Foner, *Organized Labor and the Black Worker*, 243.

"The Federal Government cannot with clear conscience . . . discrimination itself.": Foner, *Organized Labor and the Black Worker*, 240.

Chapter 46: Disloyalty . . . on Repeat

"politically dominating, economically exploiting, and socially humiliating over half of the human race": Foner, *Organized Labor and the Black Worker*, 284.

Chapter 47: A Never-Ending Red Scare

"permanent war economy": Zinn, *A People's History of the United States*, 425.

"The greatest military achievement in all history": Boyer and Morais, *Labor's Untold Story*, 333.

Chapter 48: Everybody Eating Pie Is Socialism

"We shall resist the monopolistic . . . basic wages.": Greenhouse, *Beaten Down, Worked Up*, 99.

"Labor is not fighting for a larger slice of the national pie. Labor is fighting for a larger pie." . . . "more realistic distribution of America's wealth.": Ibid.

"exposing his socialist desires": Ibid.

"If fighting for a more equal and equitable . . . being a Socialist.": Ibid.

Chapter 49: 1946 Happens

"You have during most of your life been . . . Communist Party." . . . "There is a suspicion in the record that . . . Is this true?": Goldstein, *Political Repression in Modern America from 1870 to 1976*, 299–303.

"shocking piece of legislation": "President Harry S. Truman's

Speech Regarding the Taft–Hartley Bill Veto, June 20, 1947,"
www.visitthecapitol.gov/artifact/president-harry-s-trumans-speech
-regarding-taft-hartley-bill-veto-june-20-1947.

"A New Deal for American's Employers": Boyer and Morais, *Labor's Untold Story*, 347–348.

Chapter 50: The Treaty of Detroit

"a great event in industrial history": Greenhouse, *Beaten Down, Worked Up*, 104.

"GM may have paid a billion for peace but it got a bargain.": Ibid.

Chapter 51: "Something New Is Cooking on the Freedom Train"

"creeping socialism" . . . "A union doesn't need to be . . . industrial society.": Boyer and Morais, *Labor's Untold Story*, 366–373.

"First they came for the socialists . . . to speak for me.": "Martin Niemöller: 'First they came for . . .'," U.S. Holocaust Memorial Museum, encyclopedia.ushmm.org/content/en/article/martin-niemoeller-first-they -came-for-the-socialists.

"We left the colored people out . . . are with us.": Foner, *Organized Labor and the Black Worker*, 261–262.

"We come to announce to all America . . . hope for tomorrow.": Foner, *Organized Labor and the Black Worker*, 298.

Chapter 53: The Body You're Born In

"the employment of [Black workers] . . . unheard of.": Foner, *Organized Labor and the Black Worker*, 271.

"Criticism doesn't help." . . . "These are difficult times." . . . "Now is a time for unity.": Foner, *Organized Labor and the Black Worker*, 323.

"Randolph's request is not likely to be granted.": Foner, *Organized Labor and the Black Worker*, 314.

"The fight has just begun.": Foner, *Organized Labor and the Black Worker*, 316.

"Since [the] merger did we grow in the South? . . . White Citizens' Council.": Foner, *Organized Labor and the Black Worker*, 320.

"looking only at the negative side of the picture": Ibid.

"mental deficiency, bad health, . . . insufficient education": Foner, *Organized Labor and the Black Worker*, 327.

"[B]lack labor never had a chance.": Foner, *Organized Labor and the Black Worker*, 327.

Chapter 55: I Am a Man

"You keep your back bent over, somebody's gonna ride it.": Greenhouse, *Beaten Down, Worked Up*, 111.

"My God, what the hell am I going to do with a strike in the South?": Ibid.

"What crime have they committed . . . Is that a crime?": Greenhouse, *Beaten Down, Worked Up*, 112.

"This was done to me for one reason, and that's because I was [B]lack, no other reason.": Greenhouse, *Beaten Down, Worked Up*, 113.

"If America doesn't use its vast resources . . . going to hell.": Greenhouse, *Beaten Down, Worked Up*, 114–115.

"You are demanding that this city will respect . . . a cup of coffee?": Greenhouse, *Beaten Down, Worked Up*, 115.

"King's famous espousal of non-violence was vandalism, looting, and riot.": Greenhouse, *Beaten Down, Worked Up*, 117.

"Like anybody, I would like to live . . . coming of the Lord!": Greenhouse, *Beaten Down, Worked Up*, 118.

Chapter 56: A Final Gift

"Either we go up together, or we go down together.": Greenhouse, *Beaten Down, Worked Up*, 118.

"We are not going to recognize this union.": Greenhouse, *Beaten Down, Worked Up*, 119.

"We have lost many things. But we have got the victory.": Greenhouse, *Beaten Down, Worked Up*, 120.

Chapter 57: Oil

"As one approaches nearer to the country . . . fire is applied to it.": Reuben Gold Thwaites, ed., *The Jesuit Relations and Allied Documents 1610 to 1791* (Cleveland: The Burrows Brothers Company), Vol. 43, 261.

"Corporate influence on the White House is a permanent fact of the American system.": Zinn, *A People's History of the United States*, 547.

"for $50,000 you get to talk to the President.": Zinn, *A People's History of the United States*, 548.

"had the highest volume of profits of any industrial sector": Ernest Holsendolph, "Oil Industry Uses 'Rate of Return' as Battle Cry Trying to Gauge Corporation Profits Return on Net Worth," *New York Times*, February 10, 1974.

"Those citizens who insist on driving large, unnecessarily powerful cars must expect to pay more for that luxury.": "Transcript of Carter's Address to the Nation About Energy Problems," *New York Times*, April 19, 1974.

"First we must decide that 'less' is not enough. Next we must remove government obstacles to energy production.": Meg Jacobs, "America's Never-Ending Oil Consumption," *Atlantic*, May 15, 2016.

Chapter 58: The Free Market

"President Reagan trimmed $1.46 billion from $5.66 billion earmarked for child nutrition programs": Jonathan Harsch, "Reagan Cuts Eat into School Lunches," *Christian Science Monitor*, September 17, 1981.

Chapter 59: The Unfriendly Skies

"You can rest assured that if I . . . public safety.": Greenhouse, *Beaten Down, Worked Up*, 128.

"You can't win this strike" . . . "massive damage to the labor movement.": Greenhouse, *Beaten Down, Worked Up*, 133.

"impose a tax burden on their fellow citizens": Ronald Reagan, "Remarks on the Air Traffic Controllers Strike," August 3, 1981, Miller Center of Public Affairs, University of Virginia, transcript and video, millercenter.org/the-presidency/presidential-speeches/august-3-1981 -remarks-air-traffic-controllers-strike.

"Organized labor—unionism—was essentially . . . the administration.": Greenhouse, *Beaten Down, Worked Up*, 136.

Chapter 60: Those Damn Mining Companies

"Suddenly people realized, hell, you can beat a union.": Greenhouse, *Beaten Down, Worked Up*, 137.

"Managers are discovering that strikes . . . be a dirty word.": Ibid.

Chapter 61: They've Gone Too Far

"There's a place for unions, but they've gone too far.": Greenhouse, *Beaten Down, Worked Up*, 140.

"Companies just want to get rid of unions.": Ibid.

"There's a bunch of guys in Thailand, Korea . . . market share.": Greenhouse, *Beaten Down, Worked Up*, 146.

"Corporations are chartered to serve both their shareholders and society as a whole.": Greenhouse, *Beaten Down, Worked Up*, 148.

"The paramount duty of management and boards of directors is to the corporation's stockholders.": Ibid.

"Unions are divisive." . . . "They're just a big business." . . . "Unions are just political." . . . "They cause taxes to go up.": Greenhouse, *Beaten Down, Worked Up*, 163.

Chapter 62: "Save a Logger, Eat an Owl"

"Unfortunately, strong vested interests . . . climate change.": John Theodore Houghton, "The Truth About Climate Change," *Guardian*, April 27, 2009.

"It always annoys me to leave anything . . . want it all. Now.": Judi Bari, *Timber Wars*, 12.

"Save a Logger, Eat an Owl": Bari, *Timber Wars*, 13.

"I feel sorry for Potter Valley . . . at their end.": Bari, *Timber Wars*, 23.

Chapter 63: What Happened in Vegas, Should Not Stay in Vegas

"Would You Bet a Billion Dollars on a Single Roll of the Dice?": Greenhouse, *Beaten Down, Worked Up*, 43.

"When you're in the service business . . . very quickly.": Greenhouse, *Beaten Down, Worked Up*, 44.

Chapter 64: The Tomato Wars

"These are the forgotten people, the underprotected, the undereducated, the underfed.": Greenhouse, *Beaten Down, Worked Up*, 254.

"It's not our job to tell the growers how much to pay their workers.": Greenhouse, *Beaten Down, Worked Up*, 260.

"The CIW has given the workers nothing. . . . unquestioning students.": Ibid.

"It's the time of year when you are supposed to . . . unacceptable yesterday.": Greenhouse, *Beaten Down, Worked Up*, 261.

Chapter 65: Again

"particularly the United States": Zinn, *A People's History of the United States*, 657.

"the evils of capitalism" . . . "a radical redistribution of economic and political power": Zinn, *A People's History of the United States*, 644.

"More than any other time in decades . . . poultry workers.": Zinn, *A People's History of the United States*, 671.

"Farmers from around the world . . . downtown Seattle.": Zinn, *A People's History of the United States*, 673.

"I don't think they think about people like us.": Zinn, *A People's History of the United States*, 676.

"Maybe the Court should have said, 'We're not going to take it, goodbye.'": Jeffrey Toobin, "Justice O'Connor Regrets," *New Yorker*, May 6, 2013.

Chapter 67: The Terrible, Horrible, No Good, Very Bad Law

"differences aside and find ways to work together": Scott Bauer, "Walker Wins Recall Election in Wisconsin," *State Journal-Register*, June 6, 2012.

"We can no longer live in a society . . . the have-nots.": Maddie Burakoff, "'Act 10 Took Away Our Voice': One Decade In, Public Employees still See Law's Effects," Spectrum News 1, June 29, 2021.

Chapter 69: Unions Are Communities and Communities Are Unions

"more scared of coming home and not being able to feed my child.": Greenhouse, *Beaten Down, Worked Up*, 240.

Chapter 70: Dumb Bunnies

"Now if you choose to respond to somebody . . . I won't let you down.": Brad McElhinny, "'Dumb bunnies' in WV Teacher Crowds Protest Comment by Governor Justice," MetroNews, February 25, 2018.

"Teachers want more. But it's kind of like having a teenage kid that wants a better car.": Greenhouse, *Beaten Down, Worked Up*, 313.

"I'm not voting for another stinking measure when they're acting the way they're acting.": Ibid.

"Don't make me go all West Virginia on you.": Greenhouse, *Beaten Down, Worked Up*, 316.

Chapter 71: Cool Nickname, Still Dying

"Day 1: A non-union salaried worker just crashed a tractor inside the plant. Whoops!": Jonah Furman (@JonahFurman), Twitter, 15 Oct. 2021, 11:21 a.m., twitter.com/JonahFurman/status/1449032606633299969.

"business needs": Juliana Kaplan, "Over 1,000 Nabisco Bakery

Workers Are on Strike over Twelve-Hour Shifts," *Business Insider*, August 23, 2021.

"When the government trains people to stay at home . . . people to be lazy.": Fox News Staff, "Tomi Lahren on 'Great Resignation' Survey: 'We Incentivized Laziness for Too Long'," Fox News, March 15, 2022.

Chapter 72: Gigs and Clicks

"Now, we're looking ahead and across . . . and flexible.": Lauren Feiner and Lora Kolodny, "Uber and Lyft Eye Other States after California Ballot Victory," CNBC, November 5, 2020.

"conspiracy against the good of society": Foner, *History of the Labor Movement in the United States*, Vol. 1, 78.

"Artificial intelligence is not that artificial; it's human beings that are doing the work.": Julia Carrie Wong, "'A White-Collar Sweatshop': Google Assistant Contractors Allege Wage Theft," *Guardian*, June 25, 2019.

"focus their time on what matters most": Lyft, Inc., Form S-1 Registration Statement, March 1, 2019, www.sec.gov/Archives/edgar /data/1759509/000119312519059849/d633517ds1.htm.

"Give work, not aid" . . . "the most underprivileged people in the world access to new forms of micro employment.": Phil Jones, *Work Without the Worker*, 12.

"Cramped and airless workspaces, festooned with a jumble of cables and loose wires . . .": Jones, *Work Without the Worker*, 11–12.

"Prop 22 represents the future . . . technologically-driven economy.": Kate Conger, "Uber and Lyft Drivers in California Will Remain Contractors," *New York Times*, November 4, 2020.

Chapter 73: We Are Here-ish

"Starbucks has never accepted a single proposal and never offered a single counterproposal.": Steven Greenhouse, "Calls for Starbucks Boycott Grow Amid Aggressive Union-Busting Activities," *Guardian*, September 13, 2023.

"We need to see unemployment rise. We need to see pain in the economy.": Sarah Jackson, "A Millionaire CEO Is Rooting for Higher Unemployment, Saying It's Time to 'Remind People That They Work for the Employer, Not the Other Way Around'," *Business Insider*, September 14, 2023.

"They stayed locked behind closed doors . . . 'a leck and a schmeck.'": Jason P. Frank, "The 2023 Hollywood Strike for Dummies," Vulture, November 9, 2023.

"We need to remind people that they work for the employer, not the other way around.": Tim Gurner speaking at the AFR Property Summit, September 15, 2023, www.youtube.com/watch?v=_K1tqDyN4xE.

"As the past has clearly shown, nobody wins in a strike.": Mark Reuss, "GM President Fires Back: 'Flow of Misinformation' Could Prolong UAW Strike," *Detroit Free Press*, September 20, 2023.

"Stellantis could close 18 facilities under UAW deal": Michael Wayland, "Stellantis Could Close 18 Facilities under UAW Deal," CNBC, September 18, 2023.

"Ford, GM to layoff workers due to ripple effects": Pras Subramanian, "UAW Strike: Stellantis Ups Offer; Ford, GM to Lay Off Workers Due to Ripple Effects," Yahoo!Finance, September 18, 2023.

"Looming auto workers strike could cost $5 billion in just ten days": Adam Johnson, "How Scary Headlines about 'Economic Impact' of Strikes Erode Solidarity," Real News Network, September 8, 2023.

SELECTED BIBLIOGRAPHY
(AKA FURTHER READING)

Adamic, Louis. *Dynamite: The Story of Class Violence in America.* Chico, CA: AK Press, 2008.

"African American Coal Miners: Helen, WV." National Park Service, Jan. 2020. www.nps.gov/neri/planyourvisit/african -american-coal-miners-helen-wv.htm. Accessed 4 Feb. 2020.

Aleks, Rachel. "Estimating the Effect of 'Change to Win' on Union Organizing." *ILR Review* 68, no. 3 (May 2015): 584– 605. ecommons.cornell.edu/bitstream/handle/1813/75545 /Aleks1_Estimating_the_effect_of_Change_to_Win .pdf?sequence=1. Accessed 25 Sept. 2022.

Alimahomed-Wilson, Jake, and Ellen Reese. *The Cost of Free Shipping: Amazon in the Global Economy.* London: Pluto Press, 2020.

Allegretto, Sylvia, Marc Doussard, Dave Graham-Squire, Ken Jacobs, Dan Thompson, and Jeremy Thompson. *Fast Food, Poverty Wages: The Public Cost of Low-Wage Jobs in the Fast-Food Industry.* UC Berkeley Center for Labor Research and Education, 15 Oct. 2013. laborcenter.berkeley.edu/pdf/2013 /fast_food_poverty_wages.pdf. Accessed 3 May 2022.

"An Open Letter to President Harding from 52 Members of the IWW in Leavenworth Penitentiary Who Refuse to Apply for Individual Clemency." Chicago: General Defense Committee, 1922.

Archer, Robin. *Why Is There No Labor Party in the United States?* Princeton, NJ: Princeton University Press, 2010.

Arruzza, Cinzia, Tithi Bhattacharya, and Nancy Fraser. *Feminism for the 99%: A Manifesto.* New York: Verso, 2019.

Ashby, Steven, and Robert Bruno. *A Fight for the Soul of Public Education: The Story of the Chicago Teachers Strike.* Ithaca, NY: ILR Press, 2016.

Avrich, Paul. *The Haymarket Tragedy.* Princeton, NJ: Princeton University Press, 2020.

Avrich, Paul, and Karen Avrich. *Sasha and Emma: The Anarchist Odyssey of Alexander Berkman and Emma Goldman.* Cambridge, MA: Belknap Press, 2014.

Bari, Judi. *Timber Wars.* Monroe, ME: Common Courage Press, 1994.

Berkman, Alexander. *Prison Memoirs of an Anarchist.* New York: NYRB Classics, 1999.

Bernstein, Irving. *Turbulent Years, A History of the American Worker, 1933–1941.* Boston: Houghton Mifflin, 1970.

Blanc, Eric. *Red State Revolt: The Teachers' Strike Wave and Working-Class Politics.* New York: Verso, 2019.

Bort, Ryan, and Kimberly Aleah. "Year in Review: How Black Lives Matter Inspired a New Generation of Youth Activists." *Rolling Stone*, 14 Dec. 2020. www.rollingstone.com/politics /politics-features/black-lives-matter-protests-new-generation -youth-activists-1099895. Accessed 4 Jan. 2021.

Botkin, Jane Little. *Frank Little and the IWW: The Blood That Stained an American Family.* Norman, OK: University of Oklahoma Press, 2017.

——. *The Girl Who Dared to Defy: Jane Street and the Rebel Maids of Denver*. Norman, OK: University of Oklahoma Press, 2021.

Boyer, Richard O., and Herbert M. Morais. *Labor's Untold Story: The Adventure Story of the Battles, Betrayals and Victories of American Working Men and Women*. United Electrical, Radio & Machine Workers of America, 1975.

Brecher, Jeremy. *Strike!* Boston: South End Press, 1999.

Brown, Jenny. "Workers to Starbucks: Time to Negotiate." Labor Notes, 4 May 2023. labornotes.org/2023/05/workers-starbucks -time-negotiate. Accessed 5 May 2023.

Brown, Ralph S. *Loyalty and Security: Employment Tests in the United States*. Cambridge, MA: Da Capo Press, 1972.

Cahn, William. *A Pictorial History of American Labor*. New York: Crown Publishers, 1972.

Chacón, Justin Akers. *Radicals in the Barrio: Magonistas, Socialists, Wobblies, and Communists in the Mexican-American Working Class*. Chicago: Haymarket Books, 2018.

Chafee Jr., Zechariah. *Free Speech in the United States*. Cambridge, MA: Harvard University Press, 2014.

Chibber, Vivek. "Labor's Long March." *Jacobin*, 2 Aug. 2022. jacobin.com/2021/08/labors-long-march. Accessed 9 Sept. 2022.

Christmann, Samantha. "Starbucks Keeps Firing Union Organizers, but the Fired Workers Are Undeterred." Buffalo News, 20 Sept. 2022. buffalonews.com/business/local /starbucks-keeps-firing-union-organizers-but-the-fired -workers-are-undeterred/article_d127271a-2872-11ed-9ddd -9f74cfc0273c.html. Accessed 3 Oct. 2022.

Cohn, D'Vera. "How U.S. Immigration Laws and Rules Have Changed through History." Pew Research Center, 30 Sept. 2015. www.pewresearch.org/fact-tank/2015/09/30/how-u-s -immigration-laws-and-rules-have-changed-through-history. Accessed 10 Oct. 2021.

Cole, Peter. *Ben Fletcher, The Life and Times of a Black Wobbly*. Binghamton, NY: PM Press, 2021.

D'Costa, Krystal. "Who Are the Indigenous People That Columbus Met?" *Scientific American*, 12 Oct. 2018. blogs .scientificamerican.com/anthropology-in-practice/who-are-the -indigenous-people-that-columbus-met. Accessed 5 May. 2022.

Davis, Angela Y. *Women, Race & Class*. New York: Vintage, 2011.

Debs, Eugene. "Eugene Debs's Stirring, Never-Before-Published Eulogy to John Brown at Harpers Ferry." *Jacobin*, 27 Jan. 2022. jacobin.com/2022/01/socialist-party-america-slavery -abolitionism-race-debs-unpublished. Accessed 8 Feb. 2022.

Denvir, Daniel. *All-American Nativism: How the Bipartisan War on Immigrants Explains Politics as We Know It*. New York: Verso, 2020.

Domhoff, G. William. "The Rise and Fall of Labor Unions in the U.S. from the 1830s until 2012 (but mostly the 1930s–1980s)." Who Rules America?, Feb. 2013. whorulesamerica.ucsc.edu /power/history_of_labor_unions.html.Accessed 15 Mar. 2022.

Donner, Frank. *Protectors of Privilege: Red Squads and Police Repression in Urban America*. Berkeley: University of California Press, 1992.

Dray, Philip. *There Is Power in a Union: The Epic Story of Labor in America*. New York: Anchor Books, 2011.

Du Bois, W. E. B. *Black Reconstruction in America 1860–1880*.
New York: Free Press, 1998.

Dubofsky, Melvyn, and Joseph A. McCartin. *Labor in America:
A History*. Hoboken, NJ: Wiley-Blackwell, 2017.

Dunbar-Ortiz, Roxanne. *An Indigenous Peoples' History of the
United States*. Boston: Beacon Press, 2015.

Eidelson, Josh. "Starbucks Illegally Refused to Negotiate with
Union, US Labor Board Rules." Bloomberg News, 22 Nov.
2022. www.bloomberg.com/news/articles/2022-11-30
/starbucks-sbux-violated-labor-law-in-refusing-to-bargain
-with-union-nlrb-says?embedded-checkout=true. Accessed
14 Dec. 2022.

Engler, Mark. "Why Are Unions Popular with Young People?"
Morningside Center for Teaching Social Responsibility.
5 Sept. 2021. www.morningsidecenter.org/teachable-moment
/lessons/why-are-unions-popular-young-people. Accessed
5 June 2020.

Finnegan, William. "Child Labor Is on the Rise." *New Yorker*,
4 June 2023. www.newyorker.com/magazine/2023/06/12
/child-labor-is-on-the-rise. Accessed 4 June 2023.

Foner, Philip S. *History of the Labor Movement in the United
States*. New York: International Publishers, 1979. 11 vols.

——. *Organized Labor and the Black Worker, 1619–1981*. New
York: International Publishers, 1982.

——. *Women and the American Labor Movement: From Colonial
Times to the Eve of World War I*. New York: Free Press, 1979.

Franklin D. Roosevelt Presidential Library and Museum. "Great
Depression Facts." www.fdrlibrary.org/great-depression-facts.
Accessed 2 Feb. 2023.

Fraser, Nancy. *The Old Is Dying and the New Cannot Be Born.* New York: Verso, 2019.

Fraser, Steve. "1919: The Year the World Was on Fire." *Jacobin,* 13 Jan. 2019. jacobinmag.com/2019/01/john-reed-emma -goldman-big-bill-haywood-russian-revolution-1919 -bolsheviks. Accessed 5 Jan. 2020.

Freeman, Richard B., and James L. Medoff. *What Do Unions Do?* New York: Basic Books, 1985.

Furman, Jonah. "'Bro, How Do I Fix This?': Home Depot Workers Form Independent Union." Labor Notes, 21 Sept. 2022. labornotes.org/2022/09/bro-how-do-i-fix-home-depot -workers-form-independent-union. Accessed 22 Sept. 2022.

——. "GEICO Workers Launch Union Effort, Management Says Call the Cops." Labor Notes, 28 Sept. 2022. labornotes .org/2022/09/geico-workers-launch-union-effort-management -says-call-cops. Accessed 2 Oct. 2022.

Gage, Beverly. *The Day Wall Street Exploded: A Story of America in Its First Age of Terror.* New York: Oxford University Press, 2010.

——. *G-Man: J. Edgar Hoover and the Making of the American Century.* New York: Viking, 2022.

Geismer, Lily. *Left Behind: The Democrats' Failed Attempt to Solve Inequality.* New York: PublicAffairs, 2022.

Geoghegan, Thomas. *Only One Thing Can Save Us: Why America Needs a New Kind of Labor Movement.* New York: The New Press, 2014.

Goldman, Emma. "The Reckoning." *Mother Earth* IX, no. 7 (September 1914): 209–212.

Goldstein, Robert J. *Political Repression in Modern America from 1870 to 1976*. Champaign, IL: University of Illinois Press, 2001.

Goodwyn, Lawrence. *The Populist Moment: A Short History of the Agrarian Revolt in America*. New York: Oxford University Press, 1978.

Graeber, David. *Bullshit Jobs: A Theory*. New York: Simon & Schuster, 2018.

Greenhouse, Steven. *Beaten Down, Worked Up: The Past, Present, and Future of American Labor*. New York: Anchor, 2020.

——. "Starbucks' Aggressive Union-Busting Is a New Model for American Corporations." *Slate*, 3 Nov. 2022. slate.com /news-and-politics/2022/11/starbucks-union-busting-tactics -workers-labor-wave-nlrb.html. Accessed 4 Nov. 2022.

——. *The Big Squeeze: Tough Times for the American Worker*. New York: Anchor, 2009.

Grubbs, Donald H. *Cry from the Cotton: The Southern Tenant Farmers' Union and the New Deal*. Fayetteville, AR: University of Arkansas Press, 2000.

Gruenberg, Mark. "Starbucks Workers Win in S.C. as Drive Widens Nationwide." *People's World*, 2 June 2022. www .peoplesworld.org/article/starbucks-workers-win-in-s-c-as-drive -widens-nationwide. Accessed 4 July 2022.

Gurley, Lauren Kaori. "New Penalties for Companies That Illegally Fire Workers Who Unionize." *Washington Post*, 13 Dec. 2022. www.washingtonpost.com/business/2022/12/13 /unions-nlrb-firings-unions. Accessed 15 Dec. 2022.

Hall, Rebecca. *Wake: The Hidden History of Women-Led Slave Revolts*. New York: Simon & Schuster, 2021.

Henwood, Doug. "Take Me to Your Leader: The Rot of the American Ruling Class." *Jacobin*, 4 Apr. 2021. www .jacobinmag.com/2021/04/take-me-to-your-leader-the-rot-of -the-american-ruling-class. Accessed 3 May 2021.

Hochschild, Adam. "When America Tried to Deport Its Radicals." *New Yorker*, 4 Nov. 2019. www.newyorker.com /magazine/2019/11/11/when-america-tried-to-deport-its -radicals. Accessed 4 May 2019.

Hull, Elizabeth. *Taking Liberties: National Barriers to the Free Flow of Ideas*. Westport, CT: Praeger, 1990.

Hunter, Brooke. "Wheat, War, and the American Economy during the Age of Revolution." *William and Mary Quarterly* 62, no. 3 (July 2005): 505–26. doi.org/10.2307/3491533. Accessed 23 May 2023.

Hyclak, Thomas. *Rising Wage Inequality: The 1980s Experience in Urban Labor Markets*. Kalamazoo, MI: Upjohn Press, 2000.

Isidore, Chris. "Here's Why Car Prices Are So High, and Why That Matters." CNN Business, 8 July 2021. www.cnn .com/2021/07/08/business/car-prices-inflation/index.html. Accessed 3 Oct. 2022.

Jackson, Holly. *American Radicals: How Nineteenth-Century Protest Shaped the Nation*. New York: Crown, 2019.

Jones, Phil. *Work Without the Worker: Labour in the Age of Platform Capitalism*. New York: Verso, 2021.

Kelley, Robin D. G. *Hammer and Hoe: Alabama Communists during the Great Depression*. Chapel Hill: University of North Carolina Press, 2015.

Kelly, Jack. *The Edge of Anarchy: The Railroad Barons, the Gilded Age, and the Greatest Labor Uprising in America.* New York: St. Martin's Press, 2019.

Kelly, James. "'This iniquitous traffic': The Kidnapping of Children for the American Colonies in Eighteenth-Century Ireland." *The Journal of the History of Childhood and Youth* 9, no. 2 (Spring 2016): 233-246, muse.jhu.edu/article/619017/summary.

Kelly, Kim. *Fight Like Hell: The Untold History of American Labor.* New York: Atria/One Signal Publishers, 2022.

Kersten, Andrew E., and Clarence Lang. *Reframing Randolph: Labor, Black Freedom, and the Legacies of A. Philip Randolph.* New York: NYU Press, 2015.

Kim, E. Tammy. "How to Unionize at Amazon." *New Yorker*, 7 Apr. 2022. www.newyorker.com/news/dispatch/how-to-unionize-at-amazon. Accessed 5 May 2022.

——. "The Upstart Union Challenging Starbucks." *New Yorker*, 2 Aug. 2022. www.newyorker.com/news/dispatch/the-upstart-union-challenging-starbucks. Accessed 7 Sept. 2022.

——. "Inflation Is Obscuring Biden's Pro-labor Achievements." *New Yorker*, 31 Oct. 2022. www.newyorker.com/news/daily-comment/inflation-is-obscuring-bidens-pro-labor-achievements. Accessed 31 Oct. 2022.

Kornbluh, Joyce L. *Rebel Voices: An IWW Anthology.* Binghamton, NY: PM Press, 2011.

Lee, Ann Marie. "New Bill Would Crack Down on Companies That Break Child Labor Laws." CBS News, 26 Apr. 2023. www.cbsnews.com/news/child-labor-act-cory-booker-peter-welch. Accessed 27 Apr. 2023.

Leon, Luis Feliz. "Teamsters Begin Major Amazon Fight." *American Prospect*, 4 May 2023. prospect.org/labor/2023 -05-04-teamsters-begin-major-amazon-fight. Accessed 5 May 2023.

Leonard, Aaron J., and Conor A. Gallagher. *Heavy Radicals: The FBI's Secret War on America's Maoists: The Revolutionary Union/Revolutionary Communist Party 1968–1980*. Zero Books, 2015.

Lichtenstein, Nelson. *State of the Union: A Century of American Labor*. Princeton, NJ: Princeton University Press, 2013.

——. *Walter Reuther: The Most Dangerous Man in Detroit*. Champaign, IL: University of Illinois Press, 1997.

Lipsitz, George. *Rainbow at Midnight: Labor and Culture in the 1940s*. Champaign, IL: University of Illinois Press, 1994.

Magda, Matthew S. *Monessen: Industrial Boomtown and Steel Community 1898–1980*. Harrisburg, PA: Pennsylvania Historical and Museum Commission, 1985.

Magoon, Kekla. *Revolution in Our Time: The Black Panther Party's Promise to the People*. Somerville, MA: Candlewick Press, 2021.

Marx, Karl. *Capital: A Critique of Political Economy, Volume One*. New York: Vintage, 1977.

——. *Wage-Labour and Capital and Value, Price, and Profit*. New York: International Publishers, 2021.

Mayer, Jane. *Dark Money: The Hidden History of the Billionaires Behind the Rise of the Radical Right*. New York: Doubleday, 2016.

McAlevey, Jane F. *No Shortcuts: Organizing for Power in the New Gilded Age*. New York: Oxford University Press, 2016.

McAlevey, Jane F., and Bob Ostertag. *Raising Expectations (and Raising Hell): My Decade Fighting for the Labor Movement.* New York: Verso, 2012.

McGarr, Kathryn J. *City of Newsmen: Public Lies and Professional Secrets in Cold War Washington.* Chicago: University of Chicago Press, 2022.

Minchin, Timothy J. "Gigantic Struggles: The Battle to Build the United States Automobile Workers after the Sit-Down Strikes, 1937–1945." *Labor History* 65, no. 1 (January 2024): 1–22.

Montgomery, David. *The Fall of the House of Labor: The Workplace, the State, and American Labor Activism, 1865–1925.* Cambridge, UK: Cambridge University Press, 1987.

Moody, Kim. *An Injury to All: The Decline of American Unionism.* New York: Verso, 1988.

——. *In Solidarity: Essays on Working-Class Organization in the United States.* Chicago: Haymarket Books, 2014.

Murray, Robert K. *Red Scare: A Study in National Hysteria, 1919–1920.* Minneapolis: University of Minnesota Press, 1955.

Olton, Charles S. "Philadelphia's Mechanics in the First Decade of Revolution 1765–1775." *The Journal of American History* 59, no. 2 (September 1972): 311-326, www.jstor.org/stable/1890192.

O'Reilly, Kenneth. *Hoover and the Un-Americans: The FBI, HUAC, and the Red Menace.* Philadelphia: Temple University Press, 1983.

Orleck, Annalise. *Common Sense and a Little Fire: Women and Working-Class Politics in the United States, 1900–1965.* University of North Carolina Press, 1995.

Peck, Emily. "Amazon Workers' Union Victory Is Turbocharging a New Labor Movement." Axios, 6 Apr. 2022. www.axios .com/amazon-union-vote-starbucks-labor-jobs-1473630d -f313-4ce5-a7c2-296c8864a237.html. Accessed 23 May 2022.

Picketty, Thomas. *A Brief History of Equality.* Cambridge, MA: Belknap Press, 2022.

Pitkin, Daisy. *On the Line: A Story of Class, Solidarity, and Two Women's Epic Fight to Build a Union.* Chapel Hill: Algonquin Books, 2022.

Piven, Frances Fox, and Richard Cloward. *Poor People's Movements: Why They Succeed, How They Fail.* New York: Vintage, 1978.

Press, Alex N. "Amazon Is Trying to Destroy Its Staten Island Union by Firing Union Supporters." The Real News Network, 13 June 2022. therealnews.com/amazon-is-trying-to-destroy -its-staten-island-union-by-firing-union-supporters. Accessed 30 June 2022.

Preston, William, Jr. *Aliens and Dissenters: Federal Supression of Radicals, 1903–1933.* Champaign, IL: University of Illinois Press, 1994.

Putnam, Robert D. *Bowling Alone: The Collapse and Revival of American Community.* New York: Simon & Schuster, 2001.

Reséndez, Andrés. *The Other Slavery: The Uncovered Story of Indian Enslavement in America.* Boston: Houghton Mifflin Harcourt, 2016.

Robeson, Paul, and Philip S. Foner. *Paul Robeson Speaks: Writings, Speeches, Interviews, 1918–1974*. New York: Brunner/Mazel, 1978.

Rosenberg, Eli M. "As Major Companies Shut Down Stores with Active Union Drives, Workers File More Complaints of Retaliation." NBC News, 4 Nov. 2022. www.nbcnews.com /business/corporations/worker-complaints-alleging-anti-union -shutdowns-surge-organizing-rcna55057. Accessed 5 Nov. 2022.

Ruiz, Vicki L. *Cannery Women, Cannery Lives: Mexican Women, Unionization, and the California Food Processing Industry, 1930–1950*. Albuquerque, University of New Mexico Press, 1987.

Russell, Marta. *Capitalism and Disability*. Chicago: Haymarket Books, 2019.

Sanchez, George J. *Becoming Mexican American: Ethnicity, Culture, and Identity in Chicano Los Angeles, 1900–1945*. New York: Oxford University Press, 1995.

Scheiber, Harry N. *The Wilson Administration and Civil Liberties, 1917–1921*. Quid Pro Books, 2013.

Scheiber, Noam. "The Revolt of the College-Educated Working Class." *New York Times*, 28 Apr. 2022. www.nytimes.com /2022/04/28/business/college-workers-starbucks-amazon -unions.html. Accessed 5 July 2022.

——. "Labor Regulators Find Merit in Accusations by Unions at Amazon and Starbucks." *New York Times*, 6 May 2022. www .nytimes.com/2022/05/06/business/economy/nlrb-amazon -starbucks.html. Accessed 4 June 2022.

Schrecker, Ellen W. *No Ivory Tower: McCarthyism and the Universities*. New York: Oxford University Press, 1986.

Sengupta, Somini. "Protesting Climate Change, Young People Take to Streets in a Global Strike." *New York Times*, 20 Sept. 2019. www.nytimes.com/2019/09/20/climate/global-climate -strike.html. Accessed 2 Oct. 2019.

Smith, Morgan. "'Our Friends Are Dying so We March': Students Rally to Fight Gun Violence." *Washington Post*, 14 Mar. 2019. www.washingtonpost.com/local/education /our-friends-are-dying-so-we-march-students-rally-to -fight-gun-violence/2019/03/14/f86cce94-4692-11e9-aaf8 -4512a6fe3439_story.html. Accessed 12 Apr. 2020.

Stein, Jason, and Patrick Marley. *More Than They Bargained For: Scott Walker, Unions, and the Fight for Wisconsin*. Madison: University of Wisconsin Press, 2013.

Strang, Dean. *Keep the Wretches in Order: America's Biggest Mass Trial, the Rise of the Justice Department, and the Fall of the IWW*. Madison: University of Wisconsin Press, 2019.

Taylor, Kerry. "Deep South Baristas Strike Starbucks." Labor Notes, 28 May 2022. labornotes.org/2022/05/deep-south -baristas-strike-starbucks. Accessed 14 June 2022.

Treuer, David. "Do We Have the History of Native Americans Backward?" *New Yorker*, 7 Nov. 2022. www.newyorker .com/magazine/2022/11/14/do-we-have-the-history-of -native-americans-backward-indigenous-continent?. Accessed 8 Nov. 2022.

Varg, Paul A. "The Political Ideas of the American Railway Union." *Historian* 10, no. 2 (1948): 85–100. www.jstor.org /stable/24436032. Accessed 23 May 2023.

Vargas, Zaragosa. *Labor Rights Are Civil Rights: Mexican American Workers in Twentieth-Century America*. Princeton, NJ: Princeton University Press, 2005.

White, Ahmed. "100 Years Ago, the First Red Scare Tried to Destroy the Left." *Jacobin*, 23 Dec. 2019. jacobin.com/2019/12/red-scare-industrial-workers-of-the-world-iww. Accessed 12 May 2020.

Working Class History. *Working Class History: Everyday Acts of Resistance & Rebellion*. Edited Collectively. Binghamton, NY: PM Press, 2020.

Yarbro, E. Paul. *Forged in the Fires: How Providence, Purpose, and Perseverance Shaped America*. Meadville, PA: Christian Faith Publishing, 2019.

Zaveri, Mihir. "'I Need People to Hear My Voice': Teens Protest Racism." *New York Times*, 23 June 2020. www.nytimes.com/2020/06/23/us/teens-protest-black-lives-matter.html. Accessed 24 June 2020.

Zinn, Howard. *A People's History of the United States*. New York: Harper Perennial Modern Classics, reissue, 2015.

INDEX

Nevada, 309–11
New Deal, US, 205–6, 212, 253
New Hampshire, 53
New Jersey, 53, 147
New York, 20, 38–39, 53, 97, 118, 128, 143–44, 245
New York Communities for Change (NYCC), 336, 338
New York Times, 65, 67, 85, 101, 182, 202, 320
Niemöller, Martin, 253–54
Nixon, Richard M., 265
No Child Left Behind Act, US, 334
Non-Intercourse Act, US, 26
Nordlund, Willis J., 296
Norris–La Guardia Act, US, 205, 209, 246
North American Free Trade Agreement (NAFTA), 302
North Carolina, 259, 293

Obama, Barack, 327, 334
Occupational Safety and Health Act (OSHA), 283, 291, 307
Ohio, 147, 159, 182–83, 210, 214–15, 224–25, 264
oil industry, 64, 162, 254, 265, 286–90
Oklahoma, 343–44
Operation Wetback, US, 258
oppression, pyramid of, 71–72, 101, 169, 234, 273
capitalism and, 36, 114
nativism and, 48
organized crime, 133, 236
overproduction, 29–30
Owen, Robert, 42–43

Pacific Tomato Growers, 316–17
Palmer, A. Mitchell, 179–81, 183–84, 185–86, 188–90
Parks, Rosa, 258, 268
Parsons, Albert, 83–84
patriarchy, 227, 264
patriotism, 36, 48, 155–56, 161, 167, 175, 246
Pennsylvania, 31–32, 35, 38–39, 53, 64, 68, 90–95
Pennsylvania Railroad Company, 68–69, 196
Perkins, Frances, 125, 127, 206, 209, 220
Phelps Dodge, 297–99
picket lines, 91, 124, 140–41, 209–10, 217, 273, 277–78
Pinkerton National Detective Agency, 87–88, 91–92, 141–42
pneumonia, 137–38, 189
police, 64, 66, 76, 83–85, 139, 182, 260
anarchists and, 94
Chicago, 224, 264

IWW strikes and, 140–44
Jim Crow laws and, 254–55
Memphis, 278, 280
private, 87, 187, 210–12
sharecropping and, 186–87
violence, 141–44, 147, 187, 202, 211–12, 224–25, 261–62
women and, 125
pollution, 283, 293
Poor People's Campaign, 279–80
Popular Party, 19
Populists (People's Party), 106–9
poverty, 78, 190–203, 267, 269, 271, 291, 319
power, 19–20, 28–29, 47, 70, 179, 240–41
Prager, Robert, 161
Presidential Mediation Commission, US, 167
press, 19–20, 33, 64, 83–84, 93–94, 116, 156–57. *See also* propaganda; *specific newspapers*
Civil War coverage in, 56
corporate controlled, 29, 38–39, 40, 131–33, 171, 181–83, 195
freedom of the, 20, 33, 47, 233
on free market, 292
on homelessness, 97
on IWW strikes, 142–44
merchant capitalist control of, 36
Pentagon Papers in the, 264
Pinkerton Agency in, 87–88
railroad strikes in the, 69, 103–4
Red Scares promoted by, 245–46
on sanitation strikes, 278, 280
steel strikes in, 188
union newspapers and, 37, 45, 49, 52–53
World War I in the, 159
prices, 16–17, 21, 28–29, 105, 288
wages and, 243–44, 245, 250–51
private property, 41–43
privatization, 323–24, 332–34
Professional Air Traffic Controllers Organization (PATCO), 294–96
profits, 5–6, 7–8, 40–41, 98, 152
corporations and, 28, 77, 200, 232, 238–39, 241–42, 305
during COVID-19 pandemic, 346–48
fur trade, 11, 21
General Motors, 243–44
slavery and, 9, 10, 26–27

speedups and, 44–45
Progressive Era, 112–14, 134, 150, 269–70
propaganda, 7, 52, 86, 116, 148, 157, 174
anti-union, 298–99
about immigrants, 48–49
Proposition 22, California, 350, 353
Prosser, Gabriel, 51
proxy wars, 247–48
public
education, 37, 39, 43, 332–35, 336, 345
libraries, 37, 39, 333
Pullman, George Mortimer, 98–99
Pullman Palace Car Company, 98–104

Race to the Top Act, US, 334
racism, 77, 169, 255, 261, 328
railroad industry, 58, 59, 72–74, 96, 98, 105–6, 245
Adamson Act impacting, 146–47
B&O Railroad, 66–68
monopolies, 29
Pennsylvania Railroad Company, 68–69, 196
strikes, 66–69, 80–81, 100–104, 245–46
wages, 66, 68, 101
Randolph, A. Philip, 198, 234–35, 268–71
Reagan, Ronald, 289, 292, 294–96, 298, 302, 330
recessions, 29–30, 200, 288, 295–96, 297, 300–301, 326–27. *See also* depressions, economic
Red Scares, 43, 179–83, 185–90, 240, 253, 255
Cold War related, 245–46, 269
around World War II, 237–38
R. E. Funsten Company, 208–10
religion, 113–14, 227–28, 320
Republican Party, 53–55, 107–9
Republic Steel Company, 224–25
Reuther, Walter, 216–17, 219, 221–24, 243–44, 250–52
revolts, riots and, 17, 47, 53–54, 261–64
slave, 13–14, 51–52
Revolutionary War, US, 13, 27–28, 53
Revolutions of 1848 (Springtime of the Peoples), 47–48
Rhode Island, 27
rights, 23, 28, 33, 77, 178, 314
of corporations, 28, 327